Ambrose Bierce and the Dance of Death

Ambrose Bierce and the Dance of Death

Sharon Talley

The University of Tennessee Press / Knoxville

First Edition.

The paper in this book meets the requirements of American National Standards Institute / National Information Standards Organization specification Z39.48-1992 (Permanence of Paper). It contains 30 percent post-consumer waste and is certified by the Forest Stewardship Council.

Library of Congress Cataloging-in-Publication Data

Talley, Sharon, 1952–
Ambrose Bierce and the dance of death / Sharon Talley.
p. cm.
Includes bibliographical references and index.
ISBN-13: 978-1-57233-680-3
ISBN-10: 1-57233-680-3
1. Bierce, Ambrose, 1842–1914?—Criticism and interpretation.
2. Death in literature.
3. Fear of death in literature.
4. United States—History—Civil War, 1861–1865—Literature and the war.
5. War stories, American—History and criticism.
6. War in literature.
I. Title.

PS1097.Z5T34 2009
813'.4—dc22
2009010600

I call everyone to this dance,
Pope, emperor and all creatures,
Poor, rich, great and small.
Step forward because grieving doesn't help you!
—Lübeck

Contents

Acknowledgments ix
Abbreviations xi
Introduction xiii

1. Childhood and the Fear of Death in *The Parenticide Club* and "Visions of the Night" 1
2. The Failed Journey to Self-Understanding in "The Death of Halpin Frayser" 17
3. Scared to Death: Tales of Terror from *In the Midst of Life* 29
4. Doubling Death: Seeking the Immortal Self in Stories from *Can Such Things Be?* 43
5. Courage and Cowardice: Facing Death in Bierce's Early Civil War Writings 53
6. Death before Dishonor: Seasoned Soldiers and the Burden of Heroism 69
7. Collateral Damage: Civilians and the Human Cost of War 83
8. Seeking Death: Tales of Suicidal War Heroes 97
9. Surviving War: "Phantoms of a Blood-Stained Period" and Posttraumatic Stress Disorder 113
10. Bierce's Final Dance of Death 127

Notes 135
Bibliography 143
Index 153

Acknowledgments

I gratefully acknowledge the support and assistance of those who have contributed to the completion of this book. In particular, I am grateful to Peter Rudnytsky and S. T. Joshi, who read the entire manuscript and gave thoughtful feedback to strengthen my argument and its presentation. The original version of chapter 1 and part of chapter 4 appeared in *American Imago,* volume 66, issue 1, 2009, pages 41–69 (copyright © 2009 The Johns Hopkins Press) and is reprinted with permission of The Johns Hopkins Press. The original version of chapter 2 appeared in the *Journal of Men's Studies,* volume 14, issue 2, 2006, pages 161–72 (copyright © 2006 Men's Studies Press, LLC) and reprinted with the permission of Men's Studies Press. I appreciate the early confidence in this work that the editors of these two journals showed, as well as their mentoring.

The generous fellowship that I received from the Paul and Mary Haas Foundation enabled me to dedicate the necessary time to complete this study. Without this assistance, the project would have been much longer in coming to fruition.

I am also thankful to everyone at Texas A&M University–Corpus Christi who supported my work. The encouragement of Richard Gigliotti, dean of the College of Liberal Arts, helped to keep me focused throughout the project. Most of all, the example of my colleagues in the Department of English, all of whom excel in scholarship, creative activity, and collegiality, was invaluable in inspiring me to strive for excellence. My students also motivated me to think about Bierce in new ways through their responses to and insights about his writings. In addition, I am indebted to Robert Rios and the staff of the Interlibrary Loan Department of the university's Bell Library for facilitating the research for this book. They never failed to respond to me with courtesy, efficiency, and dedication even when they must have wearied of my seemingly endless requests and inquiries for more information.

I am fortunate to have had the opportunity to publish this book with the University of Tennessee Press. Special thanks go to Scot Danforth for his belief in the project, Stan Ivester for his deft editorial touch, and the production staff for their efficiency and expertise.

Finally, I thank my family and especially my husband, Terry, who has always been my first and most valued reader.

Abbreviations

For ease of reference, the following abbreviations are used in citing primary sources parenthetically within the text.

CW	*The Collected Works of Ambrose Bierce* (1909–12)
LAB	*The Letters of Ambrose Bierce* (1922)
MM	*A Much Misunderstood Man: Selected Letters of Ambrose Bierce* (1998)
SF	*The Short Fiction of Ambrose Bierce: A Comprehensive Edition* (2006)
SS	*A Sole Survivor: Bits of Autobiography* (1998)
UDD	*The Unabridged Devil's Dictionary* (2000)

Introduction

In one of his lesser-known short stories, Ambrose Bierce depicts the autobiographical figure of a "harmless skeleton" from the Civil War who refrains from his accustomed dance of death to fulfill his audience's preference for a life affirming "peace-dance" ("The Major's Tale" SF 709). Earlier in his career, he also used the title *Dance of Death* to create a literary hoax in which he jestingly decried the evils of the waltz.[1] Although Bierce usually did not directly invoke this long-standing allusion, his writings are so replete with themes and images of violent death that they can be seen to constitute a dance in which death is the leading participant. One critic has even famously suggested that death is "Bierce's only real character" (Wilson 622).

To explain why Bierce was so obsessed with death, critics and scholars without exception have pointed to the author's Civil War experiences. The War Between the States was undoubtedly the pivotal event in the writer's life and the focus of his best short fiction; however, such a reductive explanation for this pervasive and complex motif reflects the longstanding negligence of Biercian scholarship to make the complicated contextual links necessary to resolve the seeming contradictions and extremes in Bierce's personality and fiction. Unable otherwise to synthesize these elements, the early conclusion was that the fiction, though powerful, was hopelessly flawed and so only deserving of minor literary status. Writing in 1929, Carey McWilliams set the tone by speculating that "the ultimate judgment will be that he [Bierce] was more interesting as a man than he was important as a writer" (*Ambrose Bierce* 335). Subsequent biographers have usually agreed with this assessment, often signaling their interest in the personal over the artistic by their choice of titles: *Bitter Bierce: A Mystery of American Letters, Ambrose Bierce: The Wickedest Man in San Francisco, Ambrose Bierce: The Devil's Lexicographer,* and most recently, *Ambrose Bierce: Alone in Bad Company.*[2]

Although literary critics increasingly have insisted that Bierce's short stories, and in particular his Civil War fiction, have been undervalued, the author's place in literary history remains unsettled. In 1964, with his publication of the first significant book-length study of Bierce's fiction, Stuart C. Woodruff rightly observed, "It is difficult to understand Bierce as a writer without reference to his divided sensibility and to his contradictory responses to experience" (13). Unfortunately, however, Woodruff's attempt to find a meaningful connection between the biographical and the literary failed because his thesis was flawed by its oversimplification, positing a polarity of temperament and belief inconsistent with the complexities both in Bierce's life and in his fiction. Writing seven years after Woodruff, literary biographer M. E. Grenander also appreciated the need to synthesize Bierce's life and works by calling for more precise studies of the short literary forms he favored in relation to their psychological, political, social, and aesthetic motivations. Praising Bierce for expressing "[h]is view of man and the universe . . . with rigorous honesty and matchless precision," Grenander insisted that "his work ought to help readers avoid facile generalizations about the period in which he lived," and she forecast a major re-evaluation of Bierce's literary significance (*Ambrose Bierce* 168). John R. Brazil again bemoaned the state of Biercian studies in 1980, arguing that "[i]nsights remain discrete, discontinuous, the integrating principle elusive" because of the "unanalyzed interrelationships between aesthetic and political ideologies, between historical circumstance and personal psychology, and between psychological configuration and aesthetic and political ideologies" (225).

Cathy N. Davidson's 1984 book *The Experimental Fictions of Ambrose Bierce* began moving the scholarship in this direction by reassessing Bierce "as a fiction experimentalist who elaborated in his stories surprisingly modern views on the nature of language and the interrelationships between language, perception, and fictional forms" (3). Others, unfortunately, have been slow to respond; nevertheless, the recent publication of three new books on Bierce indicates that the long-overdue re-evaluation is finally occurring. The objectives of Lawrence I. Berkove's *A Prescription for Adversity: The Moral Art of Ambrose Bierce* are "to define and explain Bierce's intellectual profile—his philosophical inclination—and to show that his struggle with its demands is what made him a literary artist" (xi). To support this argument, the study draws on multiple versions of representative Bierce tales, the dating of the texts of these literary works, biography, correspondence, and especially the uncollected record of his journalism. From these sources, Berkove is able to perceive new insights about individual stories, but more importantly, he discerns the previously unrecognized pattern of Bierce's intellectual and literary development to show how the author's fiction arose not only from his Civil War experiences but also from his postwar search for meaning in classical Stoicism and Enlightenment literature. In his contextual analysis of the original nineteen stories collected and published in 1892 as *Tales of Soldiers and Civilians,* Donald T. Blume also draws heavily on contemporary contextual materials to consider each of the tales in the order in which they were published, first individually in periodical form and then together in the original collection that emerged from that complex milieu.[3] As a result of this process, he concludes that "the nineteen individual stories are much more similar in terms of thematic purpose and literary quality than has generally been assumed and that Bierce intricately fashioned these stories with considerable art into the critically neglected literary masterpiece he called *Tales of Soldiers and Civilians*" (360). In *The Devil's Topographer: Ambrose Bierce and the American War Story,* David M. Owens examines Bierce's Civil War stories chronologically according to the time of the action of the stories, arranging and plotting the location of their settings, using this geographical mapping and what he terms the "testimony of landscape" to determine previously unrecognized connections between Bierce's own war service and the stories.

Largely because of this work by Berkove, Blume, and Owens, as well as the surge of excellent primary scholarship that has recently appeared, it is now possible to recognize the rewards of joining Bierce's texts in meaningful ways with their multiple contexts.[4] The intent of this book is to contribute to this same undertaking by adding the still missing psychological dimension to the reassessment process. Grenander opened the door for a comprehensive psychoanalytic study by emphasizing the importance of the psychological perspective in studying Bierce and by providing some sound readings of a number of his short stories. Curiously, however, her biography of Bierce does not even address his early life, which makes it impossible to trace her readings back to possible biographical sources and influences from childhood. To date, only a few superficial attempts have been made to consider Bierce from a psychological perspective, most often in reductive Freudian readings of individual stories such as "An Occurrence at Owl Creek Bridge" and "The Death of Halpin Frayser," readings that are now dated and also make no effort to determine underlying sources or associations that would make it possible to join a body of these texts.[5]

This book not only updates these interpretations with insights from post-Freudian theorists but also uses contemporary death theory as a framework by which to analyze the sources and expressions of Bierce's attitudes about death and dying. As a result, it is possible for the first time to discern links among texts that resolve some of the still puzzling ambiguities and contradictions that have precluded a fuller understanding of both the man and his writings. In particular, this study draws on the theories of Ernest Becker about the fear of death and the role of the hero-system in Western society and from Gregory Zilboorg's and Franco Fornari's placement of this fear in the context of war, as well as from recent studies on attachment, object relations, posttraumatic stress, suicide, and the relationship of language to trauma.

Deepening previous psychoanalytic approaches that have been reductively biographical, chapter 1 uses post-Freudian perspectives on generative death anxiety and attachment, as well as relevant historical, cultural, and literary contexts, to consider Bierce's childhood, his subsequent commentary on his parents, and some of his nonmilitary writings that feature family violence. In particular, special attention is paid to *The Parenticide Club,* a collection of four bizarre tales of parricide, and to "Visions of the Night," Bierce's recollection of three persistent nightmares from his youth and adulthood.

Chapter 2 focuses on Bierce's short story "The Death of Halpin Frayser" to study Bierce's use of the gothic to probe the borders of consciousness, not only as a conscious attempt to appeal to his readers' absorption with this theme but also arguably as an unconscious representation of the underlying fear of death with which he struggled personally. Broadening previous Freudian interpretations, the chapter uses relevant historical and cultural contexts, as well as the post-Freudian theories of Jacques Lacan, Julia Kristeva, and Kaja Silverman, to examine how the tale works to expose the instability of masculine identity through its representation of the Oedipal project and its gendered repercussions.

Extending the study of Bierce's approach to the gothic, chapter 3 analyzes the writer's penchant for presenting fragmented and partial perspectives for the reader to weigh in interpreting deaths that could be the result of either natural or supernatural forces. To illustrate Bierce's artistic techniques and thematic concerns, this chapter examines four representative tales from the "Civilian" section of *In the Midst of Life:* "The Suitable Surroundings," "The Man and the Snake," "The Eyes of the Panther," and "The Damned Thing." All of these tales are unified by their focus on death in considering the power of the unconscious.

Drawing from the work of Otto Rank and Robert Rogers, among others, chapter 4 continues by examining Bierce's use of the double or *doppelgänger* motif to represent the fear of death associated with identity crisis. After explaining the development of the concept of the double in anthropology, folklore, and literature, the chapter considers Bierce's own experiences with this phenomenon as recounted in his essays "Visions of the Night" and "That Ghost of Mine." A discussion follows to illustrate Bierce's varied use of the motif in representative ghost stories, all of which appeared in his 1893 collection entitled *Can Such Things Be?* Included in this analysis are "A Cold Greeting," "Moxon's Master," and "One of Twins," as well as further consideration of "The Death of Halpin Frayser."

Chapter 5 contemplates significant facts about Bierce's life immediately before and during the Civil War, placing these facts in psychological, historical, and cultural context. That foundation is then used to study his writings of the early Civil War period to discern what they reveal not only about Bierce's own experiences and attitudes in facing death but also about those of other Civil War soldiers as they moved from innocence to experience in their first tests of heroism on the battlefield. The story "A Tough Tussle" and the related memoirs "On a Mountain" and "What I Saw of Shiloh" are treated in depth in this process.

Bierce's stories and memoirs of the early war feature a dreamland imagery of enchantment; however, this imagery of innocence disappears as soldiers who do not die or desert become seasoned in combat. Nevertheless, the stories continue to emphasize issues of courage and cowardice in depicting individual soldiers who battle fear of death as they struggle to meet the demands of the culture's hero-system. Chapter 6 considers the short stories "Killed at Resaca" and "Parker Adderson, Philosopher" to examine Bierce's portraits of soldiers who are severely tested as they attempt to bear the burden of society's definition of heroism while repeatedly facing the threat of violent death or dismemberment. At the same time, however, Bierce recognized that civilians were not just the perpetrators of prescriptive views of heroism but the victims of such attitudes as well. Chapter 7 considers this phenomenon by pondering the impact of war on southern civilians as represented in Bierce's two best-known tales, "An Occurrence at Owl Creek Bridge" and "Chickamauga." These two chapters also feature links to Bierce's own combat experience through discussion of his memoirs "The Crime at Pickett's Mill," "Four Days in Dixie," and "A Little of Chickamauga," as well as a lengthy letter that he wrote to his fiancée's sister Clara Wright in June 1864.

In many of Bierce's Civil War stories, the protagonist commits suicide as his final response to the pressures of war. Using insights from recent studies on war trauma and suicide, as well as Bierce's own wartime experience and his attitudes about suicide, chapter 8 probes the complex motivations behind and implications of this response to the physical and psychological stresses of war. After first reconsidering "A Tough Tussle" and "Killed at Resaca" in terms of the clinical aspects of the protagonists' reactions in these tales, this chapter analyzes the motif of suicide in three other Civil War tales: "The Story of a Conscience," "One of the Missing," and "The Mocking-Bird."

Chapter 9 examines Bierce's life after the war in the context of recent studies on posttraumatic stress disorders to argue that the author not only depicted but also suffered from the effects of delayed combat stress, a condition that may have been intensified because of his early childhood experiences. Readings of "The Other Lodgers," "George Thurston," and "The Major's Tale" figure prominently in this discussion.

The concluding chapter of the book looks at the final years of Bierce's life—including his growing detachment from friends and family, his relationship with his employer William Randolph Hearst, the disappointing publication of his *Collected Works,* and his final correspondence—in relation to the various scenarios that have been devised to explain the writer's mysterious disappearance in late 1913. In seeking to explain Bierce's state of mind and resulting plan to fashion his own death, this chapter draws from Otto Rank's ideas on the human need for immortality and Robert Jay Lifton's expansion of Rank's views into his concept of revolutionary immortality.

While this study is based on the belief that much of Bierce's writing can be interpreted from a psychoanalytic perspective, it finds no basis—and asserts none—for explaining his works as emanating from a "disordered" mind or as "evidence of his warped personality" (Berkove 141).[6] Nevertheless, as Leon Edel warns, "A writer writes out of his whole physical as well as mental being. I am not sure the work and the life can be dissociated" (21). Given the obvious autobiographical influence in his writings, it would be inexplicable not to explore fully and responsibly the possible psychological implications of Bierce's life experiences on his writing. In doing so, we learn about ourselves as much as we do about Bierce and his protagonists because the question of what makes his writing compelling—sometimes in spite of its technical deficiencies—lies not so much in what made Bierce write, but in what makes us read him and what drives so many people to write about him.[7] The terror of death that Bierce personally experienced and wrote about is a universal fear that all humans repress, sometimes more successfully than others. Thus, by giving voice to this unthinkable and unacknowledged but still strongly felt anxiety that besets all of his readers, Bierce helps them to understand the human condition. Far from reading or writing about Bierce's literature solely as a means of psychoanalyzing the author itself, this book argues that the writer's canon must be read with a sensitive understanding of all of its many contexts if it is to be appreciated fully.

Childhood and the Fear of Death in *The Parenticide Club* and "Visions of the Night"

> Now a word was brought to me stealthily, my ear received the whisper of it. Amid thoughts from visions of the night, when deep sleep falls on men, dread came upon me, and trembling, which made all my bones shake.
>
> **—Job 4:12–14, Revised Standard Version**

Biographers have long puzzled over—and sensationalized—Ambrose Bierce's alienation from his parents, and particularly his mother, as well as the apparent reflection of these tensions in the recurring theme of parricide that appears in his short fiction. Broadening previous psychoanalytic approaches that have been reductively biographical in focus, this chapter will use post-Freudian perspectives on the psychology of death and the unconscious, as well as relevant historical, cultural, and literary contexts, to consider Bierce's childhood, his subsequent commentary on his parents, and some of his non-military writings that feature family violence. In this process, special attention will be paid to *The Parenticide Club,* a collection of four bizarre tales of parricide, and to "Visions of the Night," Bierce's recollection of three persistent nightmares from his youth and adulthood. These writings suggest that in many ways Bierce anticipated the theories of psychoanalysis regarding the importance of dreams in the work of the unconscious and the primal nature of the fear of death in humanity.

As Daniel Liechty explains, "[t]he theory of Generative Death Anxiety (GDA) suggests that at the deepest level, human behavior is motivated by the unavoidable need to shield oneself from consciousness of human mortality" (x). According to this developing body of research, "death anxiety is more than just one emotion or fear among others. It is understood as the root [unconscious] anxiety. . . which literally defines humans as a species" (x–xi). Liechty and others have traced the origins of this theory back at least to Socrates, but the modern synthesis of GDA began with Nietzsche, Kierkegaard, and Freud, all of whom believed in the importance of the unconscious in human motivations. Freud's protégé Otto Rank wrote extensively about the fear of death, and a number of theorists have built upon Rank's work in this area.[1] However, the theorist most associated with GDA is cultural anthropologist Ernest Becker, who, in his Pulitzer Prize–winning book *The Denial of Death,* first gained widespread public attention for GDA by arguing that the terror of death is an innate fear that haunts humanity from birth. As Becker explains, because this fear is a defensive reaction to the omnipotent reality of creation in relation to one's own limited powers and possibilities, the individual from childhood must repress it "from the entire spectrum of his experience, if he wants to feel a warm sense of inner value and basic security" (52). From this perspective, anxiety becomes "a matter of the reaction to global helplessness, abandonment, fate" (53).[2]

In reorienting Freud's understanding of human motives, Becker echoes Norman O. Brown, who argues that the central problem of the child's life is not the narrowly sexual problem of lust and competitiveness that Freud in his early work termed the Oedipus complex but rather the Oedipal *project* of how to become an active agent in control of one's own life instead of a passive, helpless victim of fate.[3] As Brown observes,

> The Oedipal project is not, as Freud's earlier formulations suggest, a natural love of the mother, but as his later writings recognize, a product of the conflict of ambivalence and an attempt to overcome that conflict by narcissistic inflation. The essence of the Oedipal complex is the project of becoming God—in Spinoza's formula, *causa sui*. . . . By the same token, it plainly exhibits infantile narcissism perverted by the flight from death. (118)

In Becker's words, "The Oedipal project is the flight from passivity, from obliteration, from contingency: the child wants to conquer death by becoming the *father of himself,* the creator and sustainer of his own life" (36). Repression of the fear of death then "is inevitably self-generated in the child and is directed against the parents, irrespective of how the parents behave" (Brown 120).

According to both Becker and Brown, fear of death, though repressed, is natural and present in everyone. Arguing that this basic anxiety is actually an expression of the instinct for self-preservation, Gregory Zilboorg also concurs with this view, stating succinctly that "[n]o one is free of the fear of death" (466). Although it is generally agreed that children have no knowledge of the abstract idea of death until about the age of three to five and no rational understanding of the inevitability of death until age nine or ten, they do experience the anxiety of object-loss from birth. As Becker explains, the infant "is absolutely dependent on the mother, experiences loneliness when she is absent, frustration when he is deprived of gratification, irritation at hunger and discomfort, and so on. If he were abandoned to himself his world would drop away, and his organism senses this at some level . . . [as] a natural, organismic fear of annihilation" (13). Children who have positive maternal experiences generally will not be subject to morbid fears of object-loss and will gradually grow up to understand and accept death rationally as a part of their world view and to experience natural levels of related anxiety on a largely unconscious level; however, tensions in the early parent-child relationship, and especially in the child's relations with the pre-Oedipal mother, can result in heightened anxieties and even neurosis that can have life-long consequences.[4]

Arguably, the early childhood of Ambrose Gwinnett Bierce was characterized by just such tensions that can create abnormal levels of death anxiety. Bierce was born on 24 June 1842 in Meigs County, Ohio, the tenth child and sixth son of Marcus Aurelius Bierce and Laura Sherwood Bierce. For unknown reasons, his father gave all of the children names beginning with the letter "A." His mother, who married Marcus Bierce on her eighteenth birthday in 1822, was a direct descendent of William Bradford, and although his lineage also could be traced back to the *Mayflower*, it was commonly considered that Marcus Bierce had married well (Morris 10). According to biographer Paul Fatout, Bierce led a repressed childhood, "ruled by puritanical parents, who were of the sixth American generation of his godly Congregational ancestors" (4). Both parents had been raised in a fervid doctrinaire faith that they tried to pass on to their children, and although Bierce formally rejected his Calvinist roots, he was, by all accounts, nonetheless molded by them. In *The Devil's Dictionary*, he bluntly defined religion as "A Daughter of Hope and Fear, explaining to Ignorance the nature of the Unknowable" (*UDD* 196). A professed agnostic in adulthood, he viewed religion with suspicion because, in the words of C. Hartley Grattan, he believed it "a matter of the heart" (239). However, his tendency to dogmatic moral conservatism and iconoclasm suggests he was more influenced by the tenets of Calvinism than he was willing to acknowledge.

In writing about the Puritan family in early America, David E. Stannard observes that "the prescribed and common personal relationship between parents and children was one of restraint and even aloofness, mixed, with . . . an intense parental effort to impose discipline and encourage spiritual precocity" ("Death" 19). In part, this emotional restraint may have developed as a self-reflexive means to protect parents from the very real probability of losing one or more of their children to death before the age of puberty. However, as Stannard explains, "to the Puritan the child was more than a loved one extremely vulnerable to the ravages of the environment; he was also a loved one polluted with sin and natural depravity" ("Death" 20). Although the Puritans inherited the Christian "*prescription* that a peaceful death was a good death, the pessimism of the faith was contradictory to Christian tradition and caused exceptional discomfort as the devout Puritan awaited the end of his life. To the adult Puritan the contemplation of death frequently 'would make the flesh tremble.' To the Puritan child it could do no less" ("Death" 27–28).[5] Because of geographic dispersion, as well as in response to Enlightenment and Romantic thinking, the ideology of Puritan New England was gradually supplanted by a growing number of religious denominations that "increasingly stressed a loving, beneficient God" (Farrell 7). Nevertheless, remnants of this Calvinist heritage in many ways endured into the nineteenth century, and as Charles O. Jackson asserts, "The popular mind of antebellum America was [still] saturated with open concern about death," a concern prompted not only "by 'actuarial prevalence' but by 'existential proximity'" (61).

Bierce clearly was raised in an environment that carried many of these historically prevalent concerns and mindsets. In their youth, his parents had both been members of the First Congregational Church of Christ in Cornwall, Connecticut, where their spiritual upbringing had been guided by "the Reverend Timothy Stone, a Jonathan Edwards acolyte . . . [who] made up for his oratorical shortcomings with ferocious week-long revivals that literally scared hell out of his young charges, many of whom would tearfully descend on the altar, begging to know what they could do to be saved" (Morris 9). After marrying, Marcus and Laura Bierce had moved to Ohio, settling in a region that was steeped in the atmosphere of evangelical revivalism. Thoroughly fundamentalist in outlook, they were fastidious about matters of both faith and everyday life, perhaps holding themselves somewhat apart from what they saw as a lack of refinement in their frontier neighbors, but otherwise thoroughly at home with the devout and fervent faith that still evoked fear of sin and damnation as its main technique of social control and religious conversion.

Bierce's parents also carried other traits of their austere Puritanical heritage. Large families in this day were still the rule, especially in rural areas. With her children neatly spaced about twenty months apart, Laura Bierce could have had little time to devote to her tenth child. According to Fatout, "[s]he ran the household with a firm grip on the family reins, which the reticent, slow-moving Marcus was unable or unwilling to grasp with decision. . . . Although the outlines of her character are nebulous, Laura seems to have been a determined woman, given to government. . . . Faint hints suggest that she was humanly irritated by miserable houses and too little money, annoyed because her pedestrian husband was inferior to his famous younger brother, Lucius," who was a longtime and flamboyant member of the Ohio militia, a four-term mayor of Akron, and a zealous abolitionist (10). Despite his intellectual acumen and his more dynamic wife's prodding, Marcus Bierce remained essentially "an unassertive man fonder of speculation than of action. He was devoted to his children, but since he was restrained, austere, and saturnine rather than demonstrative or playful, he was a father for young ones to stand in awe of rather than to be chummy with" (11). The family struggled financially as Marcus drifted from one profession to the next. "At various times a farmer, a shopkeeper, a property assessor, and—somewhat [ironically] . . .—a county overseer of the poor, Marcus dutifully labored" but with little material success to show for his efforts (Morris 10).

Although his older siblings seem to have thrived in this setting, Bierce grew up an introverted, sensitive, suspicious child who resisted parental authority. In summarizing the perspectives of other biographers before him, Roy Morris, Jr., writes that Bierce's "impoverishment was more psychic than physical, and it appears to have been largely self-induced. Simply put—such things, of course, are never truly simple—Bierce blamed his mother for not loving him enough" (11). Nevertheless, because his sense of maternal deprivation began while he was a pre-Oedipal child who could not yet differentiate himself fully from his mother, his anxiety of object-loss may have been a factor in his failure to thrive. Further, his basic fear of separation no doubt intensified when three more children were born and died in infancy, leaving Bierce as the youngest surviving sibling. A son, Arthur, died in 1846 at the age of nine months, and twin girls, Adelia and Aurelia, died separately in 1848 within two years of their birth. Infant mortality was still common in mid-nineteenth-century America, but his parents' grief must have been magnified by the fact that they had never lost a child through the birth of Ambrose—and then lost all three children born subsequently. No doubt this prolonged period of grieving—as well as the family's relocation to Indiana in 1846—further deprived Bierce of his parents' attentions and in particular disrupted his bond with his mother at an especially vulnerable age.

The ability to form a selective and enduring attachment is a fundamental aspect of human experience that many theorists believe plays a crucial role in the process of personality development.[6] Attachment has generally been understood as one's working model of relatedness to specific significant others such as the mother and later romantic relationships.[7] Because of the emphasis on processes that determine the quality of interpersonal relatedness, many researchers believe that attachment theory overlaps into object-relations theory.[8] Whereas attachment bonds are present in some but not all relationships, object relationships are global, encompassing virtually all relationships. Conceivably, then, both theories can help to explain Bierce's personality and behavior, especially his difficulty in sustaining relationships. More importantly, in terms of this study, these factors arguably stimulated abnormal levels of death anxiety that may account for his obsessive focus on this issue in his writings.

As Fatout observes, Bierce as a boy "seems to have been a lone rebel who stood aside from the family stream like a looker-on, as if at the parental well of tenderness he were one child too many" (19). Entering adolescence, he demonstrated characteristics of avoidant attachment, growing "touchy, suspicious, introverted, and resistant to authority," all "enduring traits that made him a stormy foe and difficult friend" throughout his life (28). Withdrawing from his family and developing few friends as a youth, Bierce turned inward, burying himself in his father's extensive library and largely educating himself. Curiously, the only remnant of his early scholarship is a morbid epitaph for a child that, according to Morris, he found inscribed on a headstone in the local cemetery, and for some inexplicable reason chose to copy and preserve:

> She tasted of life's bitter cup
> Refused to drink her portion up
> But turned her little head aside
> Disgusted with the taste and died. (qtd. in Morris 15)[9]

Conceivably, Bierce's connection with this dead child and the words that memorialize her frustrated death stem from his own sense of maternal deprivation, as suggested by the image of "life's bitter cup," a metaphor for the mother's breast that fails to nurture and sustain the child. Thus, these words may reflect the unconscious anxiety that supported his decision to separate from his parents. At the age of fifteen, either shortly before or after he recorded these bleak words, Bierce left home permanently, moving first to nearby Warsaw and later to Akron.

Most biographers have insisted that Bierce never forgave his parents for their poverty, their evangelical religious zeal, or their lack of warmth and open affection. For evidence, they point to various later comments by Bierce, such as a remark from "The Love of Country": "The human heart has a definite quantity of affection. The more objects it is bestowed upon, the less each object will get" (CW 9: 255). Another often cited story that seems to reverberate from his own childhood experience is "Three and One Are One," which features the Lassiter family. The patriarch in this story, presumably patterned after Marcus Bierce, is described as having "that severity of manner that so frequently affirms an uncompromising devotion to duty, and conceals a warm and affectionate disposition. He was of the iron of which martyrs are made, but in the heart of the matrix had lurked a nobler metal, fusible at a milder heat, yet never coloring nor softening the hard exterior." Similarly, the Lassiter home, "though not devoid of domestic affection was a veritable citadel of duty, and duty—ah, duty is as cruel as death!" (SF 1041). In this instance, the association of death with childhood deprivation is perhaps subtly significant in suggesting the long-term effects of Bierce's impression of his parents as emotionally unresponsive. However, the images of parricide in the macabre group of four tales, which Bierce dubbed *The Parenticide Club* when he published them together in his *Collected Works,* are so outrageously gruesome that they have long alienated readers and critics and resisted serious scrutiny. Traditionally, the four tales have been dismissed either as evidence of irrational familial hatreds or as embarrassingly bad fiction.[10] More recently, Lawrence I. Berkove has insisted that the tales should be read as satire, categorically divorcing them from any valid biographical significance. These stores, however, arguably contain both conscious satirical content and unconscious biographical content that should be considered together for a full understanding.

The tales are unified by their use of first-person isolated narrators, as well as flat, unfeeling characters who desensitize readers to the pervasive violent imagery. As Berkove explains, "Bierce averts legitimate moral outrage in his readers by his use of gross exaggeration and by skillfully maintaining a humorous tone" (144). In the opening of the first of these stories, "My Favorite Murder," the narrator begins by stating, "Having murdered my mother under circumstances of singular atrocity, I was arrested and put upon my trial, which lasted seven years. In charging the jury, the judge of the Court of Acquittal remarked that it was one of the most ghastly crimes that he had ever been called upon to explain away" (SF 612). The remainder of the tale, however, is devoted to the narrator's testimony concerning his previous murder of his uncle. The narrator decides he must murder his uncle because the man has refused either to restore the gold watch and forty dollars he allegedly has stolen from the narrator in a highway robbery or to allow the narrator to go into secret partnership with him as compensation for the loss. Communicating his elaborate plans for the murder to his parents, the narrator's "father said he was proud" of his son while his "mother promised that although her religion forbade her to assist in taking human life [he] should have the advantage of her prayers for [his] success" (614).

Bierce obviously is having fun with the broadly drawn characters, all of whom owe their living to ill-gotten gains, and who evidence little or no sense of morality or sincere familial affection. Simultaneously, however, he may also be using his art unconsciously as a safe outlet for his own ambivalent feelings for his parents. At the end of the story, the judge is persuaded to acquit the defendant on the charge of the mother's murder on the basis of the defendant's successful rationalization of the matricide as being the less ghastly of the two crimes. It is no accident, however, that the narrator initially admits that the matricide—the unspeakable crime—occurs "under circumstances of singular atrocity," even though he then commences to discount the act and his accompanying guilt as a "comparative triviality" (SF 612, 613). While the narrator escapes society's punishment, he (and conceivably Bierce as well) still harbors the inner guilt and anxiety that accompanies any wish to kill the mother, whether or not the wish is acted upon.

In the second tale, "Oil of Dog," the narrator's father is a "manufacturer of dog-oil," while his mother keeps "a small studio in the shadow of the village church, where she disposed of unwelcome babies." The dutiful son, "trained to habits of industry," assists in both businesses by "procuring dogs" for his father to boil in his vats and by carrying away "the debris" of his mother's work in her studio (SF 754). One evening when he is unable "to throw the babes into the river which Nature had thoughtfully provided for the purpose," he instead throws a baby into a cauldron of boiling oil. The following day, the oil is deemed the "finest quality . . . that was ever seen," causing the narrator's parents zealously to revise their recipe for success. Eventually, their mounting greed for human ingredients drives them to kill each other by springing into the pot themselves, while their son has "the unhappiness to observe this disagreeable instance of domestic infelicity" and resulting "commercial disaster" (756).

Bierce's Swiftian imagery suggests that this tale can best be explained as a satire denouncing child abuse and the failure of society to acknowledge the problem and take action to protect children from parents whose practices are at odds with their professed beliefs and outward appearances. Although the overarching macabre humor of "Oil of Dog" masks the autobiographical connections and related anxieties, Bierce nonetheless shows courage in championing the cause of children who are raised by ostensibly "honest parents," who neglect and abuse their children while presenting themselves to the outside world as pillars of the church and community (SF 754). Bierce signals both his rejection of the Calvinist environment in which he was raised and his belief that children should not carry the burden for parental failures in the narrator's ironic depiction of the responsibility he bears for his parents' demise: "The holy influence of my dear mother was ever about me to protect me from the temptations which beset youth, and my father was a deacon in a church. Alas, that through my fault these estimable persons should have come to so bad an end!" (755).

Other aspects of the tale, read with an understanding of Bierce's own childhood experiences, add further psychological depth to this satirical portrait of parental dysfunction and its resulting effect on children. The mother's disposal of "unwelcome babes" suggests not only Bierce's own insecurity about his mother's love, but also the unconscious guilt he has assumed over the deaths of his three younger siblings, who competed with him for her affection and nurture. On the night he first throws a dead baby into the boiling oil, the narrator's struggle with his conflicted feelings conceivably mirrors Bierce's own: " . . . I held the naked body of the foundling in my lap and tenderly stroked its short, silken hair. Ah, how beautiful it was! Even at that early age I was passionately fond of children, and as I looked upon this cherub I could almost find it in my heart to wish that the small, red wound upon his breast—the work of my dear mother—had not been mortal" (SF 755). In this key passage, the telling "almost" clearly points to the narrator's ambivalence. These feelings are underscored by the conflicting passions of love and violence represented by Bierce's symbolic use of the color red, which he connects to the mortally wounded breast and its mingled associations with nourishment and eroticism. While the mother in the story has killed the baby on the narrator's lap, the reverberating psychic tensions manifest themselves in the now adult narrator's recollection of his own complicity in the child's death, which reveals his own guilt and fear of death. Diction and symbolism work together to suggest deeper implications than previously have been appreciated in this depiction of a fictional child's struggle to resolve ambivalent emotions that reflect the heritage of Bierce's own childhood experiences.

"An Imperfect Conflagration" features a narrator who first murders his father, when he refuses to make a fair division of the spoils of a robbery they have committed. He next kills his mother so she will not discover his crime against his father, and then, upon the advice of the chief of police, he burns the home to obliterate any evidence. In this tale, the son's irresolvable psychic conflict is represented by the title image of the "imperfect conflagration." Fire is a symbol that carries dichotomous associations with love and hate, and it serves as an agent of both destruction and purification. The son decides to destroy the bodies of his parents to avoid detection for their murder and to cleanse himself of the guilt feelings that attach to their bodies. His plan is thwarted, however, by the fact that, before lighting the fire, he conceals the corpses in a bookcase that, unknown to him, is fireproof. Although he apparently avoids punishment by society for his crimes, the suggestion once again is that the child can neither destroy his link to his parents nor escape his own guilty memories.

The final and perhaps most significant tale of the sequence, "The Hypnotist," features another son who, as a youth of fourteen, uses hypnosis to induce another student to give him her lunch basket each day and thus resolve his frustration over "the niggard economy of [his] parents in the matter of school luncheons." The parents, delighted with "the obvious advantages of the new *regime*," refuse to let their son renounce the scheme when it becomes tiresome to him, and it is only the mysterious death of the girl—while under the narrator's spell—that enables him to escape the situation (SF 848). As a result of this offense, he spends years in prison. While traveling back to his childhood home in "South Asphyxia" after his release, the now adult son comes upon his parents picnicking in a field. As the narrator explains, "The sight of the luncheon called up painful memories of my school days and roused the sleeping lion in my breast." Approaching "the guilty couple," he suggests that they "share their hospitality," but they refuse, insisting that there is only sufficient food for the two of them. Incensed by this forceful reminder of the parental deprivation of his childhood, the narrator convinces the couple through hypnosis that they are "two *broncos*—wild stallions both, and unfriendly," at which point they kick and stomp each other to death in a grisly scene that the son passively observes (849).

Berkove argues that in this tale, like in the other three, "what is revealed . . . is not Bierce's resentment of his parents, but rather his ridicule of individuals who refuse to acknowledge guilt and blame others instead of themselves for their actions, and his disgust at a legal system that bends over backward to avoid punishing criminals" (150). In reality, however, one of these readings does not preclude the other. It is true that the reader feels no sympathy for this narrator, who clearly takes no responsibility for his own horrendous acts and who, fifteen years after the double murder, is still evading conviction through legal maneuverings. Nevertheless, Bierce also imbues the story with elements that suggest his own unconscious fantasies. It is only as a result of the parents' failure to provide adequate nourishment to their son that the narrator comes to abandon reason and instead to realize and depend upon his hypnotic powers over others, powers to which he feels forced to resort for physical and emotional survival. Further, the disturbingly graphic death imagery suggests a traumatic primal-scene fantasy replete with unresolved anxiety. "At the end of it all," the son relays, "two battered, tattered, bloody and fragmentary visages of mortality attested to the solemn fact that the author of the strife was an orphan" (SF 850). Bierce's telling use of the word "author" links his own traumatic memories and desires to the narrator's experiences and actions, notwithstanding the manifest satirical commentary that operates in the tale.

Bierce's lifelong reticence both in communicating with and in commenting on his family, as well as the caustic family portraits in his fiction, suggest unresolved psychic conflicts that he masked with defensive acerbity. To argue that such turmoil underlies the satirical content in this fiction is not to suggest that Bierce felt unmitigated hatred for his parents or that he had a deranged mind, but rather to acknowledge the complexities of human nature and the conflicts with which all humans struggle to varying degrees. Two letters, recently reintroduced and quoted at length by Berkove, add important nuances to Bierce's psychological profile, suggesting that the author experienced intense guilt over his ambivalent feelings for his parents. The first of these letters, dated 13 February 1876, was occasioned by Bierce's learning from his brother Albert of his father's final illness:

> My Dear Mother,
>
> Al has shown me your letter of the fourth, and I can not tell you how deeply it has grieved me to learn that my poor Father is so low. Of course I had long expected some such news, but had, I think, never fully realized how dreadful it would be. There is nothing I can [do] to comfort you, Mother; I need comfort myself. If Father is still living when you receive this, I beg you to tell him how deeply I feel for him, how sorry I am for all the sorrow and trouble I have ever caused him, and ask him for forgive me [*sic*] for the sake of the love I have always born him. . . .
>
> My poor Mother, I cannot write as I feel; you know what I would say; you know how dreadful is this affliction to me, who have not even the consolaton [*sic*] of being a good son to so good a father. . . . Of us all, you my poor Mother, are the only one to whom the consciousness

> of having always performed your every duty with unswerving patience, gentleness and grace will come to temper the bitterness of grief.
>
> I can write no more for I am blind with tears. (qtd. in Berkove 1–2)

The second letter, dated 30 April of the same year, was written after Bierce learned of his father's February death:

> I have delayed writing you for so long since receiving your sad account of the great grief which has fallen upon us all, only because I felt it too keenly for me to trust myself to write of it. I had, and have now, no consolation to offer you, and it seems worse than useless to revive a sorrow so great, without some attempt to alleviate it. Be assured that I deeply sympathize with you in [a] loss which is only less to me than to you. (qtd. in Berkove 2)[11]

In contrast to the fiction, which reflects Bierce's unconscious fantasies, these letters show Bierce's conscious feelings, providing poignant proof of the psychic toll that resulted from the dynamics that characterized his early relationship with his parents. Bierce's insecure childhood attachment and subsequent redirection of his repressed fear of death by detachment from and hostility against his parents provide a credible explanation for the underlying anger that characterizes his fictional family portraits. As a result of the conflict between his conscious and unconscious thoughts, he may have suffered from neurotic levels of death fear and accompanying guilt, self-hatred, and isolation that he unconsciously displaced in his writings, where he was free to play out his unacceptable violent urges under the guise of fiction that featured exaggerated but thinly veiled familial themes of gothic horror laced with liberal doses of cynical irony and caustic wit.

The destructive intensity of Bierce's conflicted feelings toward his parents, as well as the eventual outlet for this ambivalence that he created in his fiction, are also reflected in a series of three recurring nightmares that originated in his youth and that he still recalled many years later, as evidenced by an essay entitled "Visions of the Night," which first appeared in the 24 July 1887 *San Francisco Examiner.* In this essay, he clearly recognizes the importance of dreams in discerning the work of the unconscious, defining a dream in the introduction as "[a] loose and lawless collection of memories—a disorderly succession of matters once present in the waking consciousness" (CW 10: 122). With this perception, Bierce anticipates Freud, whose landmark study *The Interpretation of Dreams* presented the first scientific theory of dreams. According to Freud, dreams are unconscious and disguised expressions of repressed, infantile wishes that often include features of condensation and displacement that connect the manifest content with the latent dream-thoughts. He included nightmares in his wish-fulfillment theory of dreams by suggesting that nightmares represented wishes for punishment emanating from the superego.

Recounting the first of three dreams, Bierce describes himself as "walking at dusk through a great forest of unfamiliar trees." Seemingly "the only living thing" in this unknown woods, he is "obsessed by some awful spell in expiation of a forgotten crime committed . . . against the sunrise" (CW 10: 125). The child Bierce is alone, without the protection of a mother or father, as he journeys through the forest of the unconscious, inner self, a journey that he interprets as punishment for a crime he has committed against his mother as a result of his birth, symbolized by the sunrise. As he walks on "[m]echanically and without hope," he moves with obvious phallic implications "under the arms of the giant trees along a narrow trail penetrating the . . . forest" to follow a stream of blood, symbolically the stream of life. At its source, he discovers "a deep tank of white marble. . . . filled with blood." Surrounding this cold and austere, but perfect, maternal image, and emphasizing the mother's dual role as the source of life and the cause of death, are a score of dead male bodies, "naked and arranged symmetrically around the central tank, radiating from it like spokes of a wheel. The feet were outward, the heads hanging over the edge of the tank. Each lay upon its back, its throat cut, blood slowly dripping from the wound" (125–26).

From a strictly Freudian perspective, these wounds might suggest either the infant's pre-Oedipal struggle for survival with the mother or the dreamer's Oedipal fear of castration by the father as a result of his sexual desire for the mother. In Jacques Lacan's update of Freud's views, however, psychosexual development hinges on the child's acceptance of the Law of the Father, the rules and restrictions controlling both desire (in all of its manifestations, not merely sexual) and the rules of communication. From this perspective, the cut throats would thus more clearly point to the prohibition of incest that occurs when the father intervenes between mother and child (son) to offer access to the Symbolic Order, the realm of power only available to the son who accepts his role as a male speaking subject and sacrifices consciousness of his prior state of oneness with the mother.

Continuing his recollection of the dream, Bierce comments, "I looked on all this unmoved. It was a natural and necessary result of my offence, and did not affect me; but there was something that filled me with apprehension and terror—a monstrous pulsation . . . [that] pervaded the entire forest, . . . a manifestation of some gigantic and implacable malevolence." At this point, though ostensibly unmoved by the replicated images of the dead male body, arguably representing both his father and himself, Bierce awakens "overcome by a terror which doubtless had its origin in the discomfort of an impeded circulation," the terror of death as a result of the monstrous unreconciled guilt he bears for his wish to kill his father so he can remain with his mother (CW 10: 126–27). Although Bierce attributes the cause of his awakening to physiological discomfort, the strength of his response suggests a more crucial psychological dimension to his reaction. His use of the word "terror" is perhaps especially significant here. As Anne Williams explains,

> Horror and terror concern two complementary modes of the "unspeakable." "Horror" is associated with the pre-Oedipal separation from the mother/material that both predates and impels the construction of the speaking subject. "Terror," on the other hand, is our experience of a self conscious of the ultimate failure of the Symbolic, the point where the system breaks down—when "words fail," where the idea of infinity faces the subject again to confront the literally unspeakable—and where, if the self exists *as* a speaking subject, it potentially or momentarily ceases to exist." (72–73)

Using Williams's distinction, terror would mark the point where repression fails and the fear of one's own death becomes conscious. Bierce thus awakens to a momentary awareness not only of his own mortality but also to a dim recognition of the original source of that fear, an awareness that normally resides only in his unconscious. Somewhat paradoxically, this terror of death ultimately becomes associated with the mother—and by extension to the culturally "female," the other. This occurs because of the individual's efforts to repress the fear and related guilt, as well as the desire to remain undifferentiated from the mother, who was the root source of the pre-Oedipal child's fear of separation and death.

The second dream is replete with the psychic scars of Bierce's Calvinist upbringing, and it is significant that he recollects first having it in his "early youth" when he "could not have been more than sixteen"—shortly, therefore, after he left his parents' home (CW 10: 127). In this dream, the trees—symbolic of male power, the self, and life itself—have been obliterated, seemingly by a scorching fire representative of God's wrath. Again parentless and "alone on a boundless level in the night," the abandoned child walks west through an "uncanny background of battlements and towers"—toward the death and damnation that he eventually discerns as "the lingering fire of eternity" (128, 129). At length, the child enters his father's house (i.e., God's house or, from Lacan's perspective, the earthly Symbolic realm) through an open portal and after wandering through the deserted edifice, discovers his own corpse, "dreadfully decomposed," the "vestigal fragment of a vanished race" that somehow as retribution for its unspeakable sins has remained "sentient after death of God and the angels" (130–31). This dream, in its interrelated themes of sin, guilt, death, and damnation, reverberates with echoes of the religious terror that was drilled into Bierce as a child and that undoubtedly intensified the psychic conflicts with which he struggled in his youth. It also suggests the Lacanian *otherness* of the unconscious in the dreamer's resistance to recognizing his own dead body. For Lacan, death—like God—is located in the Real, the order of subjectivity which, unlike the Imaginary and the Symbolic, involves intractable things or states that are impossible for the individual to imagine, symbolize, or know directly.

Bierce ends "Visions of the Night" with the most ambiguous of the dreams. This time, passing through woods near daybreak in early summer, he discovers "a horse, visibly and audibly cropping the herbage." The horse, which approaches him, is "milk-white, mild of mien, and amiable in look," causing the child to say to himself, "'This horse is a gentle soul.'" As he pauses "to caress it," it speaks to him "in a human voice, with human words, . . . which does not surprise, but terrifies," instantly causing Bierce to awaken without learning what the horse said (CW 10: 132). According to Ernest Jones's work on nightmare, animals often play a prominent part in children's dreams, where the feature that most attracts their personal interest "is the freedom they [the animals] display in openly satisfying needs" (68–69). Often a symbol of communication, horses are extensively connected to ideas of the supernatural, where "the female connotations are more often associated with the terrifying and erotic, while the noble and divine connotations have more often male associations" (248). In Bierce's dream, his desire to caress the feminized horse suggests his desire for his mother's nurture, which also includes accompanying Oedipal implications of sexual desire for the mother's material body and, thus, prompts his conflicted awakening.

From the perspective of Julia Kristeva, who builds upon Lacan's theories of language and the unconscious, the horse as mother terrifies the child with her maternal language because he experiences it as a semiotic overflow of the lack inherent in his relation to the death, materiality, and abject that are all associated with the otherness of the maternal body as a result of the child's separation from the mother into a separate state of being. Socialized to displace his desires and fantasies into the male language he has learned in entering the Symbolic Order, he is forever denied the state of *jouissance* signified by the mother and can instead only experience the abject, both a recognition that meaning is breaking down and the reaction to such a breakdown by reestablishing the primal repression.

The recurring dream suggests that Bierce suffered from guilt at his inability to communicate with his mother and with his conscious decision to leave home and discontinue his relationship with her. The horse/mother and the dreamer live in what the latter sees as two different worlds. As he explains, "I suppose I vanish from the land of dreams before it finishes expressing what it has in mind, leaving it, no doubt, as greatly terrified by my sudden disappearance as I by its manner of accosting me. I would give value to know the purport of its communication. Perhaps some morning I shall understand—and return no more to this our world" (CW 10: 133). In awakening, the dreamer rejects the mother and the world of the unconscious that is dominated by his repressed fear of death, associated here with his Oedipal guilt.

Just as Bierce's dreams served as an outlet for his repressed fear of death and related feelings of guilt and alienation, so did his writing of gothic fiction. As Joel Porte argues, the gothic—and especially the American gothic—expresses "a fundamentally Protestant theological or religious disquietude" in its preoccupation with primordial fear (43). Through Bierce's use of gothic conventions, he often presents what Porte calls "the personal narrative of sin, guilt, and retribution... [that] represents a kind of religious confession or exploration" (47). In creating these narratives, Bierce often probed the liminal state by taking conscious inspiration from his own dreamworks. In "The Moonlit Road," he even invokes the title of his dream visions, when, in recounting a dead wife's reappearance, he has her husband begin, "There is another dream, another vision of the night..." (SF 1019). Strongly reminiscent of the second dream that Bierce recounts in "Visions of the Night," the story "An Inhabitant of Carcosa" begins with another first-person narrator lost and wandering through a similar setting to make a similar discovery. Here, the narrator finds himself walking in an unfamiliar and long-deserted desert that he describes as "a bleak and desolate expanse of plain" with just "[a] few blasted trees here and there" (457). Eventually, after discerning many graves surrounding him, he sits "at the root of a great tree, seriously to consider what it were best to do." As he ponders his situation, a sudden wind blows to uncover the words inscribed on what he realizes with horror is his own headstone, a "stone [that] had apparently marked the grave out of which the tree had sprung ages ago" (459). Springing to his feet in the same indescribable terror of death that awakened the dreaming Bierce, the narrator realizes that he is wandering through the ancient ruins of his long-destroyed homeland. Less directly obvious are the echoes of "Visions of the Night" that reverberate in Bierce's most critically acclaimed gothic story, "The Death of Halpin Frayser." When this complex tale is considered closely, it provides perhaps the best opportunity to appreciate Bierce's understanding of dreams as representations of the unconscious, repressed fear of death that lies at the core of the human psyche.

The Failed Journey to Self-Understanding in "The Death of Halpin Frayser"

Light lie the earth upon his dear dead heart,
And dreams disturb him never.
Be deeper peace than Paradise his part
Forever and forever.
—Ambrose Bierce

In his gothic tales, as Philip M. Rubens observes, Ambrose Bierce often uses dreams "to create another world where some manifestation of man's inner terrors and desires can be accorded objective reality" (29). Of all of his short stories, "The Death of Halpin Frayser" best demonstrates Bierce's use of the gothic to probe the borders of consciousness not only as a perhaps unconscious representation of the underlying fear of death with which he struggled personally but also as a conscious attempt to appeal to his readers' absorption with this theme. The immense popularity of gothic tales such as this one suggests that the repressed fear of death is a manifestation of what Ernest Becker argues is the fundamental truth of the human condition. By representing this basic fear in the form of the gendered other, Bierce adheres to a well-known trope of anxiety in gothic fiction,[1] and by specifically defining this otherness in the figure of the mother, he also anticipates the associative link between the mother and death that Freud would forge and that other psychoanalysts would subsequently refine.

Written in 1891, "The Death of Halpin Frayser" is a complex tale that adheres almost perfectly to the five characteristics of the male gothic that Anne Williams defines. First of all, Bierce incorporates multiple points of view, as well as a confusing chronology and numerous plot dislocations, throughout the story's four sections. Then, he posits the supernatural as a premise for the fiction by prefacing it with an epigraph attributed to the hypothetical mystic "Hali," preparing the reader for a tale in which a spiritless body appears to strangle the protagonist in a dream of death that seemingly becomes his reality. The story also meets the third criterion because its isolated protagonist meets his death as a result of violating the Law of the Father. Fourth, the story has long puzzled readers because of its lack of narrative closure regarding the mysteries surrounding the death of the protagonist. And finally, as is typical of the male gothic, Bierce focuses less on the terror of death associated with the Oedipal crisis and more on its pre-Oedipal horror by depicting the primitive, gendered link between the mother and death in its more physical, "abject" manifestations.[2]

Surprisingly, although "The Death of Halpin Frayser" is typically considered one of Bierce's best stories, few concerted attempts have been made to interpret it. In their interpretations, M. E. Grenander, William Bysshe Stein, and Cathy N. Davidson all point out Bierce's use of "red herrings" in the form of supernatural elements that lead the reader to conclusions that fail to answer all of the questions posed by the text. Arguing against this consensus, S. T. Joshi more recently has insisted that the story is a kind of jigsaw puzzle for which Bierce provides all of the pieces, but that they can only be put together through recourse to the supernatural.[3] To date, Robert C. McLean stands alone in insisting that a rational explanation for the mysterious circumstances surrounding the death of Halpin Frayser is possible. However, his theory, though ingenious, cannot be proven from the evidence presented in the story itself.

It is beyond the scope of this chapter to try to explain all of the mysteries of life and death that lie at the core of this tale. The focus rather will be on how the story works to expose the instability of masculine identity through its representation of the Oedipal project and its gendered repercussions. While the sexual nature of this "crisis," as originally formulated by Freud, has been argued previously in interpreting "The Death of Halpin Frayser," post-Freudian theories, and especially Jacque Lacan's reformulation of the complex as the child's entry into language, also have applications for the tale that have been considered only recently.[4] By emphasizing the Lacanian perspective here, as well as Julia Kristeva's elaboration on Lacan's theories, an attempt will be made to complicate and deepen the psychoanalytic implications of the story, connecting it in more meaningful ways to the biographical, historical, and cultural contexts from which it sprang.

The backing for a strictly Freudian interpretation of this confusing narrative leans heavily on the Oedipal dynamics of the Frayser family that Bierce describes in the second section of the tale. Halpin Frayser, as "the youngest and not over robust" child of a "well-to-do" southern family, "had the double disadvantage of a mother's assiduity and a father's neglect." Described as "dreamy, indolent, and rather romantic," he shares with his mother "the most perfect sympathy," as well as a guilty love of poetry and admiration for a maternal ancestor, the obscure Colonial poet Myron Bayne (SF 807). As he matures, the relationship "between him and his beautiful mother—whom from early childhood he had called Katy—became yearly stronger and more tender. In these two romantic natures was manifest in a signal way that neglected phenomenon, the dominance of the sexual element in all the relations of life. . . . The two were nearly inseparable, and by strangers observing their manner were not infrequently mistaken for lovers" (808).

It would have been difficult for Bierce to have fashioned a more obvious description of the Oedipus complex. That the sexual attachment has become at least unconsciously troubling to the twenty-six-year-old son can be surmised by his desire to separate himself at least temporarily from his mother by traveling to California on business. Further, although the mother resists this separation, her underlying uneasiness is also suggested by the dream that she has had just prior to learning of his trip, a dream that she shares separately with both father and son. In this dream, a young and handsome Myron Bayne points to Frayser's portrait. A facecloth like those commonly used in covering the dead has been added to the painting, and below the edge of the cloth are visible the marks of hands on Frayser's throat. Katy Frayser interprets the dream as connected with her son's journey to California and further suggests her own feelings of guilt for strangling her son with her love when she exclaims, "'Look—my fingers feel so stiff; and I am almost sure they have been giving me great pain while I slept.'" Contrary to his mother, who believes she can keep her son safe at home, Frayser believes he is "to be garroted on his native heath," and so he flees to California in an attempt to escape her reach, as well as—presumably—the reach of the castrating father (SF 808).

The sexual nature of the relationship between this mother and her now adult son, as well as its attending anxieties, cannot be denied. However, to read this feature from a post-Freudian perspective as the secondary result—rather than the primary impetus—of the Oedipal crisis may be possible when other aspects of the story are considered. As we shall see, the male characters in the story are plagued by doubts about their masculinity, doubts that in some ways reflect historically and culturally specific conditions. These anxieties threaten what Kaja Silverman defines as "'our dominant fiction' or 'ideological reality'" (15). According to Silverman, the Oedipus complex is "the primary vehicle of insertion" into the "ideological reality through which we 'ideally' live . . . the symbolic order . . . as the 'dominant fiction,'" a fiction that "solicits our faith above all else in the unity of the [paternal] family and the adequacy of the male subject." Only through affirming traditional masculinity is it possible to maintain collective belief and sustain the governing "reality" (2, 15–16). When psychic reality contradicts ideology, as it does in "The Death of Halpin Frayser," anxieties multiply, and individuals must resort to imagination and fantasy to sustain themselves within the signification system of the Symbolic. These irreconcilable versions of reality, however, remain unresolved at the level of the unconscious, playing out in dreams such as the two in Bierce's tale of the Frayser family.

Halpin Frayser's father is a southerner who, with his society, has "survived the wreck wrought by civil war" (SF 807). For many white southern men, who interpreted the North's challenge of their right to own slaves as a denial of their own liberty and rights as free men, the Civil War became a test of their manhood. Having failed this test by military defeat, they were emasculated in their own eyes, as well as in the eyes of others. Complicating matters for these men was the fact that, "[b]y the time the war ended, women in both the North and the South had taken on new roles and had, in certain ways, challenged some of the most sacred features of male authority" (Clinton and Silber 280).[5] Having failed in the father's role of protecting his family from northern aggression, the southern man came home to find that in his absence his wife had assumed responsibilities previously denied to her through his authority as the head of the household. In addition, the bitter experience of Reconstruction further compromised the authority of the South, which was made to feel subordinate and inferior to the North in moral, economic, and political power. Accordingly, the language of the period was gendered as failure continued to be equated with femininity. After the war, editorial cartoons commonly feminized their representations of southern men, most notoriously in their cross-dressed images of Jefferson Davis in his failed attempt to evade capture after the Confederates' final surrender.[6]

By describing Frayser's father as a southern politician during Reconstruction, Bierce reflects in him the entire region's identity crisis, a crisis of paternalism that has obvious gendered implications for its children. Bierce explains that "Frayser *père* was what no Southern man of means is not—a politician. His country, or rather his section and State, made demands upon his time and attention so extracting that to those of his family he was compelled to turn an ear partly deafened by the thunder of the political captains and the shouting, his own included" (SF 807). Despite the war, this father has somehow managed to save enough of his wealth to educate his children and maintain "a good position" in southern society, but as a member of the Old South's ruling class, he has not repledged his allegiance to the country as a whole. His wounded masculine pride has not healed, which indicates the continuation of a divided house, not only on a national level but on a familial level as well. His absence from his family and "partly deafened" ear regarding their concerns suggest repressed anxiety about his position in the House of the Father, as well as his own culpability in his youngest son's identity crisis. To suppress his insecurities, he must resort to fantasy, shouting frantically with others like him in the still privileged male realm of politics, to maintain the illusion of confidence in his power that the ingrained ideology requires.

The descriptive terms associated with Myron Bayne also imply the instability of masculine identity. By lineage he is on the maternal side of Frayser's family tree. As Frayser's great-grandfather, he is further distanced from the power associated with the Law of the Father by two generations. To complete his feminization, Bierce describes Bayne as having "in his lifetime been sufficiently affected [by the glimpses of the moon] to be a poet of no small Colonial distinction" (SF

807). A writer is automatically distanced from masculine power because of the association of the written word with absence in place of the presence inherent in its masculine counterpart of speech. Separated from cognition by its emphasis on the emotions rather than reason, poetry is a discourse that challenges identity. In *Revolution in Poetic Language,* Kristeva explains that poetry's attention to sounds and rhythms in language points to the Semiotic, pre-Oedipal element in signification out of which the Symbolic comes. As a result, it reactivates the Semiotic component within language, pointing to alterity or difference within the subject's identity and thereby putting the subject on trial.

Building on these implications, Bierce emphasizes Bayne's place in the chronology of American history not only by referring to him as "Colonial" twice but also, near the end of the story, by having the detective Jaralson align him with "the early years of the nation—more than a century ago" (SF 814). In this way, Bierce connects Bayne and his poetry with the country's infancy, a time in which the American colonists chafed against the paternal rule of England. The American Revolution, as Michael Kimmel argues, was a revolt of "the Sons of Liberty against Father England. . . . Just as black slaves were 'boys,' the colonists felt enslaved by the English father, infantilized, and thus emasculated." They resolved this tension through "a symbolic patricide," leaving themselves free to fashion their own notions of manhood which were far different from the genteel, aristocratic models of Europe. However, this patricide also entailed "significant costs, including the loneliness of the fatherless son and the burden of adult responsibilities." More than anything, American men feared "that the overthrown effeminate aristocracy would return to haunt them" (18, 19, 21).

As a "Colonial" poet, Bayne, through history, becomes tainted with Oedipal anxieties because of his link to the father country, which has been translated by the metaphors of the new nation into the simultaneously tyrannical and feminine (i.e., the terrible mother). The "ancestral 'poetical works' (printed at the family expense, and long ago withdrawn from an inhospitable market)" are still ostensibly a source of pride for the Fraysers, since it is rare that a family member is not a "proud possessor of a sumptuous copy" (SF 807). However, the family ambivalence is also clear, as manifested most obviously through the pun on the name "Bayne." Their pride in their ancestor's memory is "not specifically observed" but rather just "observable" (807). To maintain the fiction of family unity and male adequacy, the clan passively honors the dead man through displaying (and privately reading) his poetry. Simultaneously, however, they fear the unmanly influence of poetical aspirations on future generations of Frayser men, who have now put such boyish pleasures behind them in assuming "the wholesome vocation of politics." Thus, in contrast to the father, who can maintain the fiction of stable masculinity by cloaking himself in the rhetorical power of the Law as a politician, the great-grandfather, as a "famous Colonial bard," would be considered an especially dangerous role model for Frayser boys to emulate (807).

Halpin, in particular, is the repository of the gendered anxieties of the Frayser family. The young man with his "dreamy, indolent, and rather romantic" nature is "somewhat more addicted to literature than law, the profession to which he was bred." Believing in the power of heredity, as did Bierce, the extended family sees him as having inherited "the character of the late Myron Bayne." As Bierce explains, though they would never part with their copy of Bayne's poems, "there was an illogical indisposition to honor the great deceased in the person of his spiritual ancestor." As a result, "Halpin was pretty generally deprecated as an intellectual black sheep who was likely at any moment to disgrace the flock by bleating in meter." For, although "he has never been known to court the muse, . . . there was no knowing when the dormant faculty might wake and smite the lyre" (SF 807).

Frayser occupies an untenable psychic position in the family dynamics. Although, as Bierce observes, he "faithfully reproduced most of the mental and moral characteristics ascribed by history and family tradition" to his ancestor, "his succession to the gift and faculty divine was purely inferential." Beset by the male obligation to maintain the family fiction of stable masculine identity by entering the House of the Father, he "could not have written correctly a line of verse to save himself" and can only share his love of poetry in secret with his mother, while outwardly maintaining the Law (SF 807). Frayser is unable to reconcile his ideological reality, which demands rejection of the Semiotic as a condition of masculinity, with his psychic reality, where he oscillates between the Semiotic and the Symbolic. The anxiety caused by the resulting fragmentation of his psyche precipitates the identity crisis that ultimately results in his death. In the story, the trajectory of this tragic fate can be traced through his mother's dream and his own.

Transcending the laws of logic, the maternal and the poetic both embody the contradictions of life and death, being and non-being, good and evil that the Symbolic Order represses into the unconscious. Though denied access to the Symbolic and potentially disruptive to its norms, the mother is still its handmaiden in her higher role of functioning to maintain its ideology and the appearance of family unity. In supporting her son's affinity for the poetic and affiliation with her grandfather not only during Frayser's childhood but also beyond the point when he begins to train for the Law as his calling, she violates her higher maternal responsibilities. Further, without the presence of the father to guide and balance the construction of the son's identity in the Symbolic realm, her influence gains ascendance, and the psychic ramifications of this imbalance are intensified by the sexual relationship that develops between the mother-without-a-husband and the son-without-a-father. Katy Frasyer's unconscious guilt surfaces in her dream about her son's portrait.

The Freudian interpretation of this dream, described previously, is valid as far as it goes. However, other nuances are now obvious given the additional contextualization that has been presented. The links between Bayne and Frayser are now strengthened and complicated by their connection to language and cultural history. Further, the father's laughter at the mother's distress about the dream suggests his refusal to abandon his fantasy of family unity to recognize the tragic implications that may result from his son's identity conflict, a conflict to which he, as well as his wife, have contributed on levels that include but are not limited to the sexual. Halpin Frayser, having a "more logical mind" than his mother, believes that the dream "foreshadow[s] a more simple and immediate, if less tragic, disaster than a visit to the Pacific Coast" (SF 808). Although he seemingly has abandoned hope of avoiding a tragic fate, by leaving home he can at least ward off the immediate disintegration of his personality that the dream suggests through the strangled throat, representing his death as a speaking subject. Frayser's trip to California, as well as his mother's staying in Tennessee, reflect their "equally odd notions of duty." The son seeks through a change of environment to fulfill his responsibility to the Law, while "the other remain[s] at home in compliance with a wish that her husband was scarcely conscious of entertaining" (809). All, thus, continue their outward efforts to maintain the family fiction despite their inner turmoil.

The description of Frayser's trip to California and what ensues seems almost as far-fetched as his subsequent dream and the story's resolution, suggesting that the unconscious may be at play throughout and certainly eliminating the need to try to resolve all of the mysteries that arise. Bierce explains that Frayser, "walking one dark night along the water front of the city" of San Francisco was suddenly "'shanghaied' aboard a gallant, gallant ship, and sailed for a far country. Nor did his misfortunes end with the voyage; for the ship was cast ashore on an island of the South Pacific, and it was six years afterward when the survivors were taken off by a venturesome trading schooner and brought back to San Francisco" (SF 809). That Frayser is walking in the dark suggests he has not resolved his dilemma. A ship is symbolic of the life journey from birth to death; whereas the "shanghaiing" suggests the traumatic separation between mother and child that birth entails to make this journey possible, a separation that according to Lacan occurs too soon. "Shanghaiing" was a nineteenth-century practice of drugging and kidnapping men for compulsory service on ships sailing from San Francisco to China. That Frayser is being forced to assume an adventurous (manly) role points to his failure to resolve his masculine anxieties, while the double emphasis on the word "gallant" implies that perhaps both meanings of this word are relevant: to be unflinching in battle (i.e., unambiguously masculine) and to be an amorous, aristocratic young man courting a woman (i.e., an ambivalent, effete image of manhood). This double-play suggests he is still trying gallantly to resist the temptation to be a gallant. That he is shipwrecked in the process further foreshadows his failure to save himself from psychic destruction. Finally rescued from the desert island and returned to San Francisco, Frayser assumes the guise of the male hunter. However, this final attempt to carry on the fantasy of masculine stability fails when he "los[es] his bearings" (804). "[U]tterly bewildered," he falls asleep in the midst of a cemetery on a grave of, if not his own biological mother (presuming she has divorced or been widowed and then remarried a man named Larue), then at least the grave of (an)other (m)other, who embodies the same horrific duality of life and death that threatens him (805).

Frayser's dream, which is replete with the abject horror associated with the male gothic, reflects his unconscious torment and the resulting disintegration of his ego. Walking down "a dusty road that showed white in the gathering darkness of a summer night," he travels the road of life, knowing not where he is going or why, although "all seemed simple and natural." The "parting of the ways" to which he comes recreates the choice between right and wrong, good and evil, male and female, life and death that he first approached in childhood. This time, however, instead of taking the road to manhood, he chooses the "road less traveled." This road appears "long abandoned, because, he thought, it led to something evil; yet he turned into it without hesitation, impelled by some imperious necessity." Frayser, in his dream, turns from the "highway" of the Symbolic back into the previously "abandoned" road of the maternal, a realm that he now finds "haunted with invisible existences whom he could not definitely figure in his mind" and "incoherent whispers in a strange tongue which yet he partly understood." He can no longer understand the Semiotic maternal language from which he has been forever separated, and so he experiences it only as a threat to the integrity of his ego and an unconscious tracing of the Lacanian Real that harbors death. Thus, Frayser hears only "fragmentary utterances of a monstrous conspiracy against his body and soul" (SF 805).

Traveling on in "the interminable forest" of the mother, he comes upon a "shallow pool in the guttered depression of an old wheel rut." Plunging his hand into it he discovers, "it was blood! Blood, he then observed, was about him everywhere." Abject images of vaginal blood cover the forest "in blots and splashes." "Defiling the trunks of the trees," these images recall the separation of birth which, for the infant, is also a death that separates him from the perfect oneness with the mother that can only be experienced in the womb (SF 805). These images of horror awaken his guilt for the crime he fears he must have committed to cause not only this first separation but the later entry into language that completed his fall from the Edenic protection of the maternal. "Vainly he sought by tracing life backward in memory, to reproduce the moment of his sin, . . . but nowhere could he catch a glimpse of what he sought." In his dream, his inability to recapture this experience in his conscious mind augments his terror, causing him to feel "as one who has murdered in the dark, not knowing whom nor why" (806).[7]

Unable to function in this lost world and overcome by "audible and startling whispers and the sighs of creatures so obviously not of earth," Frayser decides to try to break the "malign spell that bound his faculties to silence and inaction." Terrified at what he has discovered in attempting to regain the innocence of the past, he endeavors now to return to the Symbolic by reclaiming his role of speaking self. And so he "shout[s] with full strength of his lungs." However, the power of the Semiotic fragments his voice "into an infinite multitude of unfamiliar sounds, . . . babbling and stammering away into the distant reaches of the forest" and then dying "into silence." In desperation, he determines to supplicate the maternal through the language of poetry, a language in which he himself has never written, although he has long been drawn to it through the psychical and historical bonds between himself, his mother, and his great-grandfather. Thus, he declares to himself, "'I will not submit unheard. There may be powers that are not malignant traveling this accursed road. I shall leave them a record and an appeal. I shall relate my wrongs, the persecutions that I endure—I, a helpless mortal, a penitent, an unoffending poet.'" However, as Bierce observes, "Frayser was a poet only as he was a penitent: in his dream" (SF 806). Thus, his attempt to mediate his situation by appealing to the benign element of the maternal power is doomed to failure because it is neither authentic nor consciously rendered.

Taking from the maternal realm of nature a twig dipped in its own blood, Frayser writes with frantic rapidity to appease the power that threatens to annihilate him; however, the maternal is not fooled. The poem that he writes is only a counterfeit modeled after his great-grandfather's poetry. Given the pressures under which he has long labored—both in his waking and now in his sleeping life—it is no wonder that he suffers from what Harold Bloom defines as "the [male] anxiety of influence." Overwhelmed by the influence of his great-grandfather's poetry, complicated by the influence of his other forebears not to write poetry at all, Frayser is unable to produce anything from his own imagination. Because the threads of his identity are fragmented and split rather than interwoven in the texture of a healthy interplay between the Semiotic and the Symbolic, he can create no poetic voice of his own and so can only mimic his great-grandfather's poetry.

Even as Frayser records his failure to find his own voice, he feels a strange sensation taking "possession of his body and mind" as the unearthly voice of the female, "a soulless, heartless, and unjoyous laugh," momentarily fills the air. His former fears now are "forgotten or merged in the gigantic power that now held him in thrall," the power of the Real that is death, a power that inevitably appears before him in the form of the walking, spiritless body of his own dead mother (SF 806). This image of the terrible, devouring mother stirs "no love nor longing in his heart" and comes "unattended with pleasant memories of a golden past." As Bierce explains, "all the finer emotions" are "swallowed up in fear," as the mother, "regarding him with the mindless malevolence of a wild brute" springs "upon him with appalling ferocity" (809). Released by this primal act, his body instinctively responds to hers in the terrific struggle that represents all of the contradictions and dualities he has long struggled and failed to balance. Feeling her "cold fingers close upon his throat," he is "[b]orne backward to the earth," and the conflicting discourses resolve themselves into final darkness and silence, as "Halpin Frayser dreamed that he was dead" (810).

The uncanny experience presented in Frayser's dream points to the destruction of his psyche as well as his material body, which is discovered the next day by two representatives of the Law, Holker, a deputy sheriff, and Jaralson, a detective. Finding the fragment of language that Frayser has left behind, they reorder the ambiguous gothic disorder of the narrative to provide a closure that conforms with their ideological reality. In the process, these men display their own anxieties. As Bierce explains, "[t]heir business was man-hunting," and by their bumbling and somewhat incredulous resolution of the possible crimes involved in Frayser's death, their masculinity is severely compromised (SF 810). In particular, Jaralson, who takes the lead in this "investigation," displays suspiciously feminine attributes. He is described as "something of a scholar," and his knowledge of Bayne's poetry, as well as his admission that he has a copy of "his collected works" suggest his affinity with the feminine despite his avowed dismissal of Bayne's poems as "mighty dismal stuff" (814).

Notably, when the two men discover Frayser's dead body, which Bierce describes in horrific detail, they are rendered speechless: "All this the two men observed without speaking—almost at a glance" (SF 813). They are momentarily stripped of language as they face the conscious impossibility of death and the Real. To recover his equilibrium, Holker invokes religious symbolism for psychic protection, exclaiming, "'Poor devil! He had a rough deal,'" For his part, Jaralson responds to the sight of the dead body by assuming a thoroughly masculine, and aroused, posture, "making a vigilant circumspection of the forest, his shotgun held in both hands and at full cock. . . ." Seemingly without again glancing at the body, he dismisses the unspeakable act that created the scene as "'[t]he work of a maniac,'" insisting without proof or further investigation that "'[i]t was done by Branscom—Pardee'" (813). Subsequently, Holker recalls that Branscom, the murderer they are hunting, was really named Larue rather than Pardee as he had previously claimed. Then, in addition to this already remarkable coincidence, he has another mental flash, a revelation that he appends with a religious invocation, "'And—bless my soul! How it all comes to me—the murdered woman's name had been Frayser!'" (815). The fact that the men cannot even name their suspect reliably—cannot name him into existence—suggests he may not truly exist or at least may not have any convincing relation to the grisly scene before them. However, they nevertheless close the case, impelled by their unease in the presence of the abject remnants of Frayser's lost struggle.

As they leave, however, "the sound of a laugh, a low, deliberate, soulless laugh" comes "to them out of the fog—seemingly from a great distance" and then dies back again to the silence from which it had grown (SF 815). The fiction these two men construct, like Bierce's tale itself, refuses closure through the interpretive gaps that remain unanswerable by logic and reason. Bierce's tale demonizes the male lack it exposes through the inassimilable figure of the mother, a figure of death that always threatens male subjectivity. However, Halpin Frayser's unconscious journey implies his desire to return to the womb not as a sexually motivated feature of the Oedipal crisis but rather as a desperate attempt to resolve longstanding psychic tensions created by the pressure to perpetuate the fiction of the dominant ideology. This ideology, which posits the unambiguous male subject, thwarts the oscillation between the Semiotic and Symbolic that is productive and necessary to produce a speaking subject. Through his use of the gothic mode, Bierce exposes the problem but seems unable to imagine the possibility of an alternate, multiplistic identity that would solve the human tragedy he depicts. Thus, Halpin Frayser finds peace only in death.

Bierce's affinity with the male gothic and the identity issues he raises in "The Death of Halpin Frayser" suggest possible links to his own life experience. The blood imagery and the dreamer's inability to "reproduce the moment of his sin" reverberate strikingly with the recollections of his own nightmares, which he published in the essay "Visions of the Night" four years prior to the story of the fictional Halpin Frayser. Particularly interesting is the motif of poetry that appears in both writings. In "Visions of the Night," Bierce states at one point, "The dreamer is your only true poet; he is 'of imagination compact,'" anticipating his later claim in the story that "Frayser was a poet only . . . in his dream" (CW 10: 123; SF 806). In the earlier text, Bierce also muses, "Who can so relate a dream that it shall seem one? No poet has so light a touch" (CW 10: 124). Adding to these suggestions that Bierce, like Frayser, may have been conflicted about his own concept of self, a condition aggravated, again like Frayser, by his own frustrated poetic aspirations, is the fact that Bierce always disclaimed he *was* a poet, despite his having written and published two volumes of poetry.[8] As Grenander (1995) observes,

> Bierce's poetry constituted only a fraction of his total output. He did not consider himself a poet, regarding the true poet as the "king of men," whose output was the "highest ripest, richest fruit" of all human endeavors. . . . Creation of poetry was its own reward, as he noted in "To a Dejected Poet," for the "sacred ministry of song" was "rapture." Bierce's disarmingly modest little verse, "Humility," indicates the place he assigned himself. It is noteworthy, however, that he turned to poetry in one of the last things he wrote, the uncollected "My Day of Life," composed in September, 1910. . . . (Introduction xvii)

In this poem, Bierce again connects questions of identity, life, and death to his dreams, claiming,

> And, O I've dreamed so many things!
> One hardly can unravel
> The tangled web of visionings. . . . (lines 16–18)

Now pondering death as a man at the end of his creative struggle, the answers to life that he seeks from his dreams still elude him: "They scamper each into its hole, / These dreams of my begetting" (lines 36–37).[9] Beset perhaps by the anxiety of influence that Bloom describes, Bierce wrote no poetry that has ever been considered exceptional, and it is especially ironic that "The Death of Halpin Frayser" was written at the end of his most prolific period of publication, at a time when he was beginning to experience the waning of his imaginative powers. This story, thus, can be read metaphorically as representing his own fear of death as a creative artist, an anxiety in which not only he himself is reflected but also the larger world in which he lived and struggled to define himself as a man who was not unambiguously masculine as ideology would have it but who rather experienced a full range of complex human emotions and responses.

Scared to Death: Tales of Terror from *In the Midst of Life*

In the midst of life we are in death.
—*Book of Common Prayer*

Although much evidence ties Bierce's personal life with his use of the gothic and macabre, conscious manipulation of his readers is also at work in tales such as "The Death of Halpin Frayser" and *The Parenticide Club.* In the words of Gary Hoppenstand, "Bierce knew that morbid tales depicting family violence was [*sic*] one among many types of exploitative journalism that attracted and held his readers' interest" (224). He also found this mode of writing conducive to his interest in joining the seemingly disparate modes of the realistic and the romantic. Whether inciting his readers' interest with bizarrely romantic scenes of familial violence, ghostly encounters, scientific phenomena, or ironic twists of fate, Bierce favored a realistic narrative style. The common factor that made it possible for him to join the two modes of realism and romance was the focus on death.

Adhering to Edgar Allan Poe's theory of the concentrated special effect, Bierce's gothic tales are economically structured and create atmosphere most effectively by emphasizing the psychological distress experienced by his protagonists as a result of their often irrational fears, rather than by focusing on the supernatural in the Old World European settings of crumbling castles and abbeys as was the common practice in the expansive gothic novels of earlier British writers. One of the reasons that Bierce's gothic tales have been undervalued is that because of their organization they typically require close reading to discern the interpretive ambiguities and innovations that underlie the surface plot.

The most successful stories, which often incorporate grim humor, are usually divided into subsections that are presented out of chronological order, requiring the reader to reconstruct the sequence of events and carefully consider the credibility of the incomplete and disconnected perspectives they present. "Often the sum of the fragmentary views argues for the presence of the supernatural"; however, careful readers realize that this argument is rarely conclusive (Thomson 63). Of Bierce's canon, "The Death of Halpin Frayser," though an extreme example, is far from unique in this regard. An examination of four representative tales from the "Civilians" section of Bierce's 1898 collection *In the Midst of Life: Tales of Soldiers and Civilians* confirms the author's affinity with such techniques and his preoccupation with death in probing the human response to fear.[1]

When it first appeared in the 14 July 1889 edition of the *Examiner,* "The Suitable Surroundings" carried the subtitle "Instruction by Example in the Art of Reading a Ghost Story." Although the tale can be read as an anti-ghost story, it is more "important for its exposé of reason as being not only fallible but also potentially lethal to its possessor" (Joshi, Berkove, and Schultz 682). Bierce subdivides the story into five sections, labeling them with titles to help the reader sort out their disordered sequence. Reminiscent of his depiction of his own nightmares in "Visions of the Night," the first section of the tale, which is called "The Night," stimulates the reader's appetite for what at first appears to be a typical ghost story. A young boy, who is lost and alone "near midnight," follows "a bridle path through a dense and dark forest" as he attempts to find his way home. At length he notices a mysterious light shining and then comes upon its source, a long abandoned house—which he recollects as being "[t]he old Breede house" (SF 677). Recalling the house's "evil reputation of being haunted" and his own hand in vandalizing it long ago, "[h]e half expected to be set upon by all the unworldly and bodiless malevolences whom he had outraged by assisting to break alike their windows and their peace" (677, 678). Nevertheless, he pauses to look in "the blank window space and saw a strange and terrifying sight,—the figure of a man seated in the center of the room, at a table upon which lay some loose sheets of paper." Although horrified at the sight of the man, whom the boy presumes to be dead, he stares with fascination, discerning that "[t]he face showed dead-yellow in the light of a single candle" and that the "eyes were fixed upon the blank window space with a stare . . . which seemed to the lad altogether soulless." However, as the sound of a screech-owl pierces the night air, the man jumps "to his feet, overturning the table and extinguishing the candle" (678). Terrified at what he interprets as a supernatural phenomenon, the boy turns and flees.

Through this introductory section, Bierce intrigues his rational readers, who know better than to believe in ghosts, to search through the rest of the tale to discern a logical explanation for what they have just read. In the second section, which is entitled "The Day Before," Bierce moves back in time to provide background information that creates a context for understanding what occurred in the first section. The man, who is now identified as Willard Marsh, accepts a challenge by a local journalist and short-story writer named Colston to risk experiencing "fear—at least a strong sense of the supernatural" by reading one of Colston's ghost stories "with his undivided attention" and "[i]n solitude—at night—by the light of a candle" (SF 679). Having now explained why and for what purpose Marsh came to be at the Breede house, Bierce closes this section and moves forward in section three to "The Day After." In this section, he describes the boy's return to the cabin with three men in the afternoon following his midnight visit. Entering the house, they find the dead body of a man, the overturned table and candle, and "some paper with writing on it" (681). Apologizing to the boy for doubting his story, one of the men picks up the manuscript and moves to the window to read it. Following—for once—chronologically, the next section of the tale, "The Manuscript," reproduces the contents of the manuscript, which purports to be Colston's suicide note rather than a ghost story. In this note, Colston explains that he has decided to fulfill a suicide pact that he had previously made with his friend Breede by killing himself on the fourth anniversary of Breede's suicide. In an appended postscript, he revises his plan to keep this note on his person to explain the circumstances of his own death and instead claims that he is entrusting it to Marsh as a means of explaining this man's death. The writer adds that his ghost will visit Marsh after midnight to ensure that he has read the manuscript as promised. The concluding section, entitled "From 'The Times,'" reproduces a newspaper account of Colston's commitment to a mental institution after he was observed making preparations to kill himself by cutting his throat with a razor blade.

It is possible, of course, that Marsh died of fright when the owl screeched and he jumped up to see the boy's pale "white face" thrust "forward into the illuminated opening" (SF 678). This solution to the puzzle, however, is not wholly satisfying at first since it seems an extreme reaction for a man who, as a self-described "plain business man," prides himself on his reasonableness (679). On the surface, however, the only other solution to the mystery of Marsh's death requires the reader to admit that supernatural forces were involved. Since, according to the manuscript, Colston has already once betrayed Breede by not following through on their suicide pact, perhaps Breede's ghost takes revenge on Marsh when Colston appears again to be betraying their agreement.

Upon careful consideration, however, it seems impossible to give the manuscript—or the suicide pact that it describes—much credence. On its face, the manuscript purports to be a factual document, but Colston has described it previously to Marsh as a piece of fiction, and—in the end—it appears more likely to be the fantastic ravings of an unstable mind. In contrast to the sensible Marsh—the reader's surrogate—both Breede and Colston evidence signs of mental instability through their elaborate plans of suicide. The coroner's inquest ruled Breede's death was the result of "temporary insanity" (SF 681). During his meeting with Marsh, Colston is described as overly excited, and he displays "a certain wildness of the eyes, an unusual pallor, a thickness and rapidity of speech," leading Marsh to conclude that the popular rumor that the author "ate opium" must be true (680). Perhaps proving, more than anything, Marsh's inclination to believe all "writers are a queer lot," the real question becomes how such a *reasonable* man as Marsh could have put himself in the hands of such an obviously unstable personality just to prove that Colston's accusations of the businessman's cowardice are unfounded. Thus, the true center of terror in this tale turns on the depiction of Colston's psychotic obsession and the failure of reason to outdistance its reach.

Although reason fails Marsh most tragically, all the characters in the story suffer from its limitations. M. E. Grenander argues that Colston loses his sanity when he becomes consumed with guilt over his friend Breede's suicide. During the four years since his friend's death, Colston, ostensibly "has been living a normal life 'destitute of adventure and action,' writing journalism and fiction (especially tragic tales and ghost stories), and has established a local reputation as a writer." As he himself admits, however, "his 'mental career has been lurid with experiences such as kill and damn,'" driving him eventually to believe "that he must expiate Breede's death by taking his own life" (*Ambrose Bierce* 142). For their part, the disbelieving men of reason who accompany the boy back to the cabin come to accept his incredulous account as truth when they find Marsh's corpse. Nevertheless, the boy's perceptions of what happened were *not* accurate, since he believed that Marsh was already dead when he sat in his chair and that it was his ghost that sprang up. Neither the youth nor the men ever consider the more likely possibility that the boy's own ghostly appearance had a hand in frightening to death a man who was already unnerved from reading the manuscript in such an eerie setting. Finally, in attempting to solve the mystery surrounding Marsh's death, readers are left doubting the efficacy of not only the characters' rationality but also their own. In repeatedly testing their sense of reason by both the action of the story and its representation, Bierce suggests that logic may have fatal limitations.

"The Man and the Snake" is a much more straightforward tale in which Bierce again depicts the potentially lethal infallibility of reason. First appearing in the 29 June 1890 *Examiner*, this story, although subdivided into four sections, is presented chronologically. Capitalizing on the late-nineteenth-century interest in the superstition that snakes had the power to charm humans, the tale opens as the protagonist Harker Brayton, who is described as a "man of thought," relaxes on his sofa by reading in "old Morryster's *Marvells of Science*" about the snake's power to hypnotize its victims with its eyes. Discounting the veracity of the claim, Brayton remarks to himself, "'The only marvel in the matter . . . is that the wise and learned in Morryster's day should have believed such nonsense as is rejected by most of even the ignorant in ours." As he lowers his book, his eyes are attracted by "two small points of light, apparently about an inch apart" in the darkness under his bed (SF 719). At first dismissing the sight with the rational explanation that it is just a reflection from the gas jet, he becomes increasingly preoccupied with it. Deciding that the points of light have "a greenish luster that he had not at first observed" and that they "might have moved a trifle . . . nearer," he eventually determines that he is staring at the eyes of "a large serpent" coiled under his bed (719–20). As the first section of the tale concludes, Brayton realizes that the snake's "horrible head, thrust flatly forth from the innermost coil and resting upon the outermost, was directed straight toward him, the definition of the wide, brutal jaw and the idiot-like forehead serving to show the direction of its malevolent gaze." Accompanied by this understanding, the eyes that meet his own now take on "a malign significance" (720).

At this point, Bierce interrupts the action of the story in section two to interject a lengthy explanation about Brayton's living accommodations. Having luxurious tastes, he has "accepted the hospitality of his friend, Dr. Druring, the distinguished scientist," to live in his home, which also includes a wing that serves as "a combination of laboratory, menagerie and museum." Druring's "scientific sympathies," the reader is told, are "distinctly reptilian," and he particularly prides himself on his "Snakery" (SF 720). In a pointed play on words, Bierce concludes this section of the tale by noting that, "[d]espite the Snakery and its uncanny associations, . . . Brayton found life at the Druring mansion very much to his mind" (720). Now provided with a logical explanation for why a snake might have found its way under Brayton's bed, the careful reader nevertheless begins to suspect the soundness of Brayton's judgment.

Picking up the narrative thread again in the third section, Bierce describes Brayton's initial response to the snake's presence as befitting a reasonable man in control of his faculties: "Beyond a smart shock of surprise and a shudder of mere loathing, Brayton was not greatly affected." Indicating that his thought processes are still functioning logically, the man first considers pulling the nearby bell cord to summon a servant. However, he stifles this inclination out of concern for being thought cowardly. By strongly disavowing the natural response of fear, Brayton suggests that this emotion is at least unconsciously present and hampering his ability to respond effectively to his situation. In the face of mortal danger, as Ernest Becker argues, the culturally induced "urge to heroism is natural, and to admit it honest" (4). To admit this urge, however, requires acknowledging the underlying fear of death, which Brayton is unable to do. Thus, he determines to resolve his situation alone since, he reassures himself, it is "incongruous" and "revolting, but absurd" rather than legitimately fear inspiring (SF 721).

Again attempting a rational response to his situation, Brayton at this point rises to his feet, preparing to back quietly away from the snake without disturbing it. Thinking out this sensible plan, he determines that, if the snake follows him, he can even grab a sword from a nearby rack of weapons to defend himself.

Arresting himself in mid-stride, however, he checks his retreat. Although he tells himself that he remains in place as a result of his desire to prove his courage, Brayton's subsequent physical inability to control the movement of his legs seems clearly related to his growing psychic distress. Just before he freezes in place, he has observed that the eyes of the snake are now burning "with a more pitiless malevolence than before" (SF 721). As Stuart C. Woodruff argues, "[f]rom this moment until his death . . . , Brayton gives an involuntary demonstration of the ancient belief he had just been ridiculing. He is hypnotized by the snake's 'pitiless malevolence' and his own irrational imagination" (145). Taking on "an ashy pallor," the man unaccountably inches toward the snake and then crashes to the floor (SF 722).

With striking detail, Bierce describes the distortion of sensory perceptions that confirms Brayton's psychic crisis:

> The man groaned; the snake made neither sound nor motion, but its eyes were two dazzling suns. The reptile itself was wholly concealed by them. They gave off enlarging rings of rich and vivid colors, which at their greatest expansion successively vanished like soap-bubbles; they seemed to approach his very face, and anon were an immeasurable distance away. He heard, somewhere the continuous throbbing of a great drum, with desultory bursts of far music, inconceivable sweet, like the tones of an æolian harp. (SF 722)

Brayton's hallucinations culminate in his conviction that the "vast serpent" is looking at him through "his dead mother's eyes," suggesting, as Cathy N. Davidson argues, that he "has incorporated the external world into his own increasingly paranoid psyche" (SF 722; Davidson 35). At the end of this section, although the snake has not moved, Brayton continues to edge forward, crawling himself on his belly like a snake. Bleeding from the broken nose and bruised lip he suffered in his fall, he froths at the mouth and shakes convulsively in psychosomatic reaction to his extreme mental and emotional distress.

In the tale's concluding section, Druring and his wife enter Brayton's room to investigate the cries they have heard coming from the chamber. In doing so, they discover Brayton dead on the floor with his head and legs partly under the bed. After drawing out and examining the body, Druring concludes that the man "[d]ied in a fit." Reaching under the bed again, however, he pulls out the creature that has so traumatized Brayton, which turns out to be merely a stuffed snake with "two shoe button eyes" (SF 723). Although the reader has increasingly doubted the reliability of the protagonist's perceptions, this final revelation still surprises, since the reader, like Druring, still seeks a rational explanation for Brayton's fate. To this point, the reader has anticipated that, although Brayton was clearly delusional from fear, his death—if it occurred—would be attributable to the snake's poisonous bite. No longer able to fall back on this conclusion, the reader nevertheless finds Druring's medical pronouncement unconvincing because it ignores all evidence pointing to the powers of the unconscious. As Davidson explains, Brayton's perceptions have been "almost totally governed by psychological projection" rather than external reality. Already susceptible to the suggestion of a reptilian threat as a result of his physical surroundings and reading material, Brayton projects his unconscious fears onto the harmless stuffed toy, ultimately becoming what he feared as he crawls toward "the object of his abhorred desires" (35). "The Man and the Snake," thus, once again forces the reader to consider the possible deadly implication of irrational fear.

"The Eyes of the Panther," originally published in the 17 October 1897 *Examiner,* was chosen by Bierce to conclude *In the Midst of Life.* Although it has attracted little critical attention, it is one of Bierce's most successful tales. Bierce divides the story into four sections, presenting them out of chronological order and beginning each with an enigmatic title to incite reader interest: "One Does Not Always Marry When Insane," "A Room May Be Too Narrow for Three though One Is Outside," "The Theory of the Defense," and "An Appeal to the Conscience of God." The tale opens with a man and a woman sitting on a bench in conversation about the woman's refusal to marry the man. Bierce's introductory description of this pair creates an immediate contrast that implies their incongruous natures. The man, Jenner Brading, is "middle-aged, slender, swarthy, with the expression of a poet and the complexion of a pirate," while the woman, Irene Marlowe, is "young, blonde, graceful, with something in her figure and movements suggesting the word 'lithe.'" The woman's foremost feature, however, is her arresting eyes. As the narrator explains, "They were gray-green, long and narrow, with an expression defying analysis. One could only know that they were disquieting. Cleopatra may have had such eyes" (SF 904).

During their conversation, Brading becomes increasingly agitated as he seeks to learn the reason behind the woman's decision. Adding to the reader's unease about Brading, which is first raised by his physical description, the man at one point rises, "standing before her with clenched hands," looking "as if he might attempt to learn by strangling her" (SF 905). In response to his insistent demands and threatening manner, Irene finally tells Brading that, although she loves him, she cannot marry him because she is "insane." Faced by her lover's disbelief at this assertion, she then clarifies her position by explaining that, although physicians would say she was insane, she herself might "prefer to call it a case of 'possession'" (906). At this point, Irene insists that Brading sit back down so that she can tell him her story. Rather than reproducing her story directly, however, the narrator-author concludes this section by explaining that he has decided "to substitute his own version for hers," justifying this decision by claiming it is "[i]n deference to the reader's possible prejudice against the artless method of an unpracticed historian" (906). This male narrator then proceeds to relay his "version" of Irene's story in the second section of the tale.

Although Davidson observes that "The Eyes of the Panther" is unusual because it is "one of the few Bierce stories in which a female character plays a substantial role," this distinction is largely negated by the fact that the male speaker silences the female to tell her story of life and death from his own perspective (76). Davidson interprets this "substitution" as a means to accentuate the tale's concern with presenting "the devastating dialectical extremes of late-nineteenth century 'natural' masculine versus feminine modes of behavior" (81). Although this reading is valid as far as it goes, Bierce's emphasis on death suggests that deeper psychoanalytic implications reside within the story.

The interior tale narrated in section two takes place in the single-room log cabin of a woodman pioneer, his wife, and their child. In typical fashion, Bierce opens this section *in medias res,* as an unnamed woman crouches on the floor in the dark, clasping a child to her breast. Accentuating the gothic surroundings, the narrator informs the reader that "[o]utside, a dense unbroken forest extended for many miles in every direction." He also injects mystery by advising that, although "no human eye could have discerned the woman and the child" in the darkness, "[y]et they were observed, narrowly, vigilantly, with never even a momentary slackening of attention; and that," he insists, "is the pivotal fact upon which this narrative turns" (SF 906). Without identifying the watching presence, he then moves back in time to explain how the woman came to be alone in the dark with her child. The reader learns that Charles Marlowe, the woman's husband, had departed that morning to go hunting after she had unsuccessfully sought to keep him at home by pleading, "'please don't go out to-day. I dreamed last night, O, such a dreadful thing! I cannot recollect it, but I'm almost sure it will come to pass if you go out'" (907).

When Marlowe fails to return that night, the woman eventually falls asleep as the candle burns down, and she dreams again. In this second dream, the woman sits "beside the cradle of a second child. The first one was dead. The father was dead. The home in the forest was lost and the dwelling in which she lived was unfamiliar." Looking beneath the blanket that covers the child, she finds "the face of a wild animal," the sight of which awakens her, "trembling in the darkness of her cabin in the wood." To reassure herself, she now checks on "the child that was not a dream," taking the sleeping baby in her arms. Raising her eyes, she discerns the eyes of a panther looking at her through the open window, and "in the dreadful tumult of her feelings as the situation disclosed itself to her understanding she somehow knew that the animal was standing on its hinter feet," upright in a position "[t]hat signified a malign interest" (SF 908). Sinking to the floor, she assumes the position in which the reader was first introduced to her at the beginning of this section. When Marlowe returns to the cabin late that evening, he hears "a sound as of stealthy footfalls and a rustling in the undergrowth of the forest," before finding his wife laughing maniacally as she crouches still "[c]owering on the floor" and "clasping his child," who is "dead—pressed to death in its mother's embrace" (909).[2]

In section three of the tale, Bierce returns to the couple on the bench, whose conversation clarifies that Charles Marlowe is Irene's father and that the dead infant is an older sibling rather than Irene. Irene's mother was pregnant when she inadvertently killed her first child, and she subsequently died herself when Irene was born three months later. It is only with this information that the reader is able to make the associations necessary to pierce the surface layer of the story. Taken at face value, Bierce engages the reader in pondering whether the panther in the story is real or merely imagined as a result of the characters' fears, but at a deeper level, he is also once again probing possible neurotic repercussions of the child's fear of death that is associated most intimately and originally with the mother. In this tale, the panther and the woman in the log cabin represent the longstanding notion of the duality of female nature. The black panther, in its associations with the feminine and the power of darkness, symbolizes the mother's power of death, which overcomes her powers as a source of life and nurture.

Although the dead baby is not specifically identified as male or female, Bierce implies it is male not only by the Biblical order of creation but also by his use of a male to relay what turns out to be this child's story rather than Irene's. By silencing Irene, the narrator-author reveals his own psychic trauma, rather than hers, through his explanation of the baby's death, allowing Irene then to pick up the narrative herself to explain the circumstances of her own subsequent birth. In this process, the narrator's death anxiety is represented by the dead baby's suffocation, which has its roots in what Otto Rank termed the birth trauma. Although Rank has been criticized for exaggerating this trauma in the physical sense, his thesis was central in developing an understanding of birth as a painful separation from the mother that creates the child's first experience of death, an experience that Becker, Gregory Zilboorg, and others argue creates a fear of annihilation and instinct for self-preservation that underlies all human experience.[3] Furthermore, as J. Harnik explains, the oral anxiety associated with "the danger of losing one's breath is a significant and familiar one to every human being from his earliest years." Although often sinking into the unconscious, respiratory fears "must still be present in the foreground of consciousness and must certainly at times be experienced with that subjective quality of feeling" regarded "as the earliest basis of the ego's fear of extinction, of being compelled to die, and therefore as an important component of the fear of death" (487). Bierce would have been particularly conscious of such fears, since from early adulthood, if not before, he suffered from severe asthma, a complex health condition that "has long been considered a 'psychosomatic' disorder from a clinical perspective" and that often co-occurs with anxiety disorders in youths and adults (Goodwin 51). Thus, his depiction of the baby's death by suffocation may have its deepest source in his own fear of a similar fate.

While the interior tale of the baby's suffocation points to the impetus behind the male author's death anxiety, Irene's explanation of her subsequent birth and her glittering eyes suggest that her refusal to marry is based on her belief that she is "possessed" by the same feminine duality that resulted in the deaths of both her older sibling and her mother. At the end of the third section, Irene terminates her conversation with Brading, rising from the bench and "gliding away among the trees toward her father's house." Brading, who catches a "brief glimpse of shining eyes," is at first "dazed and irresolute," but then rushes into the wood to save her from the panther he believes he has seen and which may be stalking her (SF 910). A moment later, however, no panther is visible as he reaches the open ground and sees her disappear into her father's door. In the action of the concluding section, which occurs years after this night, Jenner is awakened by a noise and gleaming eyes at his window. Firing at it in the dark, he is "[b]linded by the flash and stunned by the report," but he "nevertheless heard, or fancied that he heard, the wild, high scream of the panther" (911). Two or three other men join him in searching, although all but Brading are eventually frightened away at the possibility of finding a wounded panther. At length, however, Brading's "courage had its reward" as he finds "the body of his victim," which turns out to be not the panther but rather Irene (912).

In finding the courage to avenge himself on the lover, who in rejecting his affection has awakened traumatic memories of his own Oedipal project, Brading seeks to assert his independence from her and his associated death anxiety.[4] That his unconscious association of Irene with the dark powers of motherhood predated her jilting him is clear when, in listening to her speak, he recalls "the indefinable dread with which, despite their feline beauty, her eyes always affected him" (SF 906). Similarly, his ambivalent feelings are suggested when he remembers, "vaguely, that he had never altogether cared to take her hand" (909). Thus, although it is more subtle and sophisticated than the tales of *The Parenticide Club,* "The Eyes of the Panther" can be interpreted as yet another of Bierce's tales of parricide, reflecting the unconscious and primal nature of the fear of death in humanity. That Bierce's own life experience provided at least unconscious inspiration for this tale is suggested by his frequent use of this theme and by his own asthmatic history. In addition, he links himself both to Brading and to the narrator of the interior tale by inclination and profession. Brading—like Halpin Frayser—is an attorney who is described as having "the expression of a poet," and the male narrator, who silences Irene to substitute his own account of the panther/mother in section two, identifies himself as the story's "author" (905, 906). Through this seminal account, Bierce communicates the pre-Oedipal source of the death anxiety, while Brading's response reflects the later Oedipal implications of this inherent fear of annihilation. As a result, "The Eyes of the Panther" presents a compilation of central issues that surface repeatedly throughout Bierce's writings.

Originally published in the 7 December 1893 edition of *Town Topics* and then in the 13 September 1896 *Examiner* before appearing in *In the Midst of Life,* "The Damned Thing" is another apt example of Bierce's approach and concerns in his gothic tales. Just as he did in "The Eyes of the Panther," Bierce subdivides the tale into four sections, this time using titles that illustrate his penchant for morbid humor, while intriguing the reader to read the story to determine their meaning: "One Does Not Always Eat What Is on the Table," "What May Happen in a Field of Wild Oats," "A Man Though Naked May Be in Rags," and "An Explanation from the Tomb." The tale opens as a coroner sits reading by candlelight. Beside him, laying face up on a table, is the body of a dead man, the presence of which has been foreshadowed by the section title. The account book that occupies the coroner's attention has been found among the dead man's effects in his cabin, which is the site of the inquest into the man's death. Bierce withholds the dead man's name—Hugh Morgan—until near the end of this first section, and he does not disclose any information about the contents of the book until the fourth and final section of the story. Sitting in the same room with the coroner are seven other men who compose the jury for this proceeding. A young journalist and story writer named William Harker arrives to give testimony and advises that he has just posted to his newspaper his account describing the circumstances of Morgan's death, an account that he purports "'was not written as news, for it is incredible, but as fiction.'" Harker adds, however, that he will "'also swear . . . it is true'" (SF 858).

In the second section of the tale, the reader is taken back in time, as Harker reads his account of visiting Morgan both to "'shoot and fish'" and "'to study him and his odd, solitary way of life'" as a "'model for a character in fiction'" (SF 859). It is through the journalist's narrative that the reader learns of the seemingly supernatural elements of Morgan's death. Harker explains that while the two men were on a hunting excursion he helplessly watched as an invisible entity approached through the wild oats and flailed the terrified Morgan before departing as he had arrived with the same "'mysterious movement of the wild oats'" (861). That Morgan had previous familiarity with this creature is suggested both through his reference to it as "'That Damned Thing!'" and by his terrified response as it approaches. Before being attacked, Morgan fires "'both barrels at the agitated grain,'" and then flees. Harker himself is "'thrown violently to the ground by the impact of something unseen in the smoke'" of the rifle's discharge. With such carefully worded specific details, Bierce adds ambiguity to the tale, making it difficult to conclude if the natural or supernatural, fact or fiction, sanity or insanity, is at work in Harker's account.

Harker describes the creature's subsequent attack of Morgan with characteristic Biercian attention to realistic detail:

> "Before I could get upon my feet and recover my gun, which seemed to have been struck from my hands, I heard Morgan crying out as if in mortal agony, and mingling with his cries were such savage sounds as one hears from fighting dogs. Inexpressibly terrified,

> I struggled to my feet and looked in the direction of Morgan's retreat; and may Heaven in mercy spare me from another sight like that! At a distance of less than thirty years was my friend, down upon one knee, his head thrown back at a frightful angle, hatless, his long hair in disorder and his whole body in violent movement from side to side, backward and forward. His right arm was lifted and seemed to lack the hand—at least, I could see none. The other arm was invisible. At times, as my memory now reports this extraordinary scene, I could discern but a part of his body; it was as if he had been partly blotted out—I cannot otherwise express it—then a shifting of his position would bring it all into view again." (SF 860)

After what he describes as only a momentary irresolution, Harker rushes to Morgan's side, explaining that he "'had a vague belief that he was suffering from a fit, or some form of convulsion.'" Before he can reach his friend, however, "'[a]11 sounds had ceased,'" and he finds the man prostrate on the ground. The section ends abruptly with the writer's succinct confirmation of Morgan's fate: "'He was dead'" (SF 861). Coupled with the vivid description of the attack, this unadorned statement causes the reader to rethink what has transpired.

Section three returns the reader's attention to the present with a description of the dead man's body, which the coroner exposes for the jury to see, "altogether naked and showing to the candle-light a claylike yellow." Again, Bierce uses realistic descriptive detail to impress the reader with the violence that accompanied Morgan's fate. The body is described as having "broad maculations of bluish black, obviously caused by extravasated blood from contusions. The chest and sides looked as if they had been beaten with a bludgeon. There were dreadful lacerations; the skin was torn in strips in shreds." That the jury doubts the credibility of the witness is made clear when the foreman asks the coroner, "'What asylum did yer last witness escape from?'" (SF 861). Insulted by this response to his account, the witness is excused. As he prepares to leave, he notices the book that the coroner has previously perused as being Morgan's diary. The coroner, however, refuses to let him see it, ruling that "'[t]he book will cut no figure in this matter,'" since "'all the entries in it were made before the writer's death'" (862). Left to their own devices to make sense of this violent death, the jury of seven reasonable men ultimately delivers a verdict that ignores the eyewitness's story: "'We, the jury, do find that the remains come to their death at the hands of a mountain lion, but some of us thinks, all the same, they had fits'" (862).

Bierce has carefully prepared the reader for this verdict in the first section of the tale by describing the members of the jury as "men of the vicinity—farmers and woodsmen" (SF 857). Not surprisingly, they seek to find a common-sense, rational explanation that fits their practical experience and understanding of life and death. However, this explanation is subverted by the eyewitness testimony, assuming that account is to be deemed credible rather than just the ravings of an escaped mental patient or an imaginative tale by a writer of supernatural fiction. Although the smoke from Morgan's gun might have obscured Harker's view when he himself was struck down, it did not keep him from seeing his friend's subsequent attack. As a result, the men of the jury "hedge their bets" by conceding that another—less plausible but still rational—explanation may be that Morgan's death resulted from a physical condition that caused him to convulse prior to dying. Obviously, this concession provides a reasonable answer to questions raised by Harker's vivid description of Morgan's death, but it reopens other issues, such as Harker being struck down, the moving oats, the savage sounds, and the corpse's lacerated and torn flesh. Neither of these two views, then, satisfies the reader.

At this point, Bierce concludes the tale with a final section—"An Explanation from the Tomb"—which gives the dead man a voice by relaying the diary entries that document his prior experiences with the invisible presence and his struggle to make sense of this seemingly supernatural phenomenon. Ultimately, he concludes that, just as humans cannot hear sounds of ultrahigh frequencies, there must be some colors they cannot discern. "'I am not mad,'" he writes; "'there are colors that we cannot see. And God help me! the Damned Thing is of such a color!'" (SF 863). The coroner, as a man of science, dismisses this possible explanation and withholds the evidence so as not to "confuse the jury" (862). The reader, however is left to ponder all of these partial perspectives in trying to discern the story's import.

Having already found the jury's verdict unsatisfactory, the careful reader may next consider the credibility of Harker and his narrative. Through Harker's occupation as a journalist who also writes short stories, Bierce clearly suggests his affinity with this character. Like Bierce himself, Harker may have had to depend on his career as a journalist for financial stability, while yearning to dedicate himself more fully to writing imaginative fiction so that he might achieve recognition and respect as a literary artist. In this character, then, as Steven Dimeo argues, Bierce may be projecting some of the conflicts of his own artistic consciousness. Harker is drawn to Morgan, whom he considers a potential "model" for his fiction. However, he also describes Morgan as being withdrawn and solitary, and Morgan's diary entries illustrate his practical, empirical approach to problem solving. In seeking a rational explanation for "The Damned Thing," Morgan shows that he values reason and the intellect over imagination and the emotions. Viewed as the pragmatic, journalistic side of the writer's consciousness and the readership that fails to value his more literary aspirations, Morgan may have been "murdered" by Harker as a way to escape the invisibility that he associates with his anonymity as a writer by giving fuller reign to his creative nature. As Dimeo observes, the invisible being is indeed real in representing "the cause of Bierce's failure to be recognized for his art" (24). In this symbolic depiction of the destructive forces beyond human consciousness, Bierce thus aligns fear of death with the writer's fear of the invisibility associated with literary anonymity.

Frozen at first in terror at the sight of Morgan's battle with this invisible presence, Harker ultimately lashes out at this side of himself in an impassioned response to his inner turmoil. Rather than a fantastic tale of an external supernatural phenomenon, this story is perhaps best understood as a more complex representation of internal psychic conflict. The emotion that the moment of terror evokes in Harker is terrifying not because it suggests the possibility that invisible forces of evil exist in the external world but rather that the propensity for such violence hides within each human being. The question remains, however, as to why only Morgan dies. Both the invisible presence and the jury allow Harker to go free. Only with such a resolution, however, can Bierce maintain hope that the writer will fulfill his literary ambitions and not succumb to artistic oblivion.

Considered together, these four tales from *In the Midst of Life* exemplify Bierce's approach to the gothic in terms of both his artistic techniques and thematic interests. Combining the romantic preoccupations of the gothic with realistic narrative detail and often complex plot structures, he probes the fear of death that underlies the human response to life. Forcing the reader to consider a variety of different perspectives involving both natural and supernatural possibilities, he reveals the possible deadly influence of the unconscious that can result when the human psyche falls victim to irrational fear.

Doubling Death: Seeking the Immortal Self in Stories from *Can Such Things Be?*

All creatures born by our fantasy, in the last analysis, are nothing but ourselves.
—**Friedrich Schiller**

Not only in "The Damned Thing," but also in "Visions of the Night," "The Death of Halpin Frayser," and many other writings, Bierce uses a double motif to represent the fear of death associated with identity crisis. Dating back to classical mythology and drama, the literary construct of the double or *doppelgänger* (literally "double-goer" in German) has acquired archetype status through time. As a result, the motif can descend into stereotype and parody when used or interpreted superficially. However, an understanding of the psychological underpinnings of the double—in connection with the personal, social, and literary contexts that influenced Bierce—supports the view that he used the device both consciously and unconsciously to project not only his own but also his readers' ambivalent feelings about the human mind and death. Thus, in reading his doubles from a psychoanalytic perspective, we learn not only about Bierce but about ourselves as well.

The term *doppelgänger* originated with the German writer Jean Paul Richter, who applied it to his 1796 novel *Siebenkäs.* Unsurprisingly, the subsequent romantic movements in Germany, England, and the United States, with their interest in exploring the individual self, the psyche of the artist, and the duality of nature, resulted in the creation of an abundance of gothic literature that employed the *doppelgänger* device. Although use of the literary double peaked in the first half of the nineteenth century, the figure still populates literature and film to the present day. The continued presence of the figure as a symbol of the divided nature of the human mind supports the argument of Carl Jung that the modern human's main goal is individuation—to become whole or integrated as a personality.[1] Clearly, however, the problem of self-knowledge and the associated human search for mental and spiritual wholeness transcends time, as the entire history of philosophy, religion, and literature testifies.

Early human concern with fragmentation and division links to ideas about duplication and doubling, most obviously in the anthropological documentation of beliefs that twins are "magical, reflections awesome, shadows tabued, dreams portentous and, most significant of all, that the soul itself is portable" (Hallam 6). In his landmark comparative study of folklore, magic, and religion, anthropologist Sir James George Frazer observes, "If a man moves or lives, it can only be because he has a little man or animal inside who moves him. The animal inside the animal, the man inside the man, is the soul. . . . Hence if death be the permanent absence of the soul, the way to safeguard against it is either to prevent the soul from leaving the body, or, if it does depart, to ensure that it shall return" (207). The concept of the double thus results when the inner being escapes to exist separately from its "host" being, causing the untenable separation of body and soul, conscious and unconscious. As a result, the figure is fraught with ambivalent notions of good and evil, sacred and profane, mortality and immortality.

While the data of anthropology and folklore verified the universality and power of the double, our understanding of the phenomenon has been informed by psychoanalytic theory. Drawing from Freud's breakthrough in understanding the divided nature of the human personality and applying those ideas to anthropological evidence, Otto Rank pioneered an understanding of the associated psychoanalytic and literary implications in his study entitled *The Double,* and he subsequently extended these ideas as part of *Beyond Psychology,* which was first published two years after his death. Rank explains the double as an extension of the ancestral and universal belief in the immortal self, a belief that evolved from "the ancient belief in the soul, as derived from a naïve association between the duplication of the body in the shadow and the corresponding mythic attitude towards the sun" (Hallam 14). Although the inherent duality in the subject itself permits its literary "treatment in different forms, varying from the naïve comedy of errors enacted between identical twins to the tragic, almost pathological loss of one's real self through a superimposed one," Rank observes that the symbolism remains constant: "namely, the presentation of the second self by one's own shadow or reflection" (*Beyond Psychology* 70). Within this concept, he "sees the root of man's two endeavors to preserve his self and to maintain the belief in its immorality: religion and psychology" (74). Through this belief in the immortal soul, the human being was able gradually to develop a personality that seemed to have an essential totality. However, as Rank points out, modern literature presents the figure of the double not as a symbol of immortality but rather of death, anticipating the division of the personality into two opposing forces.

Responding, in part, to Rank's 1914 study, Freud published *The "Uncanny"* in 1919. In this essay, he argues that the psychological experience of the double, as well as its literary recreation, fall under the category of feelings that he defines as *unheimlich,* the German word for *uncanny.* As he explains, "the uncanny is that class of the frightening which leads us back to what is known of old and long familiar" that has been repressed from the conscious memory (220). Themes of uncanniness, according to Freud, are all concerned with the idea of the double and may appear in various manifestations (e.g., split or recurring characters, automatons, fantasies, illusions, dreams).

Bierce recorded his own experience with the uncanny phenomenon of the double in two essays. In one of the recurring nightmares that he describes in his 1887 essay "Visions of the Night," he recounts meeting a double of himself in the figure of an aged wraith. In this dream, Bierce enters a room to find a "dreadfully decomposed" corpse on a bed. Describing the body in horrific detail, he writes, "The ribs protruded from the leathern flesh; through the skin of the sunken belly could be seen the protuberances of the spine. The face was black and shriveled and the lips, drawn away from the yellow teeth, cursed it with a ghastly grin." Gazing down on this corpse, he meets himself, an experience that he describes to the reader as beyond his ability to express in language: "Imagine my horror how you can—no words of mine can assist the conception; the eyes were my own!" (CW 10: 130–31). Bierce, within his dream, creates a visual hallucination of his physical self, an event known as autoscopy. This psychological event of seeing himself aligns with the belief in some preliterate cultures that the wraith or demon visits someone just prior to death.

In the essay "That Ghost of Mine," published originally in 1878, Bierce recorded another doubling experience, one that may have had a more profound effect on him than his dream because it occurred in his waking rather than his sleeping life. As Bierce explains, while he was living in London during the early 1870s, he struck up a close friendship with Tom Hood, the editor of *Fun,* a periodical to which Bierce contributed. Presumably in jest on the last night they spent together at Hood's home, the two men made "the usual pledge" that whoever "died first should, if possible, communicate with, or appear to, the survivor." Soon thereafter, Hood's health "began to fail rapidly," and he died on 20 November 1874 (SS 132). One evening months later, Hood appeared to Bierce on the street near Leamington, where the writer was then living. In recalling the uncanny experience, Bierce writes:

> . . . I certainly was not taking thought of Tom Hood, or anything relating to him. A tall, dark man met me on the walk, his eyes fixed on mine with a familiar look of friendly recognition. It was Tom! It did not occur to me at the moment that he was dead, nor did I feel the

> faintest surprise at meeting him there, a hundred miles away from London. All seemed perfectly natural, and it was only when he had passed me without salutation, or even so much as seeming to see my outstretched hand, that I felt a sense of surprise. And it was only when in my surprise I turned about to recall him, and found myself utterly alone—the sole occupant of the street as far as I could see in either direction—it was only then that I remembered. (SS 132–33)

Bierce's approach in writing about the event is to relay just the "facts of [his] own experience," which he somewhat unconvincingly rationalizes by attributing the episode to synaesthesia, a psychological condition in which sensory phenomena usually experienced separately are joined together (SS 131).[2] In this case, Bierce concludes that the peculiar odor of nearby shrubbery, unrecognized at the time, has triggered his memory of the same scent from Hood's garden and somehow resulted in a visual hallucination of his dead friend's presence before him.

In a defensive action to separate himself from the conflict of his opposing selves, Bierce achieves dual representation indirectly through his identification with Hood, who stands in as a representation for the self and a reflection of Bierce's own narcissistic self-love. The apparition that appears to him in a mirror or manifest image of Bierce's dead friend represents the soul separated from its body. Since the soul not only is dangerously separated from the body but also refuses to recognize Bierce, the writer is thwarted from any opportunity to achieve integration or wholeness of the divided selves, which suggests the anxiety about his own mortality that Hood's death has aroused.

That this event troubled Bierce is clear from the fact that he is still struggling to explain it years later and openly admits that his conclusion does not entirely satisfy him. In describing Hood's death, Bierce writes that he arrived in time for a last interview with his dying friend and that he "saw him off" (SS 132). Paul Fatout, however, claims that the writer "arrived too late," adding that Bierce "was so moved by the death of the gay and friendly Tom that for some time he was unable to write a line" (111). If one or both of Fatout's claims are correct, the suggestion is that unresolved feelings of guilt and grief may have played a role in triggering Bierce's hallucination or misapprehension. Regardless, however, this episode, as well as his dream of the wraith, and the written records he made as an aid to rationalize his experiences of the irrational, suggest a possible impetus and model for his preoccupation with the double in his fiction. This does not mean though that Bierce was a neurotic. As Rank observes:

> Though both the artist and the neurotic are beset by similar conflicts, it does not mean much to explain the one type by the other. The irrational forces which are operating in both types are striving for some kind of rationalized, that is, accepted form of expression. The

> neurotic fails in that attempt inasmuch as his productions remain irrational, whereas the artist is able and permitted to present his creation in an acceptable form justifying the survival of the irrational in the midst of our over-rationalized civilization. (*Beyond Psychology* 77)

Recognizing the function of this literature, rather than just its often banal content, is crucial in appreciating the artist's accomplishment. "The artist's imaginative faculty is shown not so much in the invention of new motifs as in recapturing the true spirit of popular tradition to which his irrational self is sensitive." In giving the phenomena of the double "form, that is, rational expression, the artist enables the public to feel sufficiently removed from the irrational elements to dare vicariously to participate in them" (*Beyond Psychology* 77, 83).

Arguably, then, by using the double as a device in much of his fiction that deals with the theme of death, Bierce was helping himself and his readers safely to examine their fears about mortality and their quest to define the self in immortal terms. In spite of his pervasive use of this figure, however, he goes unmentioned in most studies of it. To date the only extensive analysis of Bierce's use of doubles in his fiction is an unpublished dissertation by Stephen Damian Nacco. This chapter will build on and respond to Nacco's work by examining several of the writer's stories of the supernatural that first appeared together in the 1893 collection *Can Such Things Be?* These stories, chosen as representative rather than unique examples from Bierce's literary canon, demonstrate the function of the double in both overt and latent manifestations.

As Nacco observes, Bierce uses his own encounter with Tom Hood's ghost as a model for "A Cold Greeting," a little-noticed and admittedly flimsy tale first published in 1888, ten years after "That Ghost of Mine." This story is narrated in the first-person by Benson Foley, a resident of San Francisco, who relays an account in which two men—James Conroy and an attorney by the name of Lawrence Barting—make a pledge like the one Bierce and Hood made. When Conroy sees Barting on the street a few weeks later, he is perturbed when the attorney rebuffs his greeting by merely bowing and then passing by. In complaining to Foley of this snub, however, Conroy learns that Barting had died a few days before the incident occurred. Still skeptical of having met Barting's ghost, Conroy tries to excuse his identification as faulty since the figure who passed him on the street was clean-shaven. Foley responds only, "'Doubtless it was another man'"; however, he has a photograph in his pocket from Barting's widow that confirms the lawyer shaved off his moustache a week before he died (SF 1164). In this story, written fourteen years after his own supernatural encounter, Bierce may be no closer to explaining his own experience, but he now achieves the psychic advantage of doubly displacing his unease onto fictional characters. In doing so, he illustrates Robert Rogers's contention that when an author portrays a protagonist as seeing a double—whether of himself or another figure—"it is not simply a device or gimmick calculated to arouse the reader's interest by virtue of the strangeness of the episode but is, in fact, a result of his sense of the division to which the human mind in conflict with itself is susceptible" (29).

Doubling in latent form is typically more intriguing than in the more obvious manifest representation because it allows for more ambiguity of effect. In the 1891 story "The Death of Halpin Frayser," for instance, the protagonist, conflicted by his incestual feelings for his mother, shares with her a mutual love for her grandfather, the Colonial poet Myron Bayne, who represents a latent double for Frayser, mirroring his own love of poetry and artistic sensibilities. Nacco argues that Bayne is Frayser's "ancestral double . . . as a permutation of the genes and shared heredity has resulted in the creation of a psychological or latent second self three generations removed from the original" (53). From his reading, Frayser is killed—it hardly matters how—and discovered in a posture of symbolic incest on his mother's grave because of "his own perceptions, his guilt, his aversions, his fears, his own morbid state of mind that he inherited from Bayne" and that have passed from successive generations to himself through his mother (54). Nacco bases this interpretation on an 1888 essay by Bierce, entitled "The Ancestral Bond," in which Bierce argues flatly that "a man is the sum of his ancestors; that his character, moral and intellectual, is determined before his birth" (CW 11: 328–29). In this piece, Bierce cites the work of Herbert Spencer as support for his deterministic views of human evolution. However, whereas Spencer regarded the inheritance of emotions and personality in a positive light, Bierce takes a negative stance, asserting that such a pattern of inherited traits makes humans incapable of rational thought during times of identity crisis, as he illustrates not only in "The Death of Halpin Frayser" but also in a host of other works where the threat of death is imminent. He even once went so far as to remark, "All emotions are primitive, and all human acts originate in emotional impulses" (qtd. in Neale 376).

Nevertheless, as Lawrence I. Berkove observes, it is probably going too far to label Bierce "a social Darwinist at any time of his life" (42). Essentially a skeptic, he was unable to reconcile reason and emotion, but also "unable to resign himself to the remorseless operation of nature's processes, and unwilling to extirpate from himself all sense of sympathy and compassion. . . . Thus, the desperate situations in which he places his protagonists represent, allegorically, the insoluble dilemmas with which he himself grappled" (50). In the best of his fiction, he explores the dilemmas posed by the duality of human nature, and how humans respond to the anxiety that results when faced with the imminent threat of death. In Frayser's case, his split and incomplete psyche was unable to endure such anxiety, resulting in a psychotic break that ended his life both figuratively and literally.

Although it would be an oversimplification to read all of his writings as molded by an attitude of pessimistic hopelessness about humanity, Bierce did distrust the human mind and was influenced by the thinking of Darwin and

Spencer. The 1899 tale "Moxon's Master" also references Spencer and situates itself "within important controversies of late-nineteenth-century science and philosophy," including the debate between determinism and voluntarism (Davidson 63). As this tale opens, a naïve narrator, who used to work as an apprentice for the inventor Moxon, visits his former employer and poses the question of whether machines are capable of thought. Moxon responds that man is a machine that "thinks he thinks" and then later quotes Spencer's definition of "Life" as "'a definite combination of heterogeneous changes, both simultaneous and successive, in correspondence with external coexistences and sequences'" (SF 929, 931). Working from his belief that a machine works rhythmically and so can develop consciousness and the power of thought, Moxon creates one of these "external coexistences" in an automaton that duplicates the powers of his own mind. In doing so, the inventor believes he has found a way to suppress the flaws of human beings. Ultimately, however, the machine shows itself to be only too human by emulating human example. Losing its temper after being defeated by Moxon in a game of chess, it turns on its master and kills the inventor in an emotional rage. Moxon, having recreated only his own inherently flawed mind, causes his own demise by presuming to rise above the inherent limitations of his powers of rationality.

Typically, however, the tale contains another level of interpretation. Standing outside the shop building in a thunderstorm, the narrator has observed the chess game between Moxon and his machine, as well as the subsequent murder. Apparently sparked by a lightning bolt, a fire begins in the shop during the murder, precluding the narrator from attempting to rescue the inventor and destroying all traces of the machine. The narrator, who regained consciousness in a hospital three days later, is now retelling the story many years afterwards and admits at the end that he is no longer sure his memory of the machine and what happened is true. Both the narrator and the reader then are left to wonder if the narrator might have created the tale in his own mind as a reflection of his own irrational fears.

In the 1888 tale "One of Twins," Bierce makes overt and conscious use of the *doppelgänger* motif but with latent complications that make the story much more complex than it appears on the surface. The first-person narrative voice in this story is Henry Stevens, one of a set of maternal or identical twins. To add a sense of verisimilitude, Bierce presents the story in the form of a letter that Henry has ostensibly written to a family friend, the psychologist Mortimer Barr, and that has recently been discovered among the late doctor's effects. In beginning the letter, Henry notes that he is responding to a query of the doctor: "You ask me if in my experience as one of a pair of twins I ever observed anything unaccountable by the natural laws with which we have acquaintance" (SF 631). Taking on the doctor's challenge, Henry proceeds to relay his own experience involving his twin brother John, an account that suggests the two men have, at least in some ways, a shared consciousness.

Approached one day on the street by a stranger, who invites him to dinner, Henry deduces that the man has mistaken him for his brother. Recalling similar situations of identity confusion from childhood, Henry accepts the invitation by responding to the stranger by name, later wondering, "But how had I known that this man's name was Margovan?" When Henry informs John of the invitation later, this suggestion of a shared consciousness with his twin or second self is reinforced when John acknowledges that he had just that morning felt driven by "some singular impulse" to ask Margovan for his address (SF 632).

The darker implications of the brothers' shared consciousness surface after John becomes engaged to Margovan's daughter Julia. One day, compelled by an inexplicable impulse, Henry follows "a handsome but somewhat dissipated-looking man," who meets a "beautiful young woman" in Union Square and then proceeds with her to a house of ill repute. Although neither of the two is known to Henry, he senses that the woman would recognize him "at a glance" (SF 632–33). A week later, when he meets Julia Margovan, he realizes she is the woman that he followed. When, outside of his brother's hearing, he confronts the woman with his knowledge by remarking, "'You, too, Miss Margovan, have a double,'" she replies that she will agree to whatever terms he names (633). To this apparent attempt to blackmail him for his silence, Henry assures Julia that his intensions are honorable and that, because of his love for his brother, she need fear nothing from him "'but such opposition to this marriage as [he] can try to justify on—other grounds'" (634).

Henry does not tell his brother his concerns, but the following evening, he becomes "oppressed with a horrible presentiment of evil" and "[t]he dread of some impending calamity." In an effort "to dispel the conception of a terrible future by substituting the memory of a painful past," he recollects the death of his parents and their graves. Unaccountably hearing a sharp cry that he identifies as the voice of his brother, he somehow instinctively finds himself driven from his house and down an "unfamiliar street" to the Margovan home (SF 634). There he discovers in one room the body of Julia, "hours dead by poison," and "in another John Stevens, bleeding from a pistol wound in the chest, inflicted by his own hand" (635).

Although Bierce does not make it clear whether Julia committed suicide or was murdered, the implication is that Henry's knowledge about Julia's infidelity has been shared psychically with his twin, prompting John to a tragic confrontation. From the trauma of watching his brother die from his wound, Henry apparently suffers from a psychosomatic illness from which he recovers six weeks later as a result of the treatment of the psychologist Barr and his wife. Unlike traditional manifest doubles, Henry thus survives the death of his other self, recovering from the traumatic experience "to function in society with no suggestion of becoming a fragmented personality. And in fact, quite the opposite occurs as Henry seems somewhat stronger—even fortified—by the death of his brother as if in death the consciousness of John had somehow completely merged with his own" (Nacco 64). The fragmented nature of his identity, clear in his comment early in the epistolary tale, "I speak of my brother John, but I am not at all sure that his name was not Henry and mine John," seemingly has been healed by the merging of selves that John's death enables (SF 631).

Nevertheless, the ambiguous coda to the story suggests to the reader (and presumably to the psychologist Barr as well) what Henry himself fails to comprehend—that he is still not free of his psychological dependence on his twin brother. This truth is also reflected in the title of the story, in which the "One" of "Twins" is just half of a larger whole. In the concluding event, now several years later, Henry sits in the moonlight at the same spot where he once witnessed "that fateful assignation" that resulted in his brother's death. As he does so, he recalls his painful memories with "that unaccountable perversity which prompts us to dwell upon thoughts of the most painful character," much the same as he did previously in recalling the death of his parents. As the dissipated man, now grown haggard and deranged, approaches "the shadow" in which Henry sits, the moonlight symbolically suggests the presence of the second self. Rising "[w]ith no defined purpose," Henry again responds not from his own consciousness but from that of his dead twin. Confronting the harbinger of his own death by coming "eye to eye with a ghost," a "look of unspeakable terror" crosses the face of the stranger who believes he confronts the apparition of John Stevens (SF 635). Striking his fist feebly at Henry's face, the man falls to the ground as Henry walks away. Henry concludes his account by remarking only, "Somebody found him there, stone-dead. Nothing more is known of him, not even his name. To know of a man that he is dead should be enough" (635). From this final encounter, Henry emerges unscathed, securing revenge on behalf of his brother without any physical violence. From a Freudian perspective, as Nacco notes, the suggestion is that John's passion, the id, has joined with Henry's sense of moral responsibility, or super ego, into a now collective consciousness or ego (Nacco 70–71).

Beyond this tidy resolution, however, lurk latent repercussions. When examined closely, the story also suggests that parental loss and the subsequent search for the lost parental figures have also played a role in the identity problems that Henry suffers, resulting in latent object doubling. While object doubling, or the doubling of a figure other than the subject self, is differentiated from subject doubling for purposes of discussion and analysis, it is important to keep in mind that the dynamics are still "ultimately subjective in origin (the split symbolizing the conflicting attitudes on the part of the perceiver rather than significant dualities in the object)" (Rogers 109). In considering this possibility, Henry's brief opening description of his childhood and his recollection of the memory of his parents' deaths, as well as his relationship with Mortimer Barr and his wife, offer clues to deciphering a fuller understanding of the psychological puzzle Bierce has created.

Within the story, Bierce places two prominent passages describing Henry's happy childhood with his family and his painful memory of his parents' deaths, events that occurred within a week of each other and that caused the family home to be "broken up" (SF 632). Henry's habit of dwelling on this tragic loss in times of stress suggests his unresolved grief. Further, his acknowledgement that the memories "all seemed vague and unreal, as having occurred ages ago and to another person," reflects his detachment from life and explains his inability to pursue a family for himself in the proactive manner of his more passionate twin brother (634).

Object doubles, according to Rogers, are most commonly parental figures, reflecting the subject self's ambivalent feelings for the parent, as well as attitudes of adult life that originated in childhood (110). As one form of compensation for his loss, Henry has turned to the psychologist Barr and his wife as surrogate parents. Henry recalls Barr's friendship as being "the only good fortune" that his family found when they moved to San Jose (SF 631). After the deaths of the parents, Barr arranges for the twins to find jobs in San Francisco, and it is he and his "saintly wife" who nurse Henry "back to life . . . in [their] own beautiful home" after the trauma of John's death (635). The Barrs seem to represent an idealistic model of good parents; however, the name "Barr" itself—as well as the sense of formality and remoteness that characterizes their relationship to the twins—suggest that something—their creation solely within Henry's mind perhaps—bars them from realizing the ideal relationship that Henry ascribes to them in his letter.

In opposition to the positive but unrealizable parental model of the Barrs, Henry also creates a negative parental model that reflects his anger at his parents, who abandoned him by dying, and especially at his father, whose insolvency forced Henry's separation from his twin brother. The "handsome but somewhat dissipated-looking man" doubles the insolvent natural father, while the beautiful but sinful Julia Morgovan, who Henry himself observes to "have a double," represents the bad mother. Bierce thus creates a "whore/madonna dichotomy of mother figures," with "Julia Margovan presenting the bad alternative to the 'saintly' Mrs. Barr" (Nacco 77).[3] While this second set of parents creates a Freudian subtext within the story that reflects an Oedipal fantasy with typically tragic repercussions, just as important in understanding the story are the opposing extremes of the two sets of surrogate parents.

When an author replicates complementary parent figures—one good and one bad—he or she often is expressing "ambivalent feelings, the conjunction of which (particularly when hostility is repressed) is so intolerable that the ambivalence is dealt with defensively by decomposing the loved and hated [parent] into two separate and seemingly unrelated persons" (Rogers 5). Since what is known of Bierce's life suggests just such ambivalent feelings about his parents, it is not unreasonable to think that he unconsciously may be displacing them in these parental object doubles. In killing the bad parents and the guilty id-twin under the cover of fiction, the adult-child strives to reintegrate his ego; however, the ending of the story suggests that he is far from successful in this endeavor.

Courage and Cowardice: Facing Death in Bierce's Early Civil War Writings

What like a bullet can undeceive!
—**Herman Melville**

A consideration of what is known of Bierce's life in the years immediately following his decision to leave home at the age of fifteen indicates that he, like Henry Stevens in "One of Twins," persisted in searching for parental role models that could validate his sense of self and help repair damage to his ego development. His continued inability to find emotional stability or a purpose to which he could devote himself arguably led him to enlist when the Civil War began and made him particularly vulnerable to the trauma to which he was exposed over the ensuing four years. It is important to contemplate significant facts about Bierce's life immediately before and during the war, placing those facts in psychological, historical, and cultural context to develop a base from which to study his writings of the early Civil War period. Such an approach makes it possible to discern what these writings reveal not only about Bierce's own experiences and attitudes in facing death but also about those of other Civil War soldiers as they moved from innocence to knowledge in their first tests of heroism on the battlefield.

Whether Bierce ran away from home in 1857 or moved from the family farm into nearby Warsaw with his parents' consent is not known, although the latter circumstance seems more likely.[1] Regardless, however, the move opened new vistas and opportunities for an isolated youth with no strong ties to family or friends. By taking a job as a printer's devil for the *Northern Indianian,* an abolitionist newspaper established in 1856, Bierce not only began laying the foundation for his future career as a journalist, but he also came under the influence of radical political activists, who doubtlessly stimulated his later commitment to the Union cause when the Civil War erupted. At the same time, in keeping with the theory that a history of unsatisfactory attachments can elicit a search for substitute attachments, he unconsciously sought new parental figures to provide the emotional support he failed to find, or at least to recognize, in his own parents.[2]

Upon his arrival in Warsaw, Bierce first fell under the authority of Reuben Williams, the editor of the *Northern Indianian.* A staunch Republican, Williams had established this newspaper with G. W. Fairbrother to counter the Democratic press as political opinion regarding slavery became increasingly polarized nationwide. Williams, who was widely respected in the community, served as Bierce's mentor in his apprenticeship on the newspaper, and he also became a surrogate father when the youth moved into his home and began eating with the Williams family. Although Bierce worked for Williams for approximately two years, the relationship seems to have ended poorly with Bierce's abrupt resignation when the editor falsely accused him of theft. According to Paul Fatout, who gleaned this account from an interview with Reuben Williams's son, L. H. Williams, Bierce "was soon cleared of the charge, [but] his fierce pride would not tolerate the insult, and he left in a huff" (33). This reaction speaks obviously to Bierce's lack of maturity, but it also shows the hostile, aggressive, antisocial pattern typical of an avoidant response to attachment insecurity.

Even while he was officially living under Williams's roof, Bierce evidently tested familial constraints in his search for emotional security and parental love. His long-time friend and publisher Walter Neale asserts that the writer told him of being about fifteen years of age when he met "[h]is first mistress, who was well past seventy" herself. Bierce, who claimed to have lived with this woman "surreptitiously," characterized the relationship as both passionate and sexually intimate (129–30). Such an attachment may seem incredible; however, as Fatout observes, "it is consistent with his lifelong search for a combination of romantic and maternal love" (32). This relationship, which clearly existed in Bierce's fantasy, if not in reality, confirms his continued inability to resolve his sense of maternal deprivation. It also strongly supports the view that his own life experiences underlie the trauma that he associates with the sexualized mother-son relationship in stories such as "The Death of Halpin Frayser," "The Eyes of the Panther," and "One of Twins."

Unwilling to return home to his parents when he lost his job at the newspaper, Bierce moved to Akron to live with his Uncle Lucius, and, in this flamboyant figure, he found another substitute father whose example created a lasting imprint. "In later years Bierce frankly admitted that he had modeled his career after that of his uncle" (McWilliams, *Ambrose Bierce* 24). Larger than life, Lucius was a longtime member of the Ohio militia, as well as a leader in a secret military society known variously as the Hunters and Chasers of the Eastern Frontier, the Patriots, and the Grand Eagles. He also served as a self-styled "General" over a force of adventurers whom he recruited in 1838 to invade Windsor, Ontario, to free the country from the presumed oppression of British rule. Although Lucius was prosecuted for violating American neutrality laws, the indictments were dropped because of popular sentiment, and he returned to Ohio to receive a hero's welcome. Shortly thereafter, he was elected to the first of four terms as mayor of Akron. Taking on the cause of abolition in the 1850s, Lucius was a zealous supporter of his neighbor John Brown, who openly advocated armed revolution as a necessary means to end slavery. When Brown left Akron, Lucius supplied him with a wagon full of arms and ammunition, as well as swords left over from the Windsor escapade that Brown would use in the massacre at Pottawatomie Creek in Kansas. When Brown was subsequently hanged on 2 December 1859 for the insurrection he led at the federal arsenal at Harpers Ferry, Lucius helped organize an evening rally to commemorate what he saw as Brown's heroic sacrifice for a just cause. At the event, Lucius called Brown "the first martyr in the 'irrepressible conflict' of liberty with slavery" and publicly admitted his complicity in Brown's Kansas work by remarking, "Thank God! I furnished him with arms—as did others in Akron—and right good use did he make of them; and today Freedom in Kansas is more indebted to John Brown of Ossawatomie than to all others" (qtd. in Knepper 26–27).[3]

Such heroic, if misguided, principles and actions no doubt helped to arouse Bierce's own growing political convictions and resolve, but by late 1859 he was already in Franklin Springs, Kentucky, where he had been enrolled by his uncle at the Kentucky Military Institute, one of the South's most prestigious military schools. "It was here, presumably, that Bierce acquired his characteristic military bearing and the useful skills of draftsmanship and cartography that would stand him in good stead in the years to come." Less than a year after entering, however, he returned to Indiana, where he, "perhaps clinically depressed, drifted without energy through a series of menial—not to say demeaning—jobs" until the outbreak of the Civil War finally gave him a collective cause to join (Morris 18). According to Franco Fornari, the group ideal of war becomes a love object that replaces the original, individual love object that is represented for the child by the mother (32). War, by this theory, may have provided Bierce with a necessary defense against the internal psychic anxiety associated with his early object-loss, enabling him to translate that anxiety into real external dangers so that he could control them by projecting onto the enemy the feelings of hatred and aggression originally directed against his mother.

At the same time, the Union cause conceivably provided Bierce with yet another surrogate attachment since, as John Bowlby claims, attachment, "although in many ways transformed, underlies many of our" relationships with "country, sovereign, or church" ("Growth of Independence" 558). When Abraham Lincoln called the nation to arms in April 1861, Bierce was the second man in Elkhart County to enlist. On 19 April, he signed the enlistment rolls of Company C of the Ninth Indiana Volunteers, and he reported to Indianapolis just a week later to begin training. After only a month of drill, the regiment was sent to the front in Virginia (now West Virginia). Motivated, as most of his young comrades were, by the naïve optimism and romantic patriotism that characterized the day, Bierce had no realistic conception of heroism, war, or the sacrifices they entailed. Certainly no one could have expected much from this seemingly unexceptional youth of eighteen. "His friends and neighbors knew him only as a solitary undemonstrative boy who preferred books to games and who showed few signs of ambition or ability" (Aaron 182). By all accounts, however, Bierce was "an excellent soldier. He was to become a veteran of some of the war's bloodiest campaigns, including personal participation in three of the war's ten costliest battles: Shiloh, Stones River, and Chickamauga" (Owens 9). Recognized repeatedly for bravery, Bierce was steadily promoted through the ranks and served with distinction as a topographical engineer until his discharge in early 1865 because of the lingering effects of a severe head wound he had received at Kennesaw Mountain, Georgia, in June 1864.

Under combat conditions of severe stress and crisis, soldiers develop strong attachments to their superior officers and comrades (Kirkpatrick 813). At the battle of Shiloh in April 1862, Bierce and the Ninth Regiment first fought under the command of Colonel William B. Hazen. In Hazen, who was promoted to brigadier general shortly after Shiloh, Bierce found his most influential father figure. As David M. Owens explains,

> No person was more singularly responsible for Bierce's professional military development. If overstating the importance of military service on Bierce's life would be difficult, then overstating the importance of Hazen on Bierce's military service would be equally so. The two were, in fact, kindred spirits, both stubborn and extremely opinionated and each a sincere admirer of the other. Moreover, if elements of Bierce's war stories as essential as historical context, setting, and theme reflect his soldierly growth, then one could reasonably expect that Brigadier General Hazen's imprint would surface in them. (15)

Twelve years older than Bierce, Hazen was a highly principled, focused soldier with many characteristics for which Bierce himself later would become known. In sharp contrast to the "poetic, idealistic cast of General Lucius Bierce," the somewhat misanthropic Hazen was "taciturn, grim, and adamant." Known as a strict disciplinarian, he was feared but respected by his men, and although a strong strategist and commander, "he was always falling into unfortunate quarrels." "His career was blotched by bad luck, his ugly disposition, and the jealousy of rivals" (McWilliams, *Ambrose Bierce* 48).

In the words of Bierce himself, Hazen was "a born fighter, an educated soldier, . . . the best hated man that I ever knew, and his very memory is a terror to every unworthy soul in the service. . . . He was aggressive, arrogant, tyrannical, honorable, truthful, courageous—a skillful soldier, a faithful friend and one of the most exasperating of men. Duty was his religion . . ." ("The Crime at Pickett's Mill" SS 39). Under Hazen's command, and through his example and influence, Bierce shed the callow idealism of youth and found within himself the heroic courage to sustain himself in the face of violent death. In doing so, he at least temporarily protected himself against the pain associated with his early sense of maternal deprivation and resulting attachment insecurity.

Ernest Becker calls heroism the central problem of human life "because it is based on organismic narcissism and on the child's need for self esteem as *the* condition for his life." In his words, "heroism is first and foremost a reflex of the terror of death. We admire most the courage to face death" (7, 11). Like Becker, Herman Feifel supports the view that most human behavior of consequence is a response to the problem of death. Some clinicians and investigators have even asserted that fear of, or anxiety about, death is a universal reaction from which no one is free.[4] Gregory Zilboorg describes this omnipresent fear as an expression of the instinct for self-preservation, which functions as a positive drive to maintain life and as a negative drive to master the dangers that threaten life (467). Because humans would be unable to function normally if they were constantly conscious of this fear, it must be repressed. At the conscious, intellectual level, we typically deny the fear of death entirely under normal circumstances. For many, religion also serves as a defense against this fear by supporting the notion of immortality. Life within society, however, is so replete with dangers that additional psychological measures are necessary to help humans overcome inner fears of mortality. To maintain the conviction that we are stronger than such dangers, we must each believe that we are exceptions whom death will exempt from its grasp. Thus, we sometimes court death in dangerous sports to prove we are fearless, assuming a challenging, "Death cannot get *me*," bravado. "So strong is this propensity in us that we elevate it to the height of great virtue; we hold a 'physical coward' in contempt, and the physical coward is normally ashamed to admit that he is afraid to die" (Zilboorg 468).

In this denial process, as Becker explains, society functions as a vehicle for earthly heroism, a codified hero-system to sustain and drive humans when defused, unconscious anxiety of death is transformed into objectified fear that threatens the human psyche's normal defenses (4–5).[5] While the specific script for heroic behavior varies by culture, each cultural system determines roles for performances of various degrees of heroism, and serving the hero-system enables people to earn a feeling of primary value and usefulness to creation. The human urge to heroism is not always ennobling; however, humans are capable of the highest generosity and self-sacrifice if they believe what they are doing is truly heroic, timeless, and supremely meaningful. When these conditions do not exist, however, a crisis in heroism results that can have devastating effects not only for the individual but for society as well.

In the event of war within a civilized society, fear of death undergoes a crucial change. "The civilian may still utilize the mechanism that makes him feel that he is an exception. Now he becomes a real exception, in that he does not wear a uniform and is not exposed to the fatal contingencies of war." Although his sense of his own exceptionalism increases as he gains a clearer emotional realization of the dangers of war through the loss of loved ones in battle, he "begins to wrestle with an unconscious sense of guilt about those who have fallen," which he represses "with a mounting sense of anger and feeling of hatred for the enemy who kills" (Zilboorg 471). The active combatant, for his part, is motivated by the dynamics of the culture's hero-system to fulfill a role that requires that he repeatedly face the threat of violent death or dismemberment with courage, but his belief in his own exceptionalism can be severely compromised in such dangerous circumstances. As he becomes "seasoned" through participation in battle, anger over the death of comrades can enable the soldier to maintain high morale under seemingly impossible conditions by converting his fear to hatred and aggression; however, individual psychic crisis can occur if the soldier lacks sufficient training, if he does not trust his superiors or understand their overall strategies and tactics as they apply to him, or if he fails to remain convinced of the just cause for which he fights, kills, and risks his own life. Negative effects can also permeate the fabric of society if the community becomes disillusioned about the necessity and meaningfulness of the cause or the material and human costs entailed.

More than 620,000 soldiers died in the U.S. Civil War, a loss of American lives that historian James M. McPherson asserts "was as great as in all of the nation's other wars combined through Vietnam" (*Battle Cry of Freedom* 854). The Civil War "remains the nation's most costly conflict in terms of casualties and physical destructiveness. It ended slavery, created a new national identity, and set America on the road to industrial domination of the western world" (Lundberg 374). Nevertheless, it also has been condemned as an unjust conflict, the result of the North's determination to expand and eventually dominate the continent and fueled more by its apocalyptic judgment against the South than by its devotion to Union or the cause of abolition.[6] In the face of such previously unimaginable carnage, and magnified by the fratricidal nature of the conflict itself, existing models for interpreting heroism and the meaning of death were severely tested. In resolving the crisis of meaning involved with the mass death experienced during the Civil War, "images of sacrifice, heroism, and glory were not abandoned by most, but the American imagination had yet to develop ways of satisfactorily mythologizing persons and events connected with [modern] warfare" (Linenthal 75).

It took time to adjust to this new type of war, which was fought on such an enlarged and costly scale. Traditional notions of heroism had to be modified as part of this adjustment because romantic images of chivalric splendor and hand-to-hand combat could no longer be sustained as advances in weaponry increasingly distanced the soldier from his foe, while exponentially multiplying the number of casualties. The new art form of photography increased the tension during this transition, as grimly naturalistic scenes of human destruction for the first time were recorded and disseminated to the public. "Images of mass death brought images of mass heroism." The heroic soldier now became "one who stoically accepted his duty and endured the horrors of war. The common soldier, often before seen as a crusader, was" increasingly "seen as a man of discipline 'doing his job'" (Linenthal 75–76).

Bierce's Civil War experiences and writings reflect not only his own psychic conflict but also the related national crisis in sensibilities, marking the transition between concepts of the heroic. Critics and scholars have long struggled to reconcile the writer's views on war. John R. Brazil, for instance, claims that Bierce's war experiences "constricted his perception to the vicious in life" (226). The writer's own brother Albert blamed the head wound that Bierce received for his later misanthropic outlook and bitter, suspicious nature (Grattan 17). Nevertheless, despite the undeniable sense of horror and revulsion that permeates the mature Bierce's understanding of war, he was also exhilarated by it, and, as his memoirs attest, he himself was puzzled by his ambivalence. As Eric Solomon explains, "Bierce enjoyed the test of combat, the companionship and the excitement of war, [but] he was revolted, intellectually, by the harsh brutalities of a repellent, paradoxical world" (150).

Bierce continuously subverts romantic stereotypes of war in his stories; however, according to Giorgio Mariani, he "does not try to expose the world of war as a cultural and historical reality . . . which could be called into question by a different value-system" (222). Pondering Bierce's lifelong preoccupation with the war, Lawrence I. Berkove surmises that the writer "was endlessly obsessed with war because he was involved in life, and to him life was war, and conflict of some kind a truer and more natural state than peace" (37). Notions of heroism evolve to support the cultural hero-system, but the logic of war remains the only conceivable reality. "Every generation must have its war; that is a law of nature," Bierce insists in a column that appeared in the 23 January 1886 *Wasp* (qtd. in Blume, *Ambrose Bierce's Civilians and Soldiers* 65). Mariani and Berkove focus on the cultural implications of such a reality; however, in Bierce's case, war can be seen to have served both a personal and cultural necessity by providing a sanctioned and controllable object for internal aggression. Joanna Montgomery Byles explains that "[w]ar is a collective phenomenon that mobilizes . . . anxieties and allows . . . original sadistic fantasies of destructive omnipotence to be reactivated and projected onto 'the enemy'" (210). As he fought in the Civil War as a Union soldier, the Confederate "enemy" provided external stability for Bierce's sense of identity and inner control. Because he needed this defense to keep his conflicted self together, he grew so outwardly cynical after the war that he was often accused of misanthropy, evidencing behavior that might best—and perhaps most simply—be interpreted as his inventing an enemy when one was no longer readily available. Such matters, of course, are rarely so simple, and thus, in the end, labeling Bierce as a misanthrope is unjust, denying the complex psychic pressures that drove him to respond as he did.

Many critics have observed a strong link between Bierce's Civil War fiction and his own military career.[7] When arranged chronologically according to the time of the action depicted and then plotted by location, these stories yield "a reasonably accurate chart of Bierce's own progress through the war" (Owens 4). Ordered in this sequence, the early stories tend to feature the common, inexperienced soldier, while the later stories more often reflect upon the duties and conflicts of officers. The reading of these stories can also be supplemented and informed by considering the short memoirs or, as he called them, "bits of autobiography" that Bierce wrote about the war. This does not mean, however, that the stories can or should be read as autobiography. As David M. Owens explains, "Although Bierce was always faithful to the larger historical context of the war, he makes frequent modifications to the actual geography of the settings" and to the events and personalities that inhabit them (6).

Significantly, the forested landscape of the early stories is often described in dreamland imagery of enchantment, but the effect of the action serves to shatter the illusion and expose the nightmare realities of war, reflecting the movement from innocence to knowledge that Bierce himself experienced. "A Tough Tussle," for instance, is set during an autumn evening in 1861, as a picket guard sits "alone in the heart of a forest in western Virginia" at "the fork of an old woodrock" in "the Cheat Mountain country" (SF 619). Anticipating the forked path imagery of choice in "The Death of Halpin Frayser," this story, which was first published in 1888, features Second Lieutenant Brainerd Byring as its protagonist. Byring, at this point in the war, is "young and comparatively inexperienced . . . in the business of killing his fellow-men." Much like Bierce, "[h]e had enlisted in the very first days of the war as a private, with no military knowledge whatever" and had been promoted to sergeant and then to second lieutenant because "of his education and engaging manner," as well as because of the "lucky" death of his captain in battle. Although he finds "[t]he exhilaration of battle . . . agreeable," war is still a romantic, abstract concept characterized by "gallantry" rather than tragedy (620).

Because he has not received adequate training to prepare himself for the realities of war, Byring's bravery, which Bierce calls into question through overemphasis, is untested. Further compromising Byring's ability to withstand the pressures of war and the threat of his own mortality is the fact that his unconscious defenses against death already seem compromised. Although ostensibly a "brave and efficient officer," Byring has an irrational "horror" of dead bodies. As the narrator explains, "What others have respected as the dignity of death had to [Byring] no existence—was altogether unthinkable. Death was a thing to be hated. It was not picturesque, it had no tender and solemn side—a dismal thing, hideous in all its manifestations and suggestions" (SF 620). Historian Gerald F. Linderman explains that, during the Civil War, "[f]ear was not a feeling to be shared but a weakness to be stifled. Ordinarily no one spoke of fear" (23). Because Byring's fears contradict society's views of death at this early stage of the war, he feels compelled to hide his "reasonless antipathy" to protect his reputation as a man of courage upon which his self-esteem depends (SF 620).

Feeling "very comfortable," Byring begins his watch "with senses all alert," but the intensity of his concentration gradually awakens his fears. Using gothic imagery strikingly reminiscent of his own nightmares in "Visions of the Night," Bierce reflects Byring's growing uneasiness in the soldier's perceptions of his surroundings: "From the vast, invisible ocean of moonlight overhead fell, here and there, a slender, broken stream that seemed to plash against the intercepting branches and trickle to earth, forming small white pools among the clumps of laurel. But these leaks were few and served only to accentuate the blackness of his environment, which his imagination found it easy to people with all manner of unfamiliar shapes, menacing, uncanny, or merely grotesque." As Byring's anxiety in the darkness grows, "[t]he very silence" acquires "another quality than the silence of the day. And it is full of half-heard whispers—whispers that startle—ghosts of sounds long dead" and "living sounds, too, such as are never heard under other conditions" (SF 620). Eventually his fears escalate to the point that he forgets "the nature of his connection with the visible and audible aspects and phases of the night," as his universe becomes "one primeval mystery of darkness, without form and void, himself the sole, dumb questioner of its eternal secret" (621). It is at this point that Byring realizes he is sitting next to the corpse of a Confederate soldier, creating a phobic reaction in which his free-floating anxiety becomes objectified by what is really only one aspect of the general cause of his distress.

Byring's physical and emotional isolation from his comrades further compromises his ego defenses, decreasing his ability to repress or control his fears. He previously has placed his subordinates at some distance from himself, and his state of distress makes him oblivious to the comfort even this distanced presence might provide. As a result, the defense of exceptionalism is not readily available to him. He cannot effectively protect himself through what Becker terms "[n]atural narcissism," the feeling that the person *next* to him will die rather than himself (133). Further, as the officer in charge of the picket, he is required by the culture's hero-system to provide a model of courage for his subordinates. According to McPherson, a Civil War officer was unable to gain the respect of his men "unless he demonstrated a willingness to do everything he asked his men to do" (*For Cause and Comrades* 58). Because the "cultural values of Victorian America held each individual rather than society mainly responsible for that individual's achievements or failures," a soldier's personal courage was what counted most in defining his character and so was the ultimate test of leadership (61). Although he is tempted to leave his post, Byring's obligations to this code of conduct prevent him from alleviating his anxiety by repositioning himself. He remembers that "he had told his men in front and the officer in the rear who was to relieve him that he could at any time be found at that spot." More to the point, Byring recognizes that his situation is a "matter of pride, too." As the narrator explains, "If he abandoned his post he feared they would think he feared the corpse. He was no coward and he was unwilling to incur anybody's ridicule" (SF 622).

Bound by the dictates of the hero-system, Byring remains at his post, where his terror continues to increase beyond manageable limits. Eventually, as all of his defenses fail, he can "no longer conceal from himself the horrible fact of his cowardice." By this point he has become so frightened that he cannot run or "even cry out." In a psychic break that Bierce associates with shattering "the spell of that enchanted man" of romance and releasing Byring's "modern manhood," the soldier, who now imagines that the corpse has moved, leaps forward, "hot-hearted for action," as shots ring out from the front (SF 623). The next morning, Byring is found dead from his own sword as a result of his "'tough tussle'" with the corpse, destroyed by his inability to reconcile romantic notions of war and death with his own experience and fears (624). As Stuart C. Woodruff observes in an early interpretation, "All of the actions and images of the story point to a man driven inward upon his imperfect mental resources, undone by a fatal imbalance which causes him to react in a manner contrary to what he knows he should believe and do" (142). Unable to rationalize his fears, he succumbs to them.[8]

In the fictional account of Byring, Bierce depicts "an elemental and near-universal concern on a first-time combatant's mind: his reaction to the sight of suffering and death" (Owens 26). With only a few weeks of training to prepare them for battle, raw recruits at the beginning of the Civil War typically arrived at the front young and naïve. Though suffused with patriotic notions of cause and courage that made them outwardly eager to "join the fray" and "see the elephant," they inwardly nursed apprehensions about how they might react to their first true test on the battlefield. That these concerns were also Bierce's seems clear from his 1909 memoir "On a Mountain," which describes his early war experiences in "Cheat Mountain country," a region that he recalls "through the haze of near half a century" as "a veritable realm of enchantment" (SS 6–7).

While waiting here for the war to begin in earnest, Bierce and his fellow soldiers spent most of their time "hunting and idling," although they "had a bit of war now and again. There was an occasional 'affair of outposts'; sometimes a hazardous scout into the enemy's country, ordered," he feared, "more to keep up the appearance of doing something than with a hope of accomplishing a military result" (SS 9). With a jaunty air, Bierce recaptures their cocky assurance of their own exceptionalism, which protects them against their fear of death: "We had been in action, too; had shot off a Confederate leg at Philippi, 'the first battle of the war,' and had lost as many as a dozen men at Laurel Hill and Carrick's Ford, whither the enemy had fled in trying, Heaven knows why, to get away from us" (7). The struggle to repress anxiety, however, can be detected in the description of one minor skirmish, after which they were forced to return to their own camp, "leaving [their] dead—not many." Among the dead left behind, Bierce recalls "a chap belonging to [his] company, named Abbott" (8). Death at this point, when it occurred, was still individual and exceptional.

"How romantic it all was," Bierce reminisces, and "[t]hen there was the 'spice of danger'" (SS 9). This idealistic recollection ends, however, with the destruction of such romantic notions of war when he and his comrades come face to face with a different view of death. During a halt in their march down from the "eyrie" of Cheat Mountain, Bierce and his comrades come across "something—some things—lying by the wayside." In describing what occurred next, Bierce writes, " . . . we examined them, curiously lifting the blankets from their yellow-clay faces. How repulsive they looked with their blood-smears, their blank staring eyes, their teeth uncovered by contraction of the lips! The frost had begun already to whiten their deranged clothing. We were as patriotic as ever, but we did not wish to be that way" (9). Having lost their unrealistic visions of war through this confrontation, the men, who pass by the same spot again the following day, are now described as "a beaten, dispirited and exhausted force, feeble from fatigue and savage from defeat." Like the fictional Byring in "A Tough Tussle," some of the men are unnerved in finding that the "bodies had altered their position." Further, they find that "[t]heir expression, too, had an added blankness—they had no faces." The mystery of this gruesome scene, unlike the unresolved mystery of Byring's "tussle," is determined when the men find "a heard of galloping swine," which they execute for have eaten the fallen soldiers and destroyed their own innocence in the face of death (10). These soldiers, in meeting their horrific fate, have been transformed into an anonymous heap of corpses, stripped both of human dignity and their individual identities. Despite one's patriotism and belief in the Union cause, whose euphoria would not be dampened by confronting the possibility of such a fate for oneself? From this point forward, Bierce's reactions to war were marked by the ambivalence that accompanies his increasingly realistic understanding of the sacrifices and costs it entails.

The march down from Cheat Mountain helped to prepare Bierce for facing the mass death and destruction that occurred at Shiloh Church, where he fought on the second day of the battle waged on 6 and 7 April 1862. According to Joseph Allan Frank and George A. Reaves, "More were killed and wounded in the two days at Shiloh, than were lost in the entire Revolutionary War, the

War of 1812, and the Mexican War combined" (87). Bierce's regiment, the Ninth Indiana, which did not reach the location of the battle at Pittsburg Landing, Tennessee, until the evening of 6 April, "suffered the highest casualties of any on the Union Side" (Loyd 7). Like Bierce, most soldiers at Shiloh were volunteers who initially had signed on for only ninety days of service. As volunteers who retained a civilian outlook despite their military training, "[t]hey continued to envision their commitment to fight in the light of a mutually agreed contract between community and soldier. They were responding to a national emergency, which they believed would last only a few months" (Frank and Reaves 23–24). This first major battle in the western theater of the war brought a shocking realization by soldiers and civilians alike that the war would not end quickly. This realization, which was reinforced by subsequent battles such as Stones River and Chickamauga, forced the reevaluation of attitudes toward the war and related cultural concepts of courage and cowardice.

"What I Saw of Shiloh" is the longest and first published of Bierce's Civil War memoirs. Originally published in the April and May 1874 issue of the *London Sketch-Book*, this account is purposefully limited to his own range of vision, as emphasized in the title.[9] In it, Bierce captures the unremitting intensity of the combat at Shiloh, as well as the ambivalent emotions and tragic costs such combat elicits. As a preface to his recollection, Bierce defines his audience, as well as his relationship to that audience. "This is a simple story of a battle," he writes, "such a tale as may be told by a soldier who is no writer to a reader who is no soldier" (SS 11). With these words, Bierce recognizes the separate realms and perspectives of civilians and soldiers which this pivotal battle forced into the nation's consciousness. Then, as in "On a Mountain," he opens his account by painting a peaceful and idyllic scene in which romantic notions of war are still operating.

In the bright warmth of Sunday, 6 April, reveille was "sounded rather late" because it was to be "a day of rest" for the troops, who were "wearied with long marching." Their shocking state of unreadiness is stressed in this passage in which the men are described as "idling," "preparing breakfast," "looking carelessly to the condition of their arms," and "chatting with indolent dogmatism on that never-failing theme, the end and object of the campaign." Even the sentinels "paced up and down the confused front with a lounging freedom of mien and stride that would not have been tolerated at another time." Bierce recalls arms being stacked in this casual disarray, a short distance from the tents of the "frowsyheaded officers," who "occasionally peered [out], languidly calling to their servants." Emblematic of the pervasive spirit of the morning, the flag itself hung "limp and lifeless at headquarters" (SS 11). With this image, Bierce suggests not only the lackadaisical pre-battle posture of the troops and their leaders, but also the ultimate cost of such unprofessionalism by foreshadowing the posture of the inert bodies that would soon litter the distant field at Shiloh.

Significantly, it is this same flag, rather than the men over whom it flies, that first sensed the imminent danger beyond this tranquil scene. "[A] dull, distant sound like the heavy breathing of some great animal below the horizon" began to rise and fall in the wind, causing the flag to lift "its head to listen." Soon the men responded to the flag's "warning sign," as "the breeze bore to [their] ears the long, deep sighing of iron lungs." Using animalistic imagery, Bierce describes the opening sounds of battle, capturing the "regular throbbings—the strong, full pulse of the fever" that energized the men and the representative flag over them. Responding to the exhilaration of this call and its accompanying expectations of valor, the soldiers assembled as "[t]he flag flapped excitedly, shaking out its blazonry of stars and stripes with a sort of fierce delight" (SS 11). McPherson explains that the "pride and honor of an individual soldier were bound up with the pride and honor of his regiment, his state, and the nation for which he fought, symbolized by the regimental and national flags" (*For Cause and Comrades* 82–83). What soldier who heard such a call to patriotism, Bierce muses retrospectively, could "forget the wild intoxication of its music?" (SS 12). Protected outwardly by this sense of frenzied patriotism and inwardly by their pride, the Indianians marched toward Grant's army at Pittsburg Landing, as the groaning sounds of this "great animal" became increasingly distinct and continuous.

Arriving across the riverbank from the battlefield as night falls, the men showed signs of the physical and mental toll of this "terrible race," during which "some regiments had lost a third of their number from fatigue, the men dropping from the ranks as if shot, and left to recover or die at their leisure." Bierce observes that "moral confidence" was also fading at this point. With "the air full of thunder and the earth . . . trembling beneath their feet," their "eyes reported only matter for despair." Since by this time darkness cloaked their view of all but "[f]leeting streaks of fire" and "blinding flashes," imagination had to provide a visual canvas to accompany the still reverberating sounds of battle (SS 13). To Bierce himself, the occasional black figures he could discern seemed "ludicrously like the figures of demons in old allegorical prints of hell." Nevertheless, he writes of a feeling of "impotent rage" as characterizing the response of those "who had the good fortune to arrive" too late to join that day's fighting (14). Bierce here depicts the contradictory feelings with which soldiers in such situations must struggle. Though anxious for their own safety—imagining, for instance, the possibility of stray shots hitting the engine-room of a nearby steamer—they yearned also to prove themselves heroic by coming to the aid of their comrades across the river.

According to Linderman, "Courage had for Civil War soldiers a narrow, rigid, and powerful meaning: heroic action undertaken without fear." In simple terms, "[a] failure of courage in war was a failure in manhood" (17). Bierce, in this memoir, reflects upon the psychic toll of trying to meet such a humanly impossible standard of conduct. Like the fictional Brainerd Byring, the soldiers at

Shiloh were unable to voice their fears of death or accept them as natural when the normal defense of denial failed. As a result, some of them broke under the pressure of such an untenable situation. Bierce describes the cowards of Shiloh in stark terms: "These men were defeated, beaten, cowed. They were deaf to duty and dead to shame. A more demented crew never drifted to the rear of broken battalions" (SS 15). Face to face with the war's first horrific test of their manhood and unable, even at gunpoint, to force themselves up the bank to the battlefront, these men illustrate to Bierce one of the ironies of courage. "An army's bravest men," he recognizes, "are its cowards. The death which they would not meet at the hands of the enemy they will meet at the hands of their officers, with never a flinching" (15). Although his comments here are not unmixed with contempt, Bierce would probe the ironies of courage and cowardice repeatedly over the next thirty years in his stories of the war. On a personal level, such an obsessive interest in this subject suggests his own unresolved feelings. From a cultural perspective, it also reflects his recognition of the unfair demands that the hero-system placed on the individual soldier's psyche as romantic concepts of warfare proved incompatible with the new techniques and accompanying mass casualties of modern warfare that the Civil War introduced.

Since the fighting had ended by the time that Bierce's regiment had crossed the river, they were forced to pass the night listening to others recount "the depressing incidents of the day" (SS 15–16). They also observed the hospital tents, which "were constantly receiving the wounded, yet were never full; they were continually ejecting the dead, yet were never empty. It was as if the helpless had been carried in and murdered, that they might not hamper those whose business it was to fall to-morrow." Forced to pass the night at the rear among the dead, the dying, and the cowards of war, Bierce took strength and comfort from the companionship of those around him, whatever their condition, as the "long night wore away" (16). His experience confirms McPherson's research of Civil War soldiers' letters and diaries, which found that "[n]early all soldiers agreed that the time of utmost anxiety occurred *before* the actual fighting, as the tension mounted while they waited to go into action" (*For Cause and Comrades* 38).

Again, however, with the coming of morning light, the illusion of peaceful enchantment returned:

> . . . as the glimmer of morning crept in through the forest we found ourselves in a more open country. But where? Not a sign of battle was here. The trees were neither splintered nor scarred, the underbrush was unmown, the ground had no footprints but our own. It was as if we had broken into glades sacred to eternal silence. I should not have been surprised to see sleek leopards come fawning about our feet, and milk-white deer confront us with human eyes. (SS 16)

As if by magic, in the "raw morning air," a single bugle note ended the false sense of tranquility, replacing it with an "electric" charge of animalistic energy, much stronger than had first lured them toward Shiloh the day before: "The men thrust forward their heads, expanded their eyes and clenched their teeth. They breathed hard, as if throttled by tugging at the leash. If you had laid your hand in the beard or hair of one of these men," Bierce writes, "it would have crackled and shot sparks" (SS 17). In this electric pulse lies the secret appeal of war that persisted for Bierce even after he was seasoned to its brutal realities. J. Glenn Gray observes that the appeal of "[w]ar as a spectacle, as something to see, ought never to be underestimated" (29). War provided Bierce, and thousands like him, with a means to escape the monotony of his unadventurous civilian life. After the unexpected tedium of a year spent mostly waiting to "see the elephant," Shiloh represented the opportunity finally to see the sublime spectacle of war firsthand. In this ecstatic rush, which persists for most soldiers beyond the first experience of going into battle, a loss of self-awareness occurs, providing the ego with a protective sense of security, in the awesome recognition of the power and grandeur of war. Gray argues that, at such moments, soldiers "are able to disregard personal danger . . . by transcending the self, by forgetting [their] separateness" (35).

In the rest of the memoir, Bierce strives to capture this sublime sight for his readers, as well as the rote, "no nonsense" business of war that also served to shield the soldiers from their fear of death. Passing out of the "singular oasis that had marvelously escaped the desolation of battle," they reached level ground and now could view the "wretched debris of the battle [that] still littered the spongy earth as far as one could see, in every direction" (SS 18–19). Exercising his discretion, Bierce recalls deploying his platoon. Then "the forest seemed all at once to flame up and disappear with a crash like that of a great wave upon the beach—a crash that expired in hot hissings, and the sickening 'spat' of lead against flesh" (19). Forced to take cover by lying on the ground as the two lines fired over their heads, Bierce writes of the situation as "inglorious" for those who were prevented from joining the "brave, hopeless task!" and so denied the opportunity to die "like men" (21). As defenses against the fear of death failed, what preoccupied many was *how* they would be viewed: as a coward or as a hero. The hero-system dictated that one must die in a heroic posture facing the enemy, rather than lying on one's belly hiding from the enemy or—worse yet—running from the enemy.

During a brief respite in the battle, Bierce acknowledges that he "obtained leave to go down into the valley of death and gratify a reprehensible curiosity" to see the piled bodies of an Illinois regiment in a deep ravine. "Death," he notes, "had put his sickle into this thicket and fire had gleaned the field" (SS 21). While some of the corpses were positioned "in the unlovely looseness of attitude denoting sudden death by the bullet," many more had been burned to death in "the tormenting flame" of fallen leaves that had ignited from the sparks of the engagement. Both irresistibly attracted to and thoroughly repulsed by the macabre horror of death before him, he describes the scene in graphic detail: "Some were swollen to double girth; others shriveled to manikins. According to degree of exposure, their faces were bloated and black or yellow and shrunken. The contraction of muscles which had given them claws for hands had cursed each countenance with a hideous grin." At this point, Bierce abruptly cuts off the horrific recollection in an exclamation of ironic revulsion, "Faugh! I cannot catalogue the charms of these gallant gentlemen who had got what they enlisted for" (22). Bierce clearly finds romantic notions of gentlemen-soldiers thoroughly incompatible with such a gruesome fate.

Eventually, their energy spent, and "profoundly disgusted with the inglorious part to which they had been condemned," Bierce's regiment "did everything doggedly. The spirit had gone quiet out of them," he observes (SS 22). At this point, only their training and dedication to duty carried them forward, as the ecstatic exhilaration with which they had first charged forward had at least for the time being waned. Gray explains that when soldiers are in mortal danger they often "enter into a dazed condition in which all sharpness of consciousness is lost. When in this state," he observes, "they can be caught up into the fire of communal ecstasy and forget about death by losing their individuality, or they can function like cells in a military organism, doing what is expected of them because it has become automatic" (102). In this case, although they had little reason to believe they would prevail, those who remained on the field continued to do their jobs as if mechanically driven. However, with the arrival of Union reinforcements, the Confederates finally retreated in the forced recognition of "the paramount importance of numbers" (SS 23). Despite their physical exhaustion and heavy losses, the men of the Indiana Ninth Regiment regained their fortitude as this turnaround occurred. Bierce relives the power of the sublime one last time as he shifts to present tense in the strength of his recollection of this moment: "We still our breathing to catch the full grandeur of the volleys that are to tear them to shreds." Instead, however, absolute silence falls, the battle ends, and human images of those who trail in its wake—"a stretcher-bearer, . . . a surgeon! Good heavens! a chaplain!"—appear to return the scene of death and destruction to order (24).

Concluding his retrospective account of Shiloh with a final section that he did not add to the essay until 1881, Bierce remains unable to reconcile his ambivalent memories. "Is it not strange," he muses, "that the phantoms of a blood-stained period have so airy a grace and look with so tender eyes?—that I recall with difficulty the danger and death and horrors of the time, and without effort all that was gracious and picturesque?" (SS 24–25). Despite his now mature and intellectualized understanding of war and the tragic costs it entails, he still yearns for the adventure and exhilaration of his youthful days as a warrior and, perhaps above all, for the opportunity it provided to join a community and dedicate himself to a cause that enabled him to earn a feeling of primary value and usefulness.

Death before Dishonor: Seasoned Soldiers and the Burden of Heroism

It is well that war is so terrible, or we should grow too fond of it.
—Robert E. Lee

In the aftermath of the transition in which green recruits, if they survive without dying or deserting, are transformed into seasoned warriors, the dreamland imagery of enchantment disappears from Bierce's Civil War writing. His fiction nevertheless remains focused on notions of courage and cowardice in depicting individual soldiers who continue to battle fear of death as they struggle both physically and psychically to adhere to the demands of the culture's hero-system. Society's code of "[c]ourage had for Civil War soldiers a narrow, rigid, and powerful meaning: heroic action undertaken without fear" (Linderman 17). Writing about his own Civil War experiences, Bierce's contemporary John William De Forest encapsulates the impossibility of adhering to such a standard when he explains that "[t]he man who does not dread to die or to be mutilated is a lunatic. The man who, dreading these things, still faces them for the sake of duty and honor is a hero" (124). In stories such as "Killed at Resaca" and "Parker Adderson, Philosopher," Bierce presents portraits of soldiers who are severely tested as they strive to bear the burden of heroism by facing possible death or dismemberment without revealing or succumbing to their fears.

First published in 1887, "Killed at Resaca" recounts the death of First Lieutenant Herman Brayle at Resaca, Georgia, where Bierce himself fought under General William B. Hazen's command on 13–15 May 1864. The narrator of the story, in opening the tale, identifies Brayle as an aide-de-camp and "[t]he best soldier of our staff." In describing the officer further, he uses an abundance of physical details that creates an ideal image of manhood: "Lieutenant Brayle was more than six feet in height and of splendid proportions, with the light hair and gray-blue eyes which men so gifted usually find associated with a high order of courage. As he was commonly in full uniform, especially in action . . . , he was a very striking and conspicuous figure. As to the rest, he had a gentleman's manners, a scholar's head and a lion's heart." No callow youth, Brayle is a mature adult of "about thirty," whose dashing looks, modest demeanor, and apparent strength of character make him a favorite with his comrades despite his "one most objectionable and unsoldierly quality: he was vain of his courage." Since joining the brigade at Stones River, Tennessee, and repeatedly since that deadly battle of 31 December 1862 to 2 January 1863, Brayle has refused to take cover under fire "except when sternly commanded to do so by the general" (SF 507). Inexplicably and without fail in such engagements, the lieutenant would "sit his horse like an equestrian statue, in a storm of bullets and grape, in the most exposed places," or "stand like a rock in the open when officers and men alike had taken to cover" (508).

His comrades know nothing of Brayle's past, but although they are unable to explain the lieutenant's disregard for his own safety by immaturity, lack of experience, or ignorance, they find themselves at times spellbound by his daring displays of what they interpret as valor. When sent on a "perilous errand," Brayle never stooped, always instead cutting a "splendid figure, accentuated by his uniform, holding the eye with a strange fascination." As the narrator explains, "We watched him with suspended breath, our hearts in our mouths" (SF 508). In an attempt to justify their emotional response to such reckless behavior, the speaker retrospectively seeks to "do justice to a brave man's memory" by clarifying that in Brayle's "needless exposures of life there was no visible bravado nor subsequent narration" (508). Further, Brayle's failure to value his own life does not mean that he failed to care about the lives of others. When the captain, who had warned him to be more careful, was "shot to rags from an ambuscade Brayle remained by the body for some time, adjusting the limbs with needless care—there in the middle of a road swept by gusts of grape and canister!" Using this act as his most compelling defense of Brayle's character, the narrator concludes, "It is easy to condemn this kind of thing, and not very difficult to refrain from imitation, but it is impossible not to respect, and Brayle was liked none the less for the weakness which had so heroic an expression" (509).

The ambivalence that characterizes this fictional response, as well as its historical prevalence, is explained by Gerald F. Linderman, who in documenting Civil War notions of heroism writes:

> The requirement that courage be a fearless courage meant that the soldier's feelings about what he was doing were as important as his actions. Particularly admired—sometimes extravagantly—were those

> who seemed to possess fearlessness as nature's gift, those so oblivious to fear that it could not exist within the range of their emotional reactions. Such men showed an absolute indifference under fire; they were those ideal officers who were perfectly brave without being aware that they were so. (20)

In Brayle, his comrades see embodied the perfect fearlessness in the face of death that they themselves lack and that, by this stage of the war, they realize they will never achieve. Through practical experience, they have gained a saner and more realistic view of war and soldiering, but they nevertheless are still not immune to the hero-system's sublime and idealistic image of courage that this enigmatic soldier seems to represent.

Although wounded several times, Brayle always returns "to duty about as good as new" until, inevitably, "the law of probabilities" catches up with him at Resaca (SF 509). Bierce depicts the lieutenant's death in a dramatic scene of a lone officer making a valiant ride on horseback against seemingly impossible odds.[1] As David E. Owens observes, "It is a motif that Bierce uses to explore the nature of individual courage in a way that stories set earlier in the war do not." A staff officer "has no soldiers to lead, nor does he typically engage the enemy directly." Thus, as in Brayle's case, "how he reacts in the face of the enemy becomes the public demonstration of his courage" (107).

Caught in his ride between lines by an impassable gully, Brayle refuses to drop into the steep ditch that miraculously could have provided him protection from the raging crossfire. As Bierce writes, "He could not go forward, he would not turn back; he stood awaiting death. It did not keep him long waiting." Almost instantaneously upon Brayle's fall from his horse, firing ceases, "as if both sides had suddenly repented of their profitless crime," and several Confederate officers and men assist in removing the "sacred burden" of the lieutenant's body (SF 510).

Bierce does not end the story with this romantic recognition of an individual officer's heroic death, however. Instead he attaches a coda in which the reader learns that Brayle's behavior had its source not in a perfect fearlessness but rather in his all too human fear of death. After the war, the narrator discovers among the dead man's possessions an 1862 love letter from a woman named Marian Mendenhall. In this letter, Marian advises Brayle that a report has reached her that he was "'seen crouching behind a tree'" during a battle in Virginia (SF 511). Although she claims not to believe the story, she admits that it would change her feelings for him if she did. Driving home her point, she warns, "'I could bear to hear of my soldier lover's death, but not of his cowardice'" (511). During the Civil War, Linderman reports, "Those who most imperatively urged enlistment were women. They no less than soldiers expected courageous behavior and anathematized cowardice. Their special weapon might with justice be called sexual intimidation" (87). Believing death to be a better fate than to be branded as a coward, Brayle seeks to prove himself to his sweetheart and others by actively seeking death on the battlefield. To ensure that the reader's sympathy will adhere to Brayle, despite the man's recklessness and loss of reason, Bierce concludes the story somewhat heavy-handedly with the woman's disdainful response when the narrator returns the letter to her, assuring her that the stain on the letter is "'the blood of the truest and bravest heart that ever beat.'" Flinging the letter into the fire, she remarks, "'Uh! I cannot bear the sight of blood!'" before even inquiring how her lover died. The narrator, who claims the woman is as beautiful as she is detestable, answers only that Brayle "'was bitten by a snake'" (511). Unable to face the concrete proof of the consequences of her romantic notions of war, Marian destroys the physical traces of her and society's complicity in her lover's tragic death as he sought to fulfill their impossible—and literally deadly—expectations.

Although not as successful because of its lack of character development, "Killed at Resaca" anticipates William Dean Howells's acclaimed 1905 story "Editha," which depicts essentially the same conflict and resolution although it is set during the Spanish-American War of 1898. In the later story, Editha convinces her fiancé George Gearson to enlist against his will. Unlike Bierce, Howells introduces a generational divide in his story through the contrast of Editha's romantic notions with the sober reflections of her mother. Upon the declaration of war, the older woman "said, 'Oh my!' and then said nothing more until she had sat down in one of the large Shaker chairs and rocked herself for some time" (260). The mother's subsequent conclusion that Editha's emotional manipulation of George was a "'wicked thing'" foreshadows George's death in the first skirmish of the war, after which George's mother confronts Editha with the moral responsibility that the young woman bears for her son's death: "'I suppose he made up his mind to go, but I knew what it cost him by what it cost me when I heard of it. I had been through *one* war before. When you sent him you didn't expect he would get killed. . . . No, girls don't; women don't, when they give their men up to their country'" (260, 266–67). In both stories, women are to blame for their soldier-lovers' deaths, and in the values that they espouse, they serve the larger communal belief system that functions under the guise of patriotism. Howells, however, suggests the cracking of the romantic code of courage in the figures of the two mothers, who, having lived through the Civil War, serve as the voice of experience in contrast to the youthful Editha's dangerous naivety. Having also survived the Civil War and writing more than twenty years after its end, Bierce suggests this same disparity in views with the irony that adheres to his chivalric portrait of the doomed Brayle and the outright contempt that tinges his depiction of the poisonous Marian.

In an autobiographical touch that he uses in several other stories as well, Bierce presents "Killed at Resaca" from the perspective of an unnamed first-person narrator who is the unit's topographical engineer and a fellow staff officer of the protagonist. Although this move, coupled with the setting of the story, led early readers such as Carey McWilliams to infer that the incidents related were factual, no evidence exists to support this position.[2] This does not mean, however, that the tale does not have both conscious and unconscious connections with Bierce's own life in its depiction of the dangers and related psychic pressures that Civil War staff officers faced in carrying out their duties and proving themselves as courageous as other soldiers in battle. Most obvious are the physical similarities between the writer and his character. Like Brayle, Bierce was tall, with striking blond hair and piercing blue eyes, and he took exceptional pride in his dress and appearance. According to C. Hartley Grattan, "He made a fetish of his personal appearance and spent an unusual amount of time and care over his toilet. His nephew, Carlton, asserted, perhaps in ridicule, that Bierce shaved all over every day" (39). Although his modesty about the human body was extreme, he had an almost perfect physical beauty. In the words of Walter Neale, "health, vitality, life, seemed to be embodied in Bierce's physical structure" (55). In describing Brayle's handsome vitality and the dashing figure he cut on the battlefield, characteristics so ironically at odds with his tragic fate, Bierce did not have to go beyond the mirror for inspiration.

Although the fictional Brayle was well respected, he—like Bierce himself—also seems to have stood apart from his comrades, whose ignorance of his past suggests they were not personally close to the man. In executing his military responsibilities, Bierce enjoyed being regarded as competent and accepted by his fellows, but he also stood aloof from them. As a result, though "[a]pproved of as a soldier, he was still regarded with some suspicion as a person" (Fatout 46). Correspondence reprinted in the Elkhart, Indiana, *Review* and related editorial comment regarding Bierce's promotion to second lieutenant in December 1862 and to first lieutenant in February 1863 indicate that he was not universally liked by his comrades. Nevertheless, although the men objected to "being deprived of the privilege of election by ballot" in deciding the appointment, they acknowledged that Bierce "has always been a good and brave soldier, who *knows no fear*" (qtd. in Fatout 47). In a comment that strikingly suggests both the writer's affinity with and distinction from Brayle, Fatout claims that Bierce "was not so much reckless of his safety as indifferent to death riding the humming missiles, and he carried out his orders with capable dispatch" (48). Though not foolish in his heroism, Bierce, like Brayle, showed little value for his own life on the battlefield.

One reason for his seeming indifference to death may have been his inability to form close or enduring attachments. During the same time period depicted in the tale, Bierce was suffering the pain of a broken love affair with a former classmate named Bernice Wright, who was known as Fatima and Tima to her friends. According to McWilliams, Bierce had delivered an anonymous love poem to Fatima when he first departed for war, and he became bold enough to profess his feelings in person when he was furloughed back to Warsaw between enlistments in December 1863.[3] Bierce's regiment was not recalled to active duty until February 1864, by which time he was apparently engaged to Fatima. Depressed by the heavy casualties of the Atlanta campaign and the failure of his fiancée to write regularly, Bierce wrote to Fatima's sister Clara on 8 June 1864, just three weeks after the Battle of Resaca. In beginning this lengthy letter, he struggles with the strength of his feelings for both Clara and Fatima:

> My Dear Clara:
>
> Will you be very much displeased to hear from me by letter?
>
> If I thought so I would never touch pen again. 'Tis true you never asked me to write to you, but the knowledge that I still live cannot be unwelcome to one who professes to regard me as a *friend*. I don't know Clare what the word *friend* means to you who have so many, but to *me* friendship has a meaning deeper than the definition of Webster or Worcester. And my friendship for you is a feeling which no language can define. Do you call this flattery? If so you do not know me and I forgive you.
>
> I have not written to you before, but my neglect was not caused by indifference. I knew Tima would sometimes mention my name to you. But I want to hear from you very much; not because you will tell me of Tima, but of yourself. . . . Clare, except our sweet Tima, I love you better than any one on this earth.
>
> Perhaps this is not right;—perhaps my mother and sister should be first in my affections,—but so it is. (MM 1)

Consciously registering guilt for not having such emotional ties to his own mother and sister, he seems desperately to be seeking an adult attachment to anchor himself. "I am getting very tired of my present life," he continues, "and weary of the profession of arms. Not because of its horrors or dangers; not because its hardships affect me, but because I wish to be with you and my darling. The pleasant weeks with you, so like a dream, have nearly spoiled the soldier to make the—pensive individual" (MM 1). Although he disavows the possibility that his prolonged exposure to violent death and dismemberment has any role in his weariness with his "present life," he contradicts himself a few paragraphs later when he turns alarmingly fatalistic:

> . . . I hardly expect to see you again, and perhaps it is better so. Every day someone is struck down who is so much better than I. Since leaving Cleveland, Tenn. my brigade has lost nearly one third its numbers killed and wounded.

> Among these were so many good men who could ill be spared from the army and the world. And yet *I* am left. But my turn will come in time. Oh, how pleasant would death be were it for you and Tima, instead of for my country—for a cause which may be right and may be wrong. Do you think I lack patriotism for talking this way? Perhaps so. Soldiers are not troubled with that sort of stuff. (MM 1)

Here Bierce registers his wavering belief in the cause for which he has been fighting for three years. By this point in the war, troop morale was low, with casualties still mounting and no apparent end in sight. "As convictions about the potency and protectiveness of courage yielded to the suspicion that special courage had become the mark of death, another of the war's original precepts—that the courageous death was the good death . . .—also failed the test of observation" (Linderman 159). The Battle of Resaca was fought to a virtual stalemate, resulting in nearly six thousand casualties evenly divided between North and South. Just twelve days later, on 27 May 1864, Bierce also fought at Pickett's Mill. In his 1888 memoir about this engagement, he reveals what he saw as a decades-long cover-up by General William Sherman and Major General Oliver Howard to minimize knowledge of their flawed judgment in this battle. Both Hazen and Bierce overheard Howard discussing the plan of attack with General Thomas Wood, which involved sending in only one brigade at a time, with Hazen's men going first to take the brunt of the Confederate force. As a result, in less than thirty minutes of fighting, "Hazen's brigade lost 467 men, about a third of whom were killed outright, an unusually high proportion, attesting to both the good marksmanship of the Confederates and the fact that once a man was wounded, he had no place to hide. After the battle, one Confederate officer found a dead Yank who had been shot forty-seven times" (Morris 85). Writing about "The Crime at Pickett's Mill" twenty-four years after it occurred, Bierce's bitter anger still reverberates as he describes their needless and virtually forgotten "acts of heroism and devotion performed in scenes of awful carnage to accomplish the impossible" (SS 37).

With convictions unraveling in the later days of the war, support from home became increasingly important in keeping soldiers from despairing of the patriotic duty to which they had committed themselves. Accordingly, "[m]ail call was the brightest part of a soldier's day—*if* he received a letter from home. If he did not, his spirits sank" (McPherson, *For Cause and Comrades* 132). Bierce's lack of close comrades in camp to sustain him and the failure of his fiancée to write made him particularly vulnerable as his patriotic resolve and moral certainty began to waiver. In his fragile state, he seems almost paranoid in his insecurity. "Ask Tima why I get no more letters from her," he instructs Clara. "Have I offended her? I may have written something as heartless and cruel as I used to say to her. If I have I hope she will forgive me. Her last letter was dated May 11th" (MM 1). Perhaps second-guessing his choice of the frivolous, fun-loving Fatima over the more subdued Clara, who had often chaperoned the two lovers on outings during Bierce's furlough, Bierce worries about his love letters becoming public: "Do you think that there is a probability of my letters getting into other hands than hers? Please tell me for the thought troubles me very much" (1). Reflecting an obsessive jealousy that has had time to fester in his loneliness, he questions not only Fatima's loyalty but also Clara's: "May I talk to you about D—? Do you love him yet? or think you do?" And he repeatedly seeks information about what is going on in his absence. "Do tell me all about yourself and Tima," he pleas. "What books you read, what society you have, and if you have lots of fun. . . . By the way is Jo Williams at W[arsaw]? The less you have to do with him the better you will please me. If you require reasons I will give them" (2). Bierce's suspicious and controlling nature surfaces repeatedly throughout this letter as he communicates his sense of personal isolation and friendlessness. In such a state of depression, he can no longer repress his fears about his own personal safety as he fights for a cause that no longer sustains him.

Closing this letter of overwrought emotions with a long postscript, Bierce admits, "It is raining very hard and I am very lonely," and he reaffirms his love of both women in a final wish that he might "renounce the whole world and all the ties of kindred" to give himself "up to the delicious intoxication of [their] society" (MM 2). His sense of approaching disaster, however, was soon realized both on the battlefield and at home. While leading a skirmish line forward at Kennesaw Mountain on 23 June 1864, Bierce was shot in the head by a Confederate sharpshooter. Although most such wounds were fatal, Bierce "somehow survived both the initial wound and the jolting two-day train ride back to Chattanooga in an open flatcar" (Morris 89). Released from the hospital, he was furloughed back to Indiana to convalesce. During this period, he and Fatima formally broke off their relationship. Having to live for about two months in the same house with his parents, while recovering from both his physical and emotional wounds, was more than enough to motivate Bierce to rejoin his brigade in mid-September, although he was still suffering from fainting spells related to his injury. Leaving Indiana and all the bad memories associated with it, he determined not to return, a promise to himself that he apparently kept.

Bierce's somewhat miraculous recovery from a severe head wound may have reinstated some sense of his own exceptionalism. Shortly after returning to duty, he also managed to escape a brief captivity by Confederate forces near Gaylesville, Alabama, in October 1864. In describing this experience in another 1888 memoir, "Four Days in Dixie," Bierce admits he was, for the most part, treated civilly. Nevertheless, at one point, he feared for his life when the guards who were transporting him to military headquarters warned that if Jeff Gatewood, a local guerrilla chief, came upon them, "he would probably take [Bierce] from them and hang [him] to the nearest tree" (SS 52). His captors actually protected Bierce from this possible fate by hiding him in the brush "once or twice, hearing horsemen approach," and Bierce managed to escape his guards that same night while they slept (52–53). His Civil War stories, however, depict characters that usually are not as fortunate in facing the possibility of death in similar circumstances. In the 1891 tale "Parker Adderson, Philosopher," for instance, he contrasts the reaction of two soldiers who contemplate their fate from different perspectives. This story is the only one that Bierce narrates from the Confederate side of the lines, and one of only a few that cannot be located more specifically in terms of either geography or time.

The title character of this tale is a Union sergeant and spy who has been captured in the evening and so, in accordance with standard military procedure, anticipates being executed by hanging the following morning. Most of the action takes place in the tent of the commanding officer, a Confederate general named Clavering. From the beginning, there is no question of Adderson's guilt. As Clavering confirms, "'You admit, then, that you are a spy—that you came into my camp, disguised as you are in the uniform of a Confederate soldier, to obtain information secretly regarding the numbers and disposition of my troops'" (SF 768). The story's interest lies in the two main characters' contrasting attitudes about death and, in particular, in how and why these attitudes change during the course of the evening.

The convicted spy's initial reaction to his capture and impending execution suggests that his psychological defenses are still operating, which enables him to mask and repress his fear of death to manageable limits. As he is questioned by Clavering, he repeatedly demonstrates the false bravado that Ernest Becker associates with "organismic narcissism" (7). When asked his name, the prisoner flippantly responds, "'As I am to lose it at daylight to-morrow morning it is hardly worth while concealing it. Parker Adderson'" (SF 768). When Clavering advises that he has just written a memorandum to guide the provost-marshal in arranging for the condemned man's execution, Adderson drolly remarks, "'I hope, General, the spectacle will be intelligently arranged, for I shall attend it myself'" (769). And, when the general asks if the sergeant would like to see a chaplain, the spy flatly rejects the protection to his psyche that religion's promise of immortality might provide by ironically observing, "'I could hardly secure a longer rest for myself by depriving him [the chaplain] of some of his'" (769).

Against Adderson's image of forced nonchalance, Clavering provides a striking contrast in both demeanor and expressed attitude. Described as an "officer of high rank and wide renown," the general is a "man of death," and, as such, he is suitably appalled by his prisoner's lack of sobriety (SF 768, 770). "'Good God, man!'" he exclaims, "'do you mean to go to your death with nothing but jokes upon your lips? Do you know that this is a serious matter?'" (769). However, Adderson, who in his denial process aligns himself only with life, continues to persevere in his defensive banter by responding, "'How can I know that? I have never been dead in all my life. I have heard that death is a serious matter, but never from any of those who have experienced it'" (770). The dignified Clavering makes several attempts to convince his prisoner to take death seriously. He explains, first of all, that death "'is at least a loss—a loss of such happiness as we have, and of opportunities for more,'" to which Adderson merely replies that since such a loss is one "'of which we shall never be conscious,'" it "'can be borne with composure and therefore expected without apprehension'" (770). Clavering next insists, "'If the being dead is not a regrettable condition, yet the becoming so—the act of dying—appears to be distinctly disagreeable to one who has not lost the power to feel.'" The condemned man turns this point on its head by admitting that, although pain is disagreeable, it is "'he who lives longest'" who is "'most exposed to it,'" since what is called "'dying is simply the last pain'" (770). With these and other allusions to Stoic philosophy, Adderson "embarks on a second line of psychological defense, rationalizations" (Grenander, *Ambrose Bierce* 86). Although Clavering insists, "'Death is horrible!,'" Adderson remains secure in his carefully constructed philosophical belief system, asserting that death is only "'horrible because we have inherited the tendency to think it so, accounting for the notion by wild and fanciful theories of another world—as names of places give rise to legends explaining them and reasonless conduct to philosophies in justification'" (SF 770).

Adderson's glib resort to fatalism as a protective device recalls Bierce's more somber assertion when he wrote to Clara Wright, "my turn will come in time" (MM 1). According to McPherson, "Soldiers quickly become fatalists as a result of war's "extreme challenge to the belief that man can control his fate" (*For Cause and Comrades* 62). However, this attitude is only one defense that soldiers use to repress their fear of death. More than an argument between two men about the proper attitude toward death, the dialogue between Adderson and Clavering reflects the internal conflict with which each soldier repeatedly struggles as he faces the possibility of violent death. The polarities of their views are those between which an individual vacillates, suggesting the enormous stress on the psyche that such conflict creates.

Clavering ends his philosophical debate with Adderson by simply asserting, "'I should not like to die, . . . not to-night'" (SF 771). Because they are interrupted at this point by the entrance of Captain Hasterlick, the provost-marshal, Adderson does not have the opportunity to respond, but if he had been afforded this chance, he quite likely would have used another witticism to reemphasize his self-professed indifference on this point, still comfortable in his assumption that he will not be executed until the following morning. Regardless, however, it is at this point that Clavering destroys Adderson's veneer of composure by instructing Hasterlick to conduct the prisoner "'at once to the parade ground and shoot him'" (771). Having adamantly denied his fear and anxiety to this point in time, Adderson has compromised his ego by not affording himself the adaptive benefits he could have derived from venting these emotions gradually over time. Nevertheless, the spy has successfully repressed his fear of death through the illusion of control that he has gained from his mistaken belief that his sentence will be executed according to standard procedure. The nature of his neurotic compromise is such that he can only control the "mounting tension as long as he feels that his death is not imminent and that he can accurately predict what will happen to him" (Kocher 123–24). With Clavering's announcement, Adderson's elaborate defense system crumbles, and repression becomes no longer possible, as becomes clear in the next exchange between the two men:

> A sharp cry broke from the spy's lips. He threw himself forward, thrust out his neck, expanded his eyes, clenched his hands.
>
> "Good God!" he cried hoarsely, almost inarticulately; "you do not mean that! You forget—I am not to die until morning."
>
> "I have said nothing of morning," replied the general, coldly; "that was an assumption of your own. You die now."
>
> "But General, I beg—I implore you to remember; I am to hang! It will take some time to erect the gallows—two hours—an hour. Spies are hanged; I have rights under military law. For Heaven's sake, General, consider how short—"
>
> "Captain, observe my directions." (SF 771)

In addition to manifesting clear, physical signs of unmanageable distress, Adderson now undergoes an expedient religious conversion, invoking God and Heaven for protection, as the comfort derived from the predictability of his fate evaporates. For his part, Clavering, who "coldly" responds to the suddenly distraught sergeant, evidences no sympathy for a man who has heretofore refused to acknowledge the fear and respect with which he believes all men should view death. As a result, the general sees fit to deny his prisoner the ceremonial death by hanging at sunrise that is the established custom for spies, substituting instead a form of military execution traditionally reserved for cases of desertion, cowardice, and mutiny. Donald T. Blume argues that "Clavering thus delivers a double blow to Adderson: he is not merely telling Adderson that he is to die immediately; he is telling the spy that he is beneath hanging, coequal with deserters and traitors" (*Ambrose Bierce's Civilians and Soldiers* 284). In his research of the letters and diaries of Civil War soldiers, McPherson found that the phrase "Death before dishonor" occurred repeatedly, confirming Samuel L. A. Marshall's conclusion that "[p]ersonal honor is the one thing valued more than life itself by the majority" of soldiers (McPherson, *For Cause and Comrades* 77; Marshall 150).[4] Thus, by denying Adderson an honorable death, Clavering eliminates the prisoner's most critical psychic defense. Further, since he is also denied any time to devise a rationale to defend against this humiliation, his already compromised ego functions collapse completely.

Bierce represents this psychological breakdown in the physical struggle that ensues between the two men. Adderson, described as a "frantic man," grabs Clavering's bowie knife and leaps "upon the general with the fury of a madman, hurling him to the ground and falling headlong upon him as he lay." Overturning the table and candle, "they fought blindly in the darkness. . . . Curses and inarticulate cries of rage and pain came from the welter of limbs and bodies; the tent came down upon them and beneath its hampering and enveloping folds the struggle went on" (SF 771). When the two men are finally separated, Adderson is described as "dazed," seemingly incognizant of what has happened. Thoroughly unmanned and reduced to only animalistic responses, "[h]e shrank away from those attending him, cowered upon the ground and uttered unintelligible remonstrances. His face, swollen by blows and stained with gouts of blood, nevertheless showed white beneath his disheveled hair—as white as that of a corpse." Following Clavering's order, just minutes later, the Union spy, "kneeling in the moonlight and begging incoherently for his life," is "shot to death by twenty men" (772). Meanwhile, the Confederate general, who inadvertently was mortally wounded in the fray by Hasterlick's sword, discovers that his own experience of dying is unmarked by terror. "Clavering," Bierce writes, "lying white and still in the red glow of the camp-fire, opened his big blue eyes, looked pleasantly upon those about him and said: 'How silent it all is!' . . . [T]hen, his face suffused with a smile of ineffable sweetness, he said faintly: 'I suppose this must be death,' and so passed away" (772–73).

Cathy N. Davidson argues that "[d]eath does not answer the question argued in 'Parker Adderson, Philosopher' . . . , despite the fact that the argument is about the nature of death and that, at the end of the story, both of the participants test experientially the validity of the theoretical premises which they earlier passionately advocated. Each one thereby discovers that he was wrong and the other right, a reversal that does not at all resolve the debate." Although the two soldiers, in effect, change positions, "neither can come to intellectual or emotional terms with his own mortality or the mortality of others" (66, 69). However, by looking at these two men and their opposing positions as a representation of an individual soldier's internal struggle to repress fear and act heroically in the face of violent death, it becomes possible to discern some truths about the burden of heroism.

To maintain one's composure in the face of death requires effective psychic defenses. Blume was the first critic to discern that Adderson's bravery "evaporates in the face of an unexpected development," rather than merely because his superficial philosophical rationalizations fail him (*Ambrose Bierce's Civilians and Soldiers* 279). Blume's interpretation serves to make Clavering the villain of the piece, arguing that the general "is a cruel, calculating, manipulative individual who sets out to destroy Adderson and succeeds" by denying the spy his right to meet his fate at the time and in the manner he expects and deserves (281–82). For the purposes of this argument, however, it is necessary to add one more layer to the tale's complexities. By seeing the superior officer Clavering, aligned with death and inured to the code of southern honor, as representing one half of Adderson's internal struggle, his act in denying the spy an honorable death becomes an act of the isolated soldier's superego, lashing out at himself for his lack of perfect heroism.

In the end, Adderson's equilibrium is destroyed not by another person but by his own fears, self-doubts, and self-inflicted guilt. His very profession as a spy brands him as someone who does not meet society's definition of heroism, which requires not only courage but uncompromised honor. Espionage, by necessity, requires covert action and misrepresentation. During the Civil War, spying on both sides "involved treachery, filching of official secrets, the skillful seduction of loyalty" (Kane 11). Bierce himself was no stranger to the reality of such work and its related psychological toll since he often served as a scout in his duties as a topographical engineer, crossing enemy lines "to gather intelligence about the lay of the land and enemy troop movements" (Blume, *Ambrose Bierce's Civilians and Soldiers* 213). Thus, in casting Adderson in this role, he perhaps probes fears and doubts that he himself experienced but repressed under a mask of stoic indifference. Unlike Bierce, Adderson, when tested, found that his own psychological defenses were ultimately insufficient to enable him to face death without succumbing to his fears. Further, Adderson's situation denied him the possibility of self-redemption that, in "Killed at Resaca," was available to Brayle, who had the opportunity to salvage his reputation by dying honorably—though recklessly—on the battlefield. Adderson's death thus represents every soldier's fear of failing the test of courage and not only dying but, far worse, dying dishonorably. Clavering's death, on the other hand, suggests each soldier's fervent wish for a peaceful and serene death that conforms to the hero-system's dictates of honor and valor.

Collateral Damage: Civilians and the Human Cost of War

... generally war is destruction and nothing else.
—**William Tecumseh Sherman**

As Bierce reflects in stories such as "Killed at Resaca" and "Parker Adderson, Philosopher," soldiers were the most obvious victims of Civil War society's hero-system. Civilians, meanwhile, supported the war effort by fulfilling the gate-keeping and recruiting functions necessary to maintain the integrity of the hero-system and its membership. Gerald F. Linderman explains that, in urging enlistment, "[t]he influence of home was profound. Soldiers' families enforced and reinforced the centrality of courage." Parents repeatedly "admonished their sons first to be brave and then to be careful." When a soldier died, family and loved ones "at home hoped desperately for last words that would confirm that their soldier had preserved his decency" (83, 86, 87). Nevertheless, as they labored to sustain the Civil War hero-system, civilians became as much its victims as its perpetrators. In her study of death during the Civil War, Drew Gilpin Faust argues,

> War victimized civilians as well as soldiers, and uncounted numbers of noncombatants perished as a direct result of the conflict. The war's circumstances created a variety of ways for ordinary Americans to die: from violence that extended beyond soldiers and battles, from diseases that spread beyond military camps, from hardships and shortages that enveloped a broad swatch of the American—and especially the southern—population. It was, in

> Abraham Lincoln's words, a "people's contest," and the people suffered its cruelties. (137)

No systematic accounting has ever been made of civilian casualties, which for the most part have remained unacknowledged; however, James M. McPherson estimates that the war resulted in fifty thousand civilian deaths in the South (*Battle Cry of Freedom* 619n53). Bierce was not blind to such suffering and loss, and it is perhaps significant that his two best-known and most-acclaimed short stories, "An Occurrence at Owl Creek Bridge" and "Chickamauga," focus on the cost in southern civilian lives that the Civil War entailed.

"An Occurrence at Owl Creek Bridge" depicts the death by hanging of Peyton Farquhar, a wealthy southern planter who has been caught trying to sabotage a railroad bridge in northern Alabama. In introducing the story, however, Bierce first provides a detailed description of the scene of the execution before formally introducing the reader to its victim. The first sentence of the original 1890 version of the tale specifically sets the event in the summer of 1862, but in later versions, Bierce edited out the dating. David M. Owens speculates that Bierce moved the location of the bridge, which actually is located near Shiloh Church in Tennessee, so that it could legitimately be presented as a railroad bridge. Bierce was himself in northern Alabama in the summer of 1862 to repair the railroad line, and critical sections of this railroad were destroyed by the Confederates in late September 1864 to prevent the Union army from using it (Owens 49–51).

Bierce first describes the scene through the perspective of an unidentified third-person observer-narrator, using precise details and military language. "A man" stands on a temporary platform on the bridge, "looking down into the swift water twenty feet below." His hands are "behind his back, the wrists bound with a cord. A rope closely encircle[s] his neck." The preparations for the hanging are carried out by "two private soldiers of the Federal army, directed by a sergeant. . . . At a short remove upon the same temporary platform [is] an officer in the uniform of his rank, armed. He [is] a Captain." In addition a sentinel is positioned "at each end of the bridge . . . with his rifle in the position known as 'support,' that is to say, vertical in front of the left shoulder, the hammer resting on the forearm thrown straight across the chest—a formal and unnatural position, enforcing an erect carriage of the body. It [does] not appear to be the duty of these two men," Bierce adds, to know what is "occurring at the center of the bridge; they merely blockaded the two ends of the foot planking that traversed it." Beyond the sentinels stand "the spectators—a single company of infantry in line, at 'parade rest,' the butts of the rifles on the ground, the barrels inclining slightly backward against the right shoulder, the hands crossed upon the stock. A lieutenant [stands] at the right of the line, the point of his sword upon the ground, his left hand resting upon his right" (SF 725). Bierce strips the scene of subjective interest or human emotion by focusing on the rituals involved, emphasizing the rigid inflexibility of the process. "Death," he claims, "is a dignitary who when he comes announced is to be received with formal manifestations of respect, even by those most familiar with him. In the code of military etiquette silence and fixity are forms of deference" (726).

Only at this point does Bierce provide a physical description of the still anonymous "man who was engaged in being hanged." Approximately "thirty-five years of age," he has strong and pleasing features: "a straight nose, firm mouth, broad forehead, from which his long, dark hair was combed straight back, falling behind his ears to the collar of his well-fitting frock-coat. He wore a mustache and pointed beard, but no whiskers; his eyes were large and dark gray, and had a kindly expression which one would hardly have expected in one whose neck was in the hemp." In short, "this was no vulgar assassin" (SF 726). Through what he reveals and what he withholds, Bierce effectively incites the reader's interest in, as well as at least provisional sympathy for, the character in such a desperate situation.

In closing the first section of the story, Bierce increases this connection between reader and protagonist by allowing the reader briefly to enter the mind of the southern gentleman, as he composes himself to meet his fate by closing "his eyes in order to fix his last thoughts upon his wife and children" (SF 726). In this attempt, the condemned man is repeatedly distracted, first by the beauty and sounds of the natural scene and then, increasingly, by the unnatural preparations going on around him. His sensory perceptions are both preternaturally sharpened and inconsistent, providing the first indication of his understandable psychic distress. The "swirling water of the stream racing madly beneath his feet" one moment is the next perceived as a "sluggish stream." He hears "a sharp, distinct, metallic percussion like the stroke of a blacksmith's hammer upon the anvil," a beat which in its regular recurrence is "slow as the tolling of a death knell." As the intervals between the strokes lengthen, "the sounds increased in strength and sharpness. They hurt his ear like the thrust of a knife; he feared he would shriek." And yet, what the man hears is just "the ticking of his watch" (726–27). In desperation, his mind fastens on a desperate fantasy of escape: "'If I could free my hands,' he thinks, 'I might throw off the noose and spring into the stream. By diving I could evade the bullets and, swimming vigorously, reach the bank, take to the woods and get away home. My home, thank God, is as yet outside their lines; my wife and little ones are still beyond the invader's farthest advance.'" As these thoughts are "flashed into the doomed man's brain rather than evolved from it," the sergeant standing next to the bound man steps off the platform (727).

Rather than continuing with the fall of the body that would logically have followed this movement and so ended the escape fantasy, Bierce begins the second section of the story by stopping the forward thrust of the narrative to identify the protagonist by name and explain his back-story. A close reading of this section suggests that Farquhar is far from a hero in the eyes of the author. First of all, this "well-to-do planter, of an old and highly respected Alabama family," is a slave owner who, for political reasons, "was naturally an original secessionist and ardently devoted to the Southern cause." Moreover, as a result of curiously unexplained "[c]ircumstances of an imperious nature," Farquhar has not joined the Confederate army to defend his land, his family, or his fellow southerners. Choosing instead to sit out the war at home on his plantation, "he chafed under the inglorious restraint, longing for the release of his energies, the larger life of the soldier, the opportunity for distinction. That opportunity, he felt, would come, as it comes to all in war time" (SF 727). The irony of this passage is undeniable, and it rings with the tone of a Union soldier's contempt for the politics of the South and especially for southerners who, after instigating the war to protect their interests, then failed to support them by serving in it. This is not to say, however, that civilians such as the fictional Farquhar did not suffer from self-guilt or that, as a result, they did not fervently wish to take action against the enemy. Gregory Zilboorg explains that, through the death of others in battle, a civilian can gain "a clearer emotional realization of the dangers of war," but he also "begins to wrestle with an unconscious sense of guilt about those who have fallen, and with a mounting sense of anger and feeling of hatred for the enemy who kills," which serve to repress his fear of death (471). It is in just such a state that Farquhar succumbs to the manipulations of a Union scout dressed as a "gray-clad soldier" of the Confederacy. The scout, while admitting that "'any civilian caught interfering with the railroad, its bridges, tunnels or trains will be summarily hanged,'" tempts Farquhar to try to set fire to the bridge, telling him that it is guarded by "'[o]nly a picket post half a mile out, on the railroad, and a single sentinel at this end of the bridge'" (SF 727).

Farquhar, waiting his opportunity to contribute to the war, might very well have hoped for such an assignment. According to Harnett Thomas Kane, the Civil War "was a spy-conscious war, and sometimes it seemed that everyone was talking volubly on the subject, in newspapers, parlors, bars, and at street corners" (11–12). American espionage during this era was still largely the work of amateurs. Civil War "spies improvised, experimented, and what they lacked in finesse they made up in energy and determination. They broke rules usually because they had never heard of them. They were a mixed crew, gentle and flamboyant, earnest and brazen, ingenious or crafty. They ranged from shoe clerks to young plantation owners, lawyers to *grandes dames,* actresses to plump housewives" (12). Although Farquhar represents the romantic notions of war that Bierce disdained, his wish to take a meaningful role and serve the South was no less common or heartfelt as a result. Accordingly, he was psychologically vulnerable to the manipulations of the Federal scout, and this vulnerability, rather than the stupidity that others (and quite likely Bierce himself) have attributed to him, was the main reason for his downfall.[1]

In the third and final section of the story, Bierce returns the reader to the scene of the bridge, picking up the action as he left it at the end of the first section. Farquhar falls "straight downward through the bridge," and in losing consciousness, he is described "as one already dead" (SF 728); however, what transpires next, before the confirmation of Farquhar's death in the story's last sentence, is an elaborate enactment of the fantasy escape from death that the condemned man imagined before his fall, a dreamlike sequence which the reader is led to believe is reality through Bierce's narrative technique. Critical controversy about the tale has centered on this technique, which some have labeled a cheap trick that is inconsistent with the truth of human experience. In originating this line of thinking in 1943, Cleanth Brooks and Robert Penn Warren argued that Farquhar's fantasized journey is psychologically unrealistic, and they faulted Bierce for withholding from the reader the knowledge that "the dying man's vision is merely a vision" (63). Reading the sequence, however, with an understanding of the theory of Generative Death Anxiety suggests that these objections are unfounded and that the story is, instead, an uncanny representation of the fundamental human need to deny death and repress fears of mortality.

Ernest Becker explains that there are three human responses to death: denial, mental illness, and heroism, and elements of all three responses are present in Farquhar's ultimately unsuccessful efforts to defy mortality. After failing in his misguided attempt to play hero by burning the bridge, he struggles to die with dignity and courage as the hero-system would have him. Unlike his military counterpart Parker Adderson, Farquhar does not resort to the psychological defense of caustic humor, but rather stands in somber silence. Further, as the tension mounts, he neither begs nor pleads for his life. Although revealing no outward signs of his distress, however, his exaggerated sense impressions have already belied his outward calm. At the point when his anxiety becomes overwhelming, Farquhar—like Adderson—experiences a psychic break with reality, but it takes place solely within his own traumatized mind. At the threshold between life and death, in what Don Asher Habibi calls a "liminal, distended time flashforward," Farquhar experiences a near-death fantasy in a mental projection of his survival and escape (85).[2]

In contrast to the rigid, matter-of-fact style associated with the reality of war that Bierce uses in section one, the language in section three is free-flowing and impressionistic as it presents the condemned man's inner turmoil. After falling into the water, Farquhar is awakened from his seemingly dead state "by the pain of a sharp pressure upon his throat, followed by a sense of suffocation." Eventually, he realizes that the rope has broken, and he struggles to untie the noose before he drowns, while congratulating himself on his heroic fight: "What splendid effort!—what magnificent, what superhuman strength! Ah, that was a fine endeavor! Bravo!" (SF 728). Since this action in reality did not happen, these thoughts would seem to be the protagonist's rather than the ironic commentary of the objective narrator. In this way, Farquhar appears to assume the role of observer more than participant in his escape, which serves to mitigate his guilt and humiliation in failing either to burn the bridge or to stand firm in the face of death.

In fact, Farquhar so completely suppresses the fact of his unavoidable death that, as Peter Stoicheff observes, "it is revised not only as an escape from death but further, into a vivid dream of birth itself" (355). Hands that are seemingly other than his own remove the noose and force him to the surface: "He watched them with a new interest as first one and then the other pounced upon the noose at his neck. They tore it away and thrust it fiercely aside," as he protests that they "'Put it back, put it back.'" The subjectively felt pain that marks this episode confirms the violence of the birth process: "His neck ached horribly; his brain was on fire. . . . His whole body was racked and wrenched with an insupportable anguish!" But still "his disobedient hands," denying his command, "beat the water vigorously with quick, downward strokes, forcing him to the surface. He felt his head emerge; his eyes were blinded by the sunlight; his chest expanded convulsively, and with a supreme and crowning agony his lungs engulfed a great draught of air, which instantly he expelled in a shriek" (SF 729). Bierce, with this description, depicts birth as an excruciatingly painful separation from the mother that creates the child's first experience of death and so connects Farquhar's wish to live with his desire to return to the safety of the womb.[3]

Once again in control of his physical senses, which remain "preternaturally keen and alert," he looks around him. At the forest that edges the bank of the stream, he discerns not only the individual trees but "the leaves and the veining of each leaf," and he can identify "the very insects upon them: the locusts, the brilliant-bodied flies, the gray spiders stretching their webs from twig to twig," all of which make "audible music" to his ears as he perceives the natural beauty of life that he has previously failed to appreciate (SF 729). After miraculously evading the volley of bullets fired upon him at the Union captain's command, Farquhar's heroic adventure continues as he first swims "vigorously with the current" but then spins "like a top" when he is "caught in a vortex and . . . whirled on with a velocity of advance and gyration that made him giddy and sick" (730). Bierce again connects life and death in the complex romantic symbol of the vortex in the midst of the flowing current, a symbol with myriad associations of insanity, creativity, and danger beyond mortal control.

The pre-Oedipal implications of Farquhar's fantasy continue as he reaches shore. Though "content to remain in that enchanting spot until retaken," grapeshot forces him instead to plunge into a surreal forest landscape that recalls Bierce's own nightmare recollections in the essay "Visions of the Night." To Farquhar, much like the lost and abandoned child in Bierce's dreams, "The forest seemed interminable; nowhere did he discover a break in it, not even a woodman's road. He had not known that he lived in so wild a region. There was something uncanny in the revelation." Bierce's use of the word "uncanny" anticipates

Freud by connecting womb and forest, life and death, as the dreamer seeks to satisfy his compulsion to return to the familiar safety of "home" despite its simultaneously terrifying associations with death.[4] After traveling all day, he at last finds a road that he knows leads in "the right direction," but "though wide and straight as a city street," it seems "untraveled" and without sign of "human habitation" (SF 731). Separated from his mother through birth, the child's sense of loss and abandonment as he searches to find and then travel the road of life again suggests the dreamer's extreme death anxiety and hints of the inevitable conclusion to come in the darkness of night that now surrounds him.

At this point, in the irrational logic so common to dreams, Farquhar's consciousness of the pain associated with the cord around his neck—and its attendant threat of suffocation—returns him again to the birth fantasy, threatening to take him out of the dream-state entirely as he can "no longer feel the roadway beneath his feet!" Suddenly, however, "[h]e stands at the gate of his own home. All is as he left it, and all bright and beautiful in the morning sunshine" (SF 731). Opening the gate and passing up the walk, he springs forward to extend his arms to his wife, who waits for him at the bottom of the steps, but in doing so, "he feels a stunning blow upon the back of the neck; a blinding white light blazes all about him with a sound like the shock of a cannon—then all is darkness and silence!" As Bierce explains in the terse one-sentence paragraph that follows to conclude the tale: "Peyton Farquhar was dead; his body, with a broken neck, swung gently from side to side beneath the timbers of the Owl Creek bridge" (732).

With these words, protagonist and reader simultaneously are jerked from their shared state of denial back to the reality of Farquhar's fate. The reader has operated throughout the fantasy "in the same cause-and-effect, space-time frame as the protagonist," and so experienced "the sensations, thoughts, and feelings of Farquhar's dream state directly" as lived experience (Ames 53). This narrative technique has capitalized on the reader's own psychic need to suspend disbelief. As a result, the reader's reaction, upon learning that Farquhar's denial of death is only a failed fantasy, stems not from the unreality of the psychic process it depicts but rather its overwhelming realism. "Everything in [Farquhar's] dream signals him, and the reader, that his time for heroic adventure is now over, and he will pay the price for his actions soon" (Fry and Chandler 12). That the reader as much as Farquhar fails to recognize these signals suggests the true human condition in times of peace as well as war. However, war magnifies the urge to heroism, as well as its tragic costs, and this burden, as Bierce shows through this experience, is one that civilians, as well as soldiers, bear.

Northern and southern soldiers alike often voiced hostility toward civilians who, like Farquhar, remained at home during the war. Linderman maintains that "[t]he men grew to resent unchanging civilian allegiance to the precepts with which the war began" and that "intense anger was directed at civilians who continued to voice the old values and to invoke the 1861 rituals that summoned them" (216–17, 218). "Those who continued to kill one another in battle," he claims, "often felt less estrangement from their victims than from those in whose behalf they had gone to fight" (239). McPherson agrees that soldiers had become more conflicted about the war by 1863 and experienced declining morale and increasing cynicism as a result; however, he qualifies Linderman's position by arguing that "[t]o generalize these sentiments into estrangement from 'those in whose behalf they had gone to fight' is misleading. And even more so is the argument that soldiers repudiated the 'old values' of courage, honor, and patriotism that civilians continued to voice. In fact, almost the opposite was true. Soldiers' anger was selectively targeted at civilians who *failed* to adhere to the values of 1861" (*For Cause and Comrades* 142). Farquhar's fear that he would be found lacking in such values arguably drove him to foolhardy action that resulted in his needless death. In "Chickamauga," however, Bierce shows the tragic collateral damage of war to that segment of civilian society that soldiers most sought to protect from harm: women and children.

The Battle of Chickamauga took place on 19–20 September 1863, and the resulting Confederate victory has often been characterized as Pyrrhic since the North ultimately retained control of the city of Chattanooga, over which the battle was principally fought. It nevertheless effectively marked the end of the military career of Union General William Rosecrans, whose retreat was blamed for the defeat. The engagement "was distinguished not only by its bloodiness but also by the peculiar topography of the area, vine-choked woods interspersed with open farmland" (Joshi and Schultz SS 29). Because of the dense woods, the clearings and cultivated fields around the small family farms in this area became central scenes of the battle. In his 1911 account of Chickamauga, Michael Hendrick Fitch explains that these farms were tilled by "the obscurest of backwoodsmen, who lived in small log cabins or small frame buildings. Their names would never have been known, even in Chattanooga nine miles away, had it not been for the accidental fighting there of the greatest battle of the west" (81). Although no civilian casualties were reported, the homes of the Brotherton, Glenn, Kelly, Poe, and Snodgrass families were all burned or destroyed in the fighting.

Bierce fought at Chickamauga in his first major battle as a staff officer under the command of General William B. Hazen, whose troops were located near four of the burned homes. Both Kelli A. Larson and Owens argue that Bierce's tale would most logically have been inspired by the home and personal situation of Eliza Glenn, or "Widow Glenn," as she was commonly known. The Glenn house, which had an unobstructed view in the center of the battlefield, was commandeered by Rosecrans as his headquarters on the first day of the battle, and it was subsequently destroyed during the fighting by an exploding shell. Glenn, her infant daughter, and her two-year-old son were not injured in the battle or the resulting fire because they had been moved to safety.[5]

While the location and surroundings of the Glenn house seem likely to have inspired Bierce, the case that he used the family itself as a model for his characters is less compelling. As his fictional protagonist, Bierce uses a six-year-old unnamed boy, who the reader does not learn is deaf until the child discovers his mother's dead body in the final paragraphs of the tale. Further, Bierce suggests that the boy's father, "a poor planter," is still living, although he is not depicted as physically present during the events of the story (SF 648). The narrator claims that, in his younger days, the man had been an Indian fighter and that he had also fought in the Mexican-American War. Now, however, "the warrior-fire" survives in his "peaceful life" at home only in his love of "military books and pictures," which he has shared with his son (648). By contrast, John Glenn, Eliza's husband, was dead, having enlisted as a Confederate soldier in 1861, only to die of illness two months later in an Alabama hospital (Cozzens 139).

More convincing is the argument that Bierce was moved by the general plight of the families who both witnessed and were displaced by the horrific events of Chickamauga. The neighbors in this area were close, and some were even related. Despite the urging of Union soldiers, some of the families refused to leave their homes. Hiram Vittetoe, whose home was not destroyed, kept watch for two days while his wife and three daughters hid in a small hole under the kitchen floor that was covered by planks. According to Peter Cozzens's account of the battle, Eliza Glenn and her children went to the Vittetoe's one-room cabin when they left their own home, but her location is not otherwise described (140). Meanwhile, at the Reed home, Mrs. Reed and her three small children also refused to leave when asked to do so. Most of the residents, however, "established a sort of refugee camp northwest of the Reed house.... Without shelter, sleeping in the open through the chilly nights, without sufficient blankets, thirsty and hungry, they suffered in common with the soldiers, though less inured to hardships" (Tucker 377).

Like the actual families who witnessed Chickamauga, Bierce's young protagonist, who wanders from his home into the nearby woods, experiences the battle and its aftermath firsthand; however, his age and inability to hear lead him—until the end—to misinterpret the experience as child's play rather than the deadly adult reality of battle. Suggesting the historical continuum of the human impulse to war, the young boy sets off to play soldier with a crude wooden sword he has fashioned for himself. "This weapon," Bierce writes, "he now bore bravely, as became the son of an heroic race, and pausing now and again in the sunny space of the forest assumed, with some exaggeration, the postures of aggression and defense that he had been taught by the engraver's art" in his father's books. Coming upon "the margin of a wide but shallow brook," he finds his advance cut off, but the little warrior still manages to vindicate himself against "his imaginary foe" by "putting all to the sword" (SF 648). While the child has been educated in war as an abstract art of killing, he has not yet absorbed the reality of violent death beyond the picture book portraits of the martial act itself.

Bierce further emphasizes the child's innocence in the boy's reaction to the first actual opponent he comes upon: "a rabbit!" Turning and fleeing without considering the direction, he calls "with inarticulate cries for his mother, weeping, stumbling, his tender skin cruelly torn by brambles, his little heart beating hard with terror—breathless, blind with tears—lost in the forest!" (SF 649). The child's exaggerated reaction to the harmless rabbit reinforces the reader's knowledge of the character's naivety. At the same time, however, the terror evoked by this confrontation also confirms that the child is not without fear of death, since he reacts with overwhelming anxiety when faced with an actual life situation that affects his perception of his own basic safety. Bierce aptly connects this fear of annihilation with the anxiety of object-loss that has its original source in separation from the mother. Eventually exhausted from his anxiety and disoriented from wandering "through the tangled undergrowth," the lost child lies down alone and sobs himself to sleep, positioned "within a few yards of the stream and still grasping his toy sword, no longer a weapon but a companion" (649).

Bierce adds poignancy and depth to his depiction by contrasting this child of the Confederacy's desolation with the cheery sounds of the birds and squirrels around him, which the author associates with a "celebration of Nature's victory over the son of her immemorial enslavers." Meanwhile, "back at the little plantation . . . white men and black" search for the boy as "a mother's heart was breaking for her missing child" (SF 649). Although the families in this area were poor, some had slaves. When John Glenn left for war, for instance, Eliza's father had sent a slave to help her maintain the farm and to protect the family (Cozzens 139). With this passage, Bierce alludes to the sectional and race divisions that, in keeping with historical precedent and human proclivity, are being resolved with lives rather than words. That this celebration of victory is unseemly and insensitive is signaled by the recognition that Nature is "unconscious of the pity of it." Further, the celebration is also clearly premature since "somewhere far away" the sounds of continuing warfare can also be inferred in the "strange, muffled thunder" (SF 649).

When the child awakens hours later, night has fallen. Just as many of the actual displaced civilians at Chickamauga suffered from the cold in sleeping out in the open during the battle, the boy feels "[t]he chill of the evening . . . in his limbs, the fear of the gloom in his heart." Nevertheless, having rested, he is now more composed and in control of the anxiety that had overwhelmed him previously: "he no longer wept." Feeling "some blind instinct which impelled to action," he struggles through the undergrowth to reach the open ground near the brook. "[F]rightened and repelled" by the "thin, ghostly mist" that rises from the water, however, he turns his back on it to proceed—away from the direction from which he had come—"forward toward the dark inclosing wood." Recalling his earlier encounter with the rabbit, the child at this point suddenly sees "before him a strange moving object" that he at first takes "to be some large animal—a dog, a pig—he could not name it; perhaps it was a bear." With curiosity now staying his fear, he stands his ground, gaining courage from his realization that "at least it had not the long menacing ears of the rabbit." Eventually he discovers there are in reality many such creatures, "the whole open space about him was alive with them—all moving toward the brook" (SF 649).

In contrast to Farquhar's preternaturally sharp senses, the child's senses are blunted by both his lack of maturity and his deafness, and so, although there is "something familiar" in the "shambling, awkward gait" of these figures, it is only at length that reader and protagonist together realize that they are men crawling on their hands and knees (SF 649).[6] Further, guided by Bierce, the reader, unlike the boy, comprehends that these men are soldiers, who have been wounded in the battle that raged around the deaf child as he slept:

> Singly, in pairs and in little groups, they came on through the gloom, some halting now and again while others crept slowly past them, then resuming their movement. They came by dozens and by hundreds; as far on either hand as one could see in the deepening gloom they extended and the black wood behind them appeared to be inexhaustible. The very ground seemed in motion toward the creek. Occasionally one who had paused did not again go on, but lay motionless. He was dead. Some, pausing, made strange gestures with their hands; spread their palms upward, as men are sometimes seen to do in public prayer. (SF 650)

In what to the reader is a horrific misapprehension, the boy surmises that the men, whose faces are "singularly white" and often "streaked and gouted with red," are painted circus clowns performing with "grotesque attitudes and movements" for his pleasure. As they creep onward, these men who crawl "like babies" seem to present "a merry spectacle," a make-believe game of "horsey" for his own entertainment, and so he mounts one of them in playful glee. In response, however, the man flings "the small boy fiercely to the ground as an unbroken colt might have done," and then turns "upon him a face that lacked a lower jaw—from the upper teeth to the throat was a great red gap fringed from hanging shreds of flesh and splinters of bone." Rising to his knees, the man shakes his fist at the child, who "terrified at last," runs to hide behind a nearby tree to take "a more serious view of the situation." Although still lacking an adult understanding of the gruesome reality before him, the lost boy's fear returns as he watches the "clumsy multitude" drag itself "slowly and painfully along in hideous pantomime" (SF 650).

Bierce imbues his extended description of this forest scene with surrealistic details reminiscent of his accounts of his own childhood nightmares, as well as those of fictional heroes such as Halpin Frayser and Peyton Farquhar, who journeyed lost and alone through similar scenes in an ultimately failed search for the safety represented by home. This, too, is a "haunted landscape" with "creeping figures," "monstrous shadows," blood that makes the water gleam "with dashes of red," "drowned bodies," and "wavering flames." In short, it is a nightmare scene of "[d]esolation everywhere! In all the wide glare not a living thing was visible" (SF 650–52). In drawing this landscape, however, Bierce also depicts the actual conditions at Chickamauga. During the battle, the only source of water within the Federal lines was a small cattle pond near the Glenn house, and "[s]o many wounded had crawled to it during the course of the fighting that the water was now fetid, its surface streaked with blood. Veterans aptly christened the pool 'Bloody Pond'" (Cozzens 281). Colonel John T. Wilder, who fought at Chickamauga, explained that some soldiers, driven to quench their agonizing thirst, "waded into the pond. Others knelt at the edge and drank beside men who had fallen dead of wounds while drinking" (qtd. in Cozzens 394). Blending fact with fiction, Bierce creates the lurid reality of war for both the soldiers and civilians at Chickamauga.

Joining the throng of bloodied, retreating soldiers now in flight from the hunters they themselves had hunted, the boy marches past "the dead who had died to make the glory" that he has been trained to expect from his picture books (SF 651). Cathy N. Davidson argues that "Chickamauga" presents "a world turned topsy-turvy" in which "[h]umans are the hunters and the hunted as the war that they have made pursues them all" (43). Bierce emphasizes this point in the concluding scene when, drawn by the light from the fire of his burning house, the still uncomprehending child returns to his home to find the body of his murdered mother: "There, conspicuous in the light of the conflagration, lay the dead body of a woman—the white face turned upward, the hands thrown out and clutched full of grass, the clothing deranged, the long dark hair in tangles and full of clotted blood. The greater part of the forehead was torn away, and from the jagged hole the brain protruded, overflowing the temple, a frothy mass of gray, crowned with clusters of crimson bubbles—the work of a shell." At last recognizing the human cost of war in this gruesome image, the young would-be warrior raises his voice in "a series of inarticulate and indescribable cries—something between the chattering of an ape and the gobbling of a turkey—a startling, soulless, unholy sound, the language of a devil" (SF 652). The dehumanizing nature of war crystallizes in Bierce's insistent animal imagery and the deafness of this symbolic citizen to all he has witnessed to this point.

By purposefully concluding this most visual of tales with a familial image of mother and child that emphasizes the deaf boy's aural response to his loss, Bierce once again interweaves fact and fiction to create the truth about war that he himself learned in battles such as this one. Many soldiers' recollections of Chickamauga were aural in character. At the end of his own 1898 memoir "A Little of Chickamauga," Bierce recalls finally retiring "in profound silence and dejection" after "two days of hard fighting, without sleep, without rest, without food and without hope" (SS 32). At night, darkness obscured much of the battlefield gore from view, but the sounds of suffering continued unabated. As one soldier wrote in his journal, "The thunder of battle has ceased . . . but, oh, a worse, more heartrending sound breaks upon the night air. The groans from thousands of wounded in our front crying in anguish and pain, some for death to relieve them, others for water. Oh, if I could only drown this terrible sound, and yet I may also lie thus ere tomorrow's sun crosses the heavens. Who can tell?" (qtd. in Cozzens 28). Bierce would have us both see and hear that in war lies the loss of our very humanity. In "Chickamauga," he shows that the path of destruction wrought by war spares no one by representing in this final image of mother and son the cost in civilian lives that must be included in calculating the toll of this most uncivil of civil wars.

8

Seeking Death: Tales of Suicidal War Heroes

If the righteous thought death what they think they think it they would search less diligently for divine ordinances against suicide.
—Ambrose Bierce

In experiencing trauma, humans evidence a wide range of reactions that reflects their different capacities and resources for handling the associated stress and anxiety. During war, soldiers are both the victims and the perpetrators of combat-related trauma, and these circumstances can have immediate as well as long-term psychological consequences. The most destructive of all wars in American history, the Civil War introduced modern technology to warfare, which resulted in increased numbers of psychiatric as well as physical casualties. "Within the military itself, there were no psychiatrists at all, and the military continued to take the traditional view that soldiers who broke down in battle were cowards or had a 'weak' character" (Gabriel 105–6). However, "there are no personality or demographic factors which are associated with psychiatric collapse in war; neither are there any factors associated with heroism" (78). Recent studies suggest that fear of failing the heroic test of combat rather than fear of death or injury itself causes the most trauma and psychiatric breakdown in combat.[1] These studies reflect the complex tensions inherent in heroism as a culturally expected response in facing death.

Humans, like other animals, have inborn instincts to recognize danger and to respond to it by fighting or fleeing. In addition, humans, unlike other animals, have intellectual faculties that make it possible for them to overrule these instinctive reactions. Thus, what humans believe and think can significantly affect how they behave when faced with danger. Jules Masserman argues that all human psychic defenses against trauma rest on three fundamental beliefs. To sustain themselves in such situations, humans must believe: first, that there is a connection between their actions and what happens to them; second, that they are not alone (i.e., "someone will save me"); and third, that they will somehow survive (180–82). Soldiers are trained to define themselves in terms of these beliefs and to act in accordance with them. In combat, however, they "are constantly confronted with stark evidence that none of the basic assumptions upon which their mental stability is premised are valid." As a result, the individual combatant "develops a constant and severe conflict between his physiology's autonomic functions designed to keep him alive and the mental pull of his beliefs, already seriously eroded by the evidence of his senses. He wants to live up to the ideals of being a good solider, but his fear pulls him in the other direction" (Gabriel 83). Further, his ability to fear not only what *is* happening but also to project what *may* happen serves to heighten his anxiety. If the soldier exceeds his ability to endure combat stress, he may manifest one or more symptoms of psychiatric breakdown, which serve to remove him from the stressful situation and relieve his anxiety.

One of the earliest acute responses to combat stress is physical and mental exhaustion. Other more severe reactions, which may develop quickly or gradually, include confusional states, conversion hysteria, obsessional and compulsive states, and character or personality disorders (Gabriel 89–93). In extreme cases, the soldier may commit suicide in response to combat-related trauma. Edwin Shneidman defines suicide from the perspective of Western thinking as "a conscious act of self-induced annihilation, best understood as a multidimensional malaise in a needful individual who defines an issue for which the suicide is perceived as the best solution" (203). Suicide, though without adaptive, or survival, value, does have functional value for the individual because it abolishes painful tension and anxiety (Kluckhohn and Murray 36). Although many people assume that suicide is almost entirely an emotional response, in reality it has both affective and cognitive elements. Typically, in suicide, the individual's cognitive state is constricted, narrowing "the range of options usually available to that individual's consciousness when the mind is not panicked into dichotomous thinking" (Shneidman 138).

Ambrose Bierce's writings suggest that he understood the complex psychic stresses of war, and he reflected this understanding in his depiction of a range of possible reactions to combat trauma. One of only two extant letters from this period, his 1864 letter to Clara Wright, the sister of his then fiancée, records his own experience with battle fatigue. In this letter, Bierce admits, "I am getting very tired of my present life and weary of the profession of arms" (MM 1). At this stage of the war, exhaustion was understandable, but the letter also suggests his depressed emotional state, and the barrage of questions he poses intimates an obsessive fixation on what is going on at home in his absence. It includes alarming evidence of his feelings of emotional isolation ("I am very lonely"), survivor's guilt ("And yet *I* am left"), and fatalism ("I hardly expect to ever see you again" and ". . . my turn will come") (1). Bierce's near fatal wounding just fifteen days later may actually have saved his life by removing him from the battlefield so that he could rest and restore his depleted physical and psychological stamina.

Bierce's memoirs also document similar symptoms of decompensation that he observed in both himself and his comrades. For example, in "On a Mountain," he recalls how, in the early days of the war, their first face-to-face confrontation with dead bodies turned them overnight into "a beaten, dispirited and exhausted force, feeble from fatigue and savage from defeat" (SS 10). Writing about the Battle at Pickett's Mill, he recalls laughing with others at an idle jest, observing that "men awaiting death on the battlefield laugh easily, though not infectiously" ("The Crime at Pickett's Mill" SS 40). Such laughter serves as a defense against anxiety, but making jokes and acting silly to ward off the horror of war can also quickly shift into a psychotic state known as Ganzer Syndrome.[2] In "What I Saw of Shiloh," Bierce describes soldiers who, when pushed beyond their limits of endurance, reacted to the trauma of battle by deserting the front lines. "These men," he writes, "were defeated, beaten, cowed. They were deaf to duty and dead to shame. A more demented crew never drifted to the rear of broken battalions. They would have stood in their tracks and been shot down to a man by a provost-marshal's guard, but they could not have been urged up that bank" (15). Although branded as cowards, the response of these men arguably suggests a truly sane response to the horrific strain of battle.

It is in his Civil War tales, however, that Bierce most extensively depicts the debilitating effects of combat-related trauma. The individual struggles of his isolated soldier protagonists document a full range of symptoms, as well as the dynamic process of decompensation that can occur when a soldier reaches his limits of endurance.[3] Often Bierce focuses on soldiers who ultimately commit suicide at the end of this struggle. In his depiction of these protagonists and their final acts, Bierce anticipates current psychological thinking in his appreciation of the incapacitating consequences of war trauma on the human psyche and the circumstances that can lead individuals to choose suicide as a solution when anxiety becomes overwhelming. After first looking again at "A Tough Tussle" and "Killed at Resaca" to consider the clinical implications of the protagonists' reactions in these tales, this chapter will examine the motif of suicide in three other Civil War stories, which originally were published between 1888 and 1891: "The Story of a Conscience," "One of the Missing," and "The Mocking-Bird."[4]

The experience of Second Lieutenant Brainerd Byring in "A Tough Tussle" is consistent with the finding that acute combat reactions can occur rapidly—even in minutes or seconds, as well as the conclusion that such responses, including the suicidal act that ends Byring's struggle, are more common in new recruits than in more seasoned combatants (Gabriel 58–59). Bierce foreshadows Byring's unraveling by recognizing the lieutenant's undisclosed but self-acknowledged fears of even the abstract notion of death. The lieutenant dwells on these fears as he sits alone at his post in the darkness, and they are exacerbated by the societal dictate that he behave heroically in the face of death. When he begins his watch in the forest, these fears excite within him "unusually acute sensibilities" that manifest themselves in peritraumatic dissociation. As the narrator explains, Byring's "imagination found it easy to people [his surroundings] with all manner of unfamiliar shapes, menacing, uncanny or merely grotesque" (SF 620). These distorted sense impressions signal the lieutenant's generalized anxiety about his duties as a newly commissioned officer and leader of men, a position that he has assumed without sufficient training or any combat experience to prepare him. Further, they escalate in intensity when he proves unable or unwilling to relieve his tension by leaving his post and availing himself of his comrades' support: "Surrounded at a little distance by armed and watchful friends, Byring felt utterly alone. Yielding himself to the solemn and mysterious spirit of the time and place, he had forgotten the nature of his connection with the visible and audible aspects and phases of the night" (621).

Confronted with the reality of violent death in the figure of the corpse of a Confederate soldier, the young officer's generalized anxiety becomes fixated on this object. Although he attempts to manage his distress, which he discerns through his physical symptoms of clenched teeth and heavy breathing, he is unsuccessful in this attempt, and his condition quickly reaches a phobic state. In his extreme state of agitation, Byring envisions the dead body as animate and, evidencing a ferocious rage, he attacks it, "hot-hearted for action" (SF 623). The ending of the tale suggests that Byring commits suicide by "a sword-thrust through the heart" after inflicting the unresisting corpse with "no fewer than five dreadful wounds" (624). Robert Jay Lifton argues that anger in such a situation, as well as the rage and violence that can result from it, suggests the individual's "struggle to assert vitality by attacking the other rather than the self" (*Broken Connection* 147). Unnerved by the social pressures of heroism and his fear of failing the heroic test, Byring externalizes and converts his anxious feelings about himself into anger against others who might judge him lacking in valor. When this frenzied attempt to vindicate his self-image fails to assuage his anxiety, he then turns the sword upon himself in what Emile Durkheim would term an altruistic suicide.

In altruistic suicide, the individual's sacrifice of life is imposed by society for social ends. In his study of nineteenth-century European society, Durkheim found that the suicidal aptitude of soldiers was much higher than that of the civilian population of the same age. As he explained, "the first quality of a soldier is a sort of impersonality not to be found anywhere in civilian life to the same degree. He must be trained to set little value upon himself, since he must be prepared to sacrifice himself upon being ordered to do so." Required often to act without question or even understanding of such orders, the soldier "must have but a weak tie binding him to his individuality, to obey external impulsion so docilely. In short, a soldier's principle of action is external to himself; which is the quality of the state of altruism" (234). Although the Civil War hero-system did not formally require suicidal sacrifice, it did promote the view that death was preferable to dishonor. Bierce's depiction of Herman Brayle in "Killed at Resaca" most clearly illustrates this precipitating social element in suicidal behavior.

Brayle's desire to vindicate himself in the face of his fiancée's suspicions of his cowardice impels him to reckless disregard of his own safety on the battlefield. In most likelihood, such behavior was preceded by depression which originated as an acute response to his fiancée's letter in which she writes, "'I could bear to hear of my solder lover's death, but not of his cowardice'" (SF 511). Although depression is a static protest against trauma that is characterized by emotional numbing and overall constriction, it can progress to despair and serve as a transitional "pathway into and out of other forms of psychological disorder" (Lifton, *Broken Connection* 198). In the case of Brayle, his inexplicable recklessness has often excited the attention of his comrades and superior officers, but no one has taken action to remove the soldier from the battlefield. His solicitous concern for the well-being of other soldiers, and even of his horse, suggests his behavior may be rooted in a suicidal ideation, while the source of his trauma is hinted in his neurotic attempt to meet society's conventional notions of heroism by always dressing in full uniform before battle. Nevertheless, although Brayle has even been wounded several times as a result of his behavior, he has repeatedly returned to duty deemed "about as good as new" (SF 509).

Because no psychiatrists were posted at the front, the psychological care of Civil War soldiers fell to military physicians who had "virtually no practical training or clinical experience. Their understanding of a soldier's symptoms was therefore based largely on superstition, custom, and a good measure of imagination and the supernatural" (Coleman 25). In the first scientific study of combat-related stress, Jacob Mendes Da Costa diagnosed the array of symptoms he documented as "irritable heart," interpreting the reactions as primarily physiological and related to the cardiovascular system.[5] Other doctors, however, diagnosed these same symptoms as insanity or sunstroke. "'Nostalgia,' which was a popular diagnostic category at the beginning of the war, implied a weakness of character neither army chose to indulge" (Coleman 25). "The emphasis was on maintaining high levels of manpower, and many efforts of disturbed or frightened soldiers to avoid further exposure to combat were regarded as malingering or shirking" (Dean 134). Since the fictional Brayle was eager to return to the front, evidenced no somatic symptoms, and displayed no abnormal behavior that could not be rationalized as his being "vain of his courage," it seems consistent with Civil War practices that no one intervened on his behalf to remove him from duty (SF 507). As a result, however, his anxiety became so deeply seated over time that his pattern of behavior became inflexible, developing into a personality disorder that led to his death, which though technically by enemy fire, was nonetheless caused by his belief that he must kill himself to prove his heroism.

In the case of Captain Parrol Hartroy, the protagonist of "The Story of a Conscience," Bierce focuses on the prolonged effects of guilt as a factor in suicide. This 1890 tale, which is set in the Cumberland Mountains of Tennessee in 1863, is patterned on the same situation depicted in "Parker Adderson, Philosopher," but with significant differences.[6] In an inversion of the sectional allegiances of the characters, Hartroy, a respected Union officer, recognizes and arrests Dramer Brune, a Confederate spy, who has used a forged pass to penetrate his lines. Unlike Clavering, the Confederate officer in "Parker Adderson, Philosopher," Hartroy adheres to the traditional military procedure in such situations, advising his prisoner, "'you shall not die until to-morrow morning,'" and for his part, Drune—unlike Adderson—goes to his death with honor and dignity (SF 715). Before the execution, however, Hartroy and Brune admit that they both recognize each other and discuss privately the details of their first encounter in Grafton, West Virginia, two years previously. As in the other tale, this conversation between the two central characters takes place in the commanding officer's tent. However, it is characterized by none of the defensive bombast that marks the debate between Adderson and Clavering, but rather serves to illuminate the stalwart character of both soldiers, as well as the root of the anxiety that afflicts Hartroy.

At the time of their first encounter, Hartroy was a private assigned to guard Drune, a captured Confederate spy who had recently deserted the Union forces after he was refused a discharge for reasons of "altered convictions" (SF 717). Exhausted from "a long, fatiguing march" that day, Hartroy fell asleep at his post beside the railway car in which Drune was confined (716). Rather than taking advantage of Hartroy's dereliction of duty, an offense punishable by execution, Drune instead stayed in his place. As Hartroy recollects, "'You had only to step from the car and leave me to take your place before the firing-squad. You had a divine compassion. You pitied my fatigue. You let me sleep, watched over me, and as the time drew near for the relief-guard to come and detect me in my crime, you gently waked me. Ah, Brune, Brune, that was well done—that was great—that—'" (716–17). At this point, "[t]he captain's voice failed him" and with tears "running down his face," he "buried his face in his arms and sobbed" (717). Not knowing that Drune subsequently escaped, Hartroy has for two years carried a crushing burden of guilt. As he explains to Drune, "'I believed you dead—thought that you had suffered the fate which through my own crime you might easily have escaped'" (716). His emotional outburst reveals his self-condemnation for what he views as a criminal failure to meet both his duty as a soldier to his country and his responsibility as a man of conscience to a fellow human being.

Still struggling with his emotions, Hartroy berates himself further: "'I ought to have confessed my fault in order to relate the story of your magnanimity; it might have procured you a pardon. A hundred times I resolved to do so, but shame prevented. Besides, your sentence was just and righteous. Well Heaven forgive me!'" (SF 717). Unable to forgive himself or resolve his conflicting allegiances, Hartroy invokes God as he seeks absolution for behavior that he cannot reconcile with the military's code of honor or with his own principles of right and wrong. Openly talking with Brune about this traumatic event might in other circumstances have had therapeutic effect, alleviating some of Hartroy's anxiety by enabling him to achieve closure about what happened. In this situation, however, Hartroy's inflexible commitment to his duties as a Union officer does not allow him this relief. Instead, he issues the expected command to the adjutant: "'This gentleman is a deserter and a spy; he is to be shot to death in the presence of the troops.'" Immediately upon hearing the "volley of musketry" that confirms his order has been carried out, Hartroy then shoots himself and so "renounced the life which in conscience he could no longer keep" (717).

In playing out this resolution, Bierce makes it clear that Hartroy recognizes the dilemma with which he is faced. Just prior to the adjutant's arrival, the captain acknowledges to his prisoner, "'Ah but if I had suffered the penalty of my crime—if you had not generously given me the life that I accepted without gratitude you would not be again in the shadow and imminence of death'" (SF 717). Confronted again with his "crime" after two years of suffering alone with his guilt feelings, Hartroy's anxiety quickly builds, creating severe psychological consequences. As his anxiety grows, his sense of responsibility becomes overwhelming, and his powers of logic become reduced to a dichotomous cognitive state that is common in suicide.[7] In spite of the extenuating circumstances, Hartroy feels forced, in his own mind, to order Brune's "just and righteous" sentence for the spy's crimes—both past and present. He thus determines that he must also take his own life as just punishment for previously evading the death penalty that he believes he himself deserved two years ago. In making this decision, he paradoxically regains some sense of control over his life, as evidenced in the narrator's observation that "Captain Hartroy had recovered his composure" (717). According to Lifton, "Killing oneself may appear to be the only way to break out of the 'trap' or 'encirclement' and assert whatever it is one feels one wants to, or must, about one's life" (*Broken Connection* 249). Through his final act, then, Hartroy ironically seeks to put his life back into equilibrium even as he ends it. Guided by the cultural dictates of the hero-system, he finds suicide the only possible way to redeem his life, not only in his own eyes but in society's as well.

Whereas Captain Parrol Hartroy reacts to trauma by increasing his commitment to the military code of conduct, Private Jerome Searing in "One of the Missing" reacts to long-term battlefield stress by abusing its tenets. Set during the summer of 1864, in the aftermath of the battle at Kennesaw Mountain, Georgia, this 1888 story recounts the death of Searing, a Union scout sent ahead of his unit's lines to determine the enemy's location. Bierce introduces Searing with an abundance of positive descriptors. Fighting in General Sherman's army, he is a "brave man," "an incomparable marksman, young, hardy, intelligent and insensible to fear." Further, he has "extraordinary daring," "sharp eyes," and a "truthful tongue" (SF 525). Nevertheless, the hyperbolic effect that is created by this introduction, coupled with the unaccountable fact that Searing is still a private this late in the war, immediately raises questions in the reader's mind about the accuracy of the description and its possible ironic thrust. The careful reader's suspicions about this soldier grow as he begins his mission by entering the forest, where, for Bierce, both in his stories and his own nightmares, death was always hiding.

Progressing carefully through the dense underbrush, Searing discovers a clearing with a line of rifle pits that the enemy has recently abandoned, as well as a nearby house that is located on an incline, providing a view of the surrounding area. Although the deserted homestead is in such poor condition that it is barely standing, Searing enters it, conceals "himself in the débris of joists and flooring," and then looks across the open ground to confirm that the entire rear guard of the enemy is indeed retreating. At this point, Searing has "learned all that he could hope to know," and duty would require him "to return to his own command with all possible speed and report his discovery." The scout finds the line of retiring Confederates "singularly tempting," however, and so decides instead to exceed his orders and send an "ounce and a quarter of lead hissing into their midst" (SF 527).

With this decision, Bierce aligns his protagonist with the role of a sharpshooter or sniper. For many Civil War soldiers, as Drew Gilpin Faust explains, "the horror of killing was exemplified by sharpshooters, whose work appeared simply to be 'cold blooded murder'" (42). As the weaponry of this first of modern wars increasingly put distance between combatants, restraints against sniping relaxed, but the morality of this covert practice was still hotly contested.[8] Bierce, who himself was nearly killed by a sharpshooter's bullet at Kennesaw Mountain, agreed with the prevailing sentiments against such tactics. In an often reprinted essay entitled "Modern Warfare" that was first published in 1888, he condemned the technological advances in weaponry by writing, "I should not like to say that this is an age of human cowardice; I say only that the men of all civilized nations are taking a deal of pains to invent offensive weapons that will wield themselves and defenses that can take the place of the human breast. A modern battle is a quarrel of skulkers trying to have all the killing done a long way from their persons" (CW 9: 233).

In his memoir, Union officer John Beatty reflects the attitude of many soldiers who opposed sniping on principle when he writes about his regret at having fired a shot at retreating Confederate soldiers. "[I]t would have been criminal to have killed one of these men," he acknowledges, "for his death could have had no possible effect on the result of the war" (30). Consistent with this perspective, Searing acknowledges to himself that firing at these men "would probably not affect the duration and result of the war," but then he immediately rationalizes his decision to do so with the conviction that "it is the business of a soldier to kill." Nevertheless, as the narrator explains, "Private Searing was not to murder anybody that bright summer morning, nor was the Confederate retreat to be announced by him" (SF 527). Before he can fire his already cocked rifle, a misdirected Confederate artillery shell hits the building in which he is hiding, collapsing the structure and trapping him in the wreckage. Bierce's use of the word "murder" in describing Searing's intended action is purposeful and calculated to communicate a negative impression of the soldier's principles. Searing's decision to shoot one or more of these Rebel soldiers in the back suggests that killing has become an enjoyable game to him rather than an unfortunate but necessary duty. Although he has "repeatedly refused promotion," Searing is "not without a certain kind of ambition," which implies that he has chosen to retain his rank because it offers enhanced killing opportunities (528). Bierce reinforces this idea by contrasting the rank and responsibilities of his protagonist with those of his brother Lieutenant "Adrian Searing who, rather than leading his men into battle, follows them, seemingly armed only with a watch" (Blume, *Ambrose Bierce's Civilians and Soldiers* 86). As Dave Grossman observes, "[w]ith the possible exception of rare self-defense situations, most officers in combat never fire a shot at the enemy" (64). Only by remaining a private, then, could Searing ensure that he would continue to have opportunities such as this to use his Springfield rifle, which is "fitted with a globe sight and hair-trigger" (SF 527).

During war, prolonged exposure to violence creates a sense of randomness and insecurity that makes each soldier aware of life's instability. Such insecurity creates a wide range of individual reactions that can precipitate an unbalanced orientation toward the life-death continuum with either aggressive or non-aggressive characteristics. In his scale of aggression subtypes, Erich Fromm categorizes war theoretically as a defensive or benign type of human aggression; however, because it typically exceeds the need for self-defense, it also includes the more malignant forms of aggression that feature elements of sadism associated with character disorder.[9] Sharpshooting and other technological advances during the Civil War increased the distance and anonymity between combatants and so allowed for an increase in the degree of aggression, making malignant forms of aggression more common than in previous wars (Shalit 68). James J. Reid identifies Searing's behavior as consistent with Fromm's "destroyer-nihilist" type, which is defined as sadistic aggression caused by nihilistic alienation and lack of feeling.[10] In searching where to aim his shot before the house collapsed, Searing "considered where he could plant his shot with the best hope of making a widow or an orphan or a childless mother,—perhaps all three" (SF 527). Such hopes clearly suggest a sadistic orientation. Although Searing does not yet show the obsession with death itself that is associated with necrophiliac sadism, Fromm's most extreme category of malignant aggression, the soldier's behavior does suggest that he has become fixated on causing death and derives enjoyment from inflicting pain on others. Fearing the uncertainty of his own life, he feels powerless and so attempts to compensate by having power over the lives of others.

Pinned under the rubble of the collapsed building but not seriously injured, Searing regains consciousness to find the muzzle of his rifle "aimed at the exact center of his forehead" and only his right arm partly free (SF 529). Mistakenly believing that the rifle is still cocked and finding that some loose boards touch the trigger, he feels "caught like a rat in a trap" as he struggles to maintain his composure (528). Bierce's description of the private's distorted sense impressions creates the first signal of the man's state of confusion and anxiety. He mistakes nearness for distance, becomes conscious of "an insufferable light," and hears a rhythmic sound in his ears, followed by "a great silence, a black darkness, an infinite tranquility" (528). Not knowing that the gun discharged when the building fell and so is actually harmless, Searing attempts to repress his fears through denial: "Private Searing was affected with a feeling of uneasiness. But that was as far as possible from fear; he was a brave man, somewhat familiar with the aspects of rifles from that point of view, and of cannon too" (529). He recalls previous combat situations in which he behaved courageously and evaded injury and reminds himself that "[t]o face firearms is one of the commonest incidents in a soldier's life—firearms, too, with malevolent eyes blazing behind them. That is what a soldier is for" (530). In this case, however, Bierce would have the reader see that Searing's only enemy is himself, and the rest of the story plays out how Searing succumbs to his inner turmoil.

As his analytical faculties fail, Searing enters "a mental trap where rational thought is rendered powerless to effectively reassert control" (Blume, *Ambrose Bierce's Civilians and Soldiers* 90). Although he attempts to act rationally to relieve his tension, first by ignoring the gun and then by trying to sleep, his thoughts continually return to the rifle and its threat of death. Even as he tries to distract himself with "pleasant memories of his childhood," he is unable to escape this reality. After racing with his brother and sister "across the fields," he recalls entering "the somber forest beyond" and following "the faint path to Ghost Rock, standing at last with audible heart-throbs before the Dead Man's Cave and seeking to penetrate its awful mystery." Now, "[f]or the first time he observed that the opening of the haunted cavern was encircled by a ring of metal. Then all else vanished and left him gazing into the barrel of his rifle as before" (SF 530). In his distressed state, he interprets his headache, which in reality resulted from flying debris hitting his head, as foreshadowing his fate. Each time he closes his eyes, he "instantly" feels "the poignant pain in his forehead—the prophecy and menace of the bullet" (531).

Because of the character disorder that has developed from Searing's prolonged exposure to the trauma of war, he is continually motivated by sadistic impulses to control the lives of others. Stripped by his circumstances of the ability to exercise such power, his fears about the uncertainty of life, which he typically represses through aggression, are exacerbated beyond manageable limits. Totally helpless, unable even to move without fear of activating the trigger, death gains dominance in his psyche as he assumes a fatalistic outlook that prevents him from even considering the possibility of either rescue or his own heroism in the face of death. He acknowledges that he is "a plain, common soldier," with "no religion and not much philosophy; he could not die like a hero, . . . but he could die 'game,' and he would." However, this conviction dissolves immediately in the unbearable tension of not knowing "when to expect the shot!" As rats scamper about the debris, he becomes unnerved by the possibility that they will "attack his face, gnaw away his nose, cut his throat," and he wishes only to be dead before they do so (SF 531).

At this point, thoroughly broken in spirit, Searing becomes the physical embodiment of death in life, revealing the psychological condition of the sadist that he has previously concealed beneath his aggressive veneer: "Jerome Searing, the man of courage, the formidable enemy, the strong, resolute warrior was as pale as a ghost. His jaw was fallen; his eyes protruded; he trembled in every fiber; a cold sweat bathed his entire body; he screamed with fear. He was not insane—he was terrified" (SF 531–32). In his last struggle, he manages to thrust a strip of board against the trigger. Although this action does not result in the rifle firing, since it had previously discharged, it does result in Searing's death, which occurs literally from the fright of his ordeal, a "psychic suicide" that represents "the final measure of how little he could cope with his realization that he did fear death and his discovery of his own cosmic insignificance" (Davidson 32–33). The story concludes when Searing's brother Adrian arrives just moments later. Failing to recognize the dead body as belonging to his brother, or even to the Union forces, the lieutenant estimates from its condition that the soldier, wearing a uniform so dusty that it looks "Confederate gray," has been "[d]ead a week" (SF 533). With this postscript, Bierce emphasizes the traumatic impact of the private's psychic ordeal, which actually took only twenty-two minutes according to his brother's watch, and especially Searing's alienation from himself and others who might have loved and sustained him, a condition of enmity that ultimately caused his self-inflicted death.

In arranging his stories about soldiers in the collected *Tales of Soldiers and Civilians,* Bierce chose to conclude with "The Mocking-Bird," a tale that returns his readers to the early days of the war to relate the circumstances in which a soldier commits suicide after discovering that he has inadvertently killed his twin brother. With this tale, which was first published in 1891, Bierce underscores the self-destruction on both an individual and societal scale that he suggests is unavoidable in war by using a *doppelgänger* motif and the fratricidal nature of the Civil War to make his point. The protagonist in "The Mocking-Bird" is twenty-four-year-old Private William Grayrock, another isolated and previously untested soldier whose psychological resources fail him in an ordeal with death that once again turns the enchanted forest imagery of West Virginia into the wildly surreal, almost primal "gloom of a moonless night" (SF 791).

At the beginning of the story, which has marked similarities to "A Tough Tussle," Grayrock is introduced as a Union sentinel sitting "comfortably at the root of a great pine tree" on "a pleasant Sunday afternoon in the early autumn of 1861." His post, like that of Brainerd Byring, is "at a considerable distance from those to right and left." Unlike his relaxed posture, however, his mind is characterized by a "perturbation of spirit" as he reflects on what occurred the previous night during his watch at this same location (SF 790). At that time, disoriented in the darkness, Grayrock heard approaching footsteps but was unable to tell from which direction they came. Hearing no response to his command to halt, he fired his rifle into the night. This shot set off "a sympathetic fusillade" from the other sentinels, who then retreated, leaving only the lost "Grayrock, who did not know in what direction to retreat" (791). Certain that his bullet had hit its intended—though unseen—mortal target, Grayrock unsuccessfully searched for the body, but he then remained silent when, two hours later, the officer of the guard discovered and commended him for his courage in remaining at his post.

Now back at his post in clear daylight, after having again searched unsuccessfully for a body, Grayrock suffers from feelings of guilt. He knows that he failed in his duties as a sentinel by losing his bearings and shooting without adequate knowledge or provocation and that he then compounded his dereliction by not telling his superior officer what had transpired. Further, his careless act may have caused the death of an innocent person. Bierce's depiction of Grayrock's state suggests that the soldier is experiencing an acute reaction to trauma. "[S]omewhat fatigued," he directs a barrage of questions at himself that reveals his agitation, confusion, and disordered thought processes:

> "Do I . . . really wish that I had taken life in the performance of a duty as well performed without? What more could I wish? If any danger threatened, my shot averted it; that is what I was there to do. No, I am glad indeed if no human life was needlessly extinguished by me. But I am in a false position. I have suffered myself to be complimented by my officers and envied by my comrades. The camp is ringing with praise of my courage. That is not just. . . . What, then, shall I do? Explain that I saw an enemy and fired? . . . Shall I tell a truth which, discrediting my courage, will have the effect of a lie? Ugh! It is an ugly business altogether. I wish to God I could find my man!" (SF 792)

With these last words, Grayrock links his own manhood with that of the person he believes he has shot, foreshadowing the mutual loss of life that will ultimately transpire from his act.

Significantly, Grayrock, though distressed, falls asleep almost immediately after uttering these words. Seeking to escape from his turmoil, he escapes into sleep, commonly known as "death's brother," a self-imposed death-like state that serves to terminate, at least temporarily, his conscious thought processes. While asleep, he experiences a dream vision, which forms the heart of the tale.[11] In his dream, Grayrock returns to the "fair, fair land" of childhood that he shared with his twin brother John, who was "[w]ith him always, at his side," the "one to whom he gave his heart and soul in love." Strolling together through this seemingly idyllic paradise, the boys look beyond their fields to the "Realm of Conjecture," and further southward, they catch "glimpses of the Enchanted Land." Throughout these "golden days," a caged mockingbird sings in a "clear melody" that "*seemed,* indeed the spirit of the scene, the meaning and interpretation to sense of the mysteries of life and love" (SF 792–93, emphasis added). Eventually, after their mother's death, the twins are separated. Grayrock, who is identified as "the dreamer," is sent to live with family in the Realm of Conjecture, while John, taking the pet mockingbird with him, is sent to other family members who reside in the Enchanted Land (793).

Awakening to the song of another mockingbird, Grayrock still fails to realize the bird's falseness—signaled by its very name—and momentarily becomes overwhelmed by the fullness of his memories as "[f]or the moment he was, indeed, a child, in spirit and in memory, dwelling again by the great river, over-against the Enchanted Land!" The narrator, who is not deluded by the bird's song, observes that "[t]here was little in that—it was only to open the bill and breathe." Nevertheless, Grayrock dissolves into tears of loss, and it is only "with an effort of the will" that he is able to pull himself together and go onward (SF 794). When he does, however, he discovers, within a small thicket and marked by the bird's notes, the body of his dead twin. His simultaneous recognition of his lost brother—his second-self—and his lost innocence stills the song of the bird as it glides into the sunset and presumably provokes his suicide, for "[a]t roll-call that evening in the Federal camp the name William Grayrock brought no response, nor ever again thereafter" (794). Although the story is usually interpreted as ending with Grayrock's literal suicide, the ambiguity of Bierce's concluding sentence, coupled with the mockingbird imagery of flight, does not preclude the possibility that the private, instead, responded to his traumatic experience by deserting the army.[12] Desertion was not an uncommon occurrence, especially during the early days of the war when new recruits were first exposed to the brutal realities of actual or threatened death to themselves or others. "It is impossible to know how many of the almost 400,000 deserters (about 10 percent of both armies) were running from personal demons, but it was the only recourse, short of execution or suicide, available to those most acutely afflicted" (Coleman 24).

Whether or not this fatal encounter ends in Grayrock's literal suicide, the conclusion has a subtle "kind of symbolic logic which appears to originate in

Bierce's sense of his own lost youth and defeated ideals" (Woodruff 72). The imagery of Grayrock's dream vision closely resembles that of Bierce's stirring conclusion to his memoir "What I Saw of Shiloh." In this passage, seeking to reconcile his ambivalent feelings about war, he registers a poignant exclamation of loss: "O days when all the world was beautiful and strange; when unfamiliar constellations burned in the Southern midnights, and the mocking-bird poured out his heart in the moon-gilded magnolia; when there was something new under a new sun" (SS 24). He again expresses these same sentiments in a later letter when he writes "of a certain 'enchanted forest' hereabout to which I feel myself sometimes strongly drawn as a fitting place to lay down 'my weary body and my head'" (LAB 204). With these words, his affinity with Grayrock's experience seems palpable, and the letter continues with an explanation that suggests more parallels:

> The element of enchantment in that forest is supplied by my wandering and dreaming in it forty-one years ago when I was a-soldiering and there were new things under a new sun. It is miles away, but from a near-by summit I can overlook the entire region—ridge beyond ridge, parted by purple valleys full of sleep. . . . Can you guess my feelings when I view this Dream-land—my Realm of Adventure, inhabited by memories that beckon me from every valley? I shall go; I shall retrace my old routes and lines of march; stand in my old camps; inspect my battlefields to see that all is right and undisturbed. I shall go to the Enchanted Forest. (LAB 204)

Bierce's romantic illusions about life and war, like Grayrock's, were destroyed by the reality of his experiences, and, as a result, he sometimes fell victim to depression, yearning to follow the symbolic mockingbird into the sunset valley of death by taking his own life.

In the end, however, Grayrock succumbed to his fears by either killing himself or deserting, while Bierce did not, suggesting their different individual capacities to endure and respond to trauma. The story charts several moments of acute anxiety from which Grayrock recovers. Although he becomes lost in the darkness, daylight follows, enabling him to regain his bearings and his composure. Similarly, when he hears the mockingbird upon awakening, he eventually manages to recollect himself and move forward again. Ultimately, however, Grayrock is undone by his own imperfect psychic resources, capitulating in a moment of overwhelming anxiety. Grayrock's act—whether suicide or desertion—was reflexive. Although some suicides are meticulously planned, if he did take this most extreme measure to resolve his dilemma, it would support Shneidman's hypothesis that "suicide is often a metacritical act, representing a reverberating crisis, . . . a need to do something and to do it quickly, thoughtlessly, recklessly, in order to discharge the pressure of the psychological pain" (60). By concluding his tales of soldiers with Grayrock's experience, Bierce argues that, although the world certainly contributes to our undoing, we, in the end, are our own worst enemies.

Although Bierce did not always sympathize with the human frailties that prompt his protagonists to take their own lives, he believed that suicide was a heroic act of human will. In the 1893 essay "Taking Oneself Off," he argues that "[s]uicide is always courageous. We call it courage in a soldier merely to face death—say to lead a forlorn hope—although he has a chance of life and a certainty of 'glory.' But the suicide does more than face death; he incurs it, and with a certainty, not of glory, but of reproach. If that is not courage we must reform our vocabulary." Nevertheless, he also admits that "there may be a higher courage in living than in dying" and that "[t]he ethics of suicide is not a simple matter." In the end, he argues that "each case is to be judged, if judged at all, with a full knowledge of all the circumstances, including the mental and moral make-up of the person taking his own life—an impossible qualification of judgment" (CW 11: 341–42). Such views were quite controversial in his time, and even today, "religious doctrines still largely cleave to the belief that suicide is a sin," although the fields of law and social science "have taken the lead in advocating for more compassionate paradigms" (Coleman 136). Recognizing the complexities involved and the impetus that human isolation can add to the proclivity to see suicide as one's only solution to unbearable psychological pain, Bierce's writings count suicide as part of the tragic price of the Civil War hero-system.

Surviving War: "Phantoms of a Blood-Stained Period" and Posttraumatic Stress Disorder

Then with the knowledge of death as walking one side of me,
And the thought of death close-walking the other side of me,
And I in the middle as with companions, and as holding
the hands of companions. . . .
—Walt Whitman

Bierce's Civil War tales and memoirs depict soldiers on the battlefield who suffer both acute and chronic psychological effects of combat trauma. Some of these soldiers, like Private William Grayrock in "The Mocking-Bird," either desert the battlefield or take the extreme measure of causing their own deaths to resolve their dilemmas and end their suffering. Others, like Bierce, are able to marshal their psychic defenses to withstand their own fears and the societal pressures of the hero-system as they repeatedly face the brutal realities of actual or threatened death to themselves and others. For many of the survivors, however, the psychic effects of such exposure to violence do not end on the battlefield but rather continue long after they return home and resume their lives as civilians. Because there was little recognition or understanding of the psychological effects of war in the nineteenth century, the stress responses of Civil War veterans received even less attention or study than the similar symptoms of combatants in the field. As a result, even today, the myth persists that Civil War veterans were able to recover from whatever combat-related psychological problems they may have developed because of the warm welcome home they received by appreciative civilians. However, as recent studies have shown, Civil War veterans suffered from many of the same debilitating stress symptoms that veterans of more recent armed conflicts have experienced.[1]

In his analysis of the case histories of 291 Civil War veterans who, between 1861 and 1920, were committed to the Indiana Hospital for the Insane, Eric T. Dean, Jr., determined that "[m]any of these men continued to suffer from the aftereffects of the war and, along with their families, often lived in a kind of private hell involving physical pain, the torment of fear, and memories of killing and death" (100). Although no officially recognized diagnosis for the phenomenon existed at the time, these veterans all suffered from symptoms that would today be diagnosed as posttraumatic stress disorder. A formal diagnostic category only since the 1980 publication of the third edition of the American Psychiatric Association's *Diagnostic and Statistical Manual of Mental Disorders* (DSM-III), posttraumatic stress disorder (PTSD) is now widely recognized as "an occupational hazard of military life. Intense combat is perhaps the best-known and most powerful risk factor for PTSD" (Jones and Wessely 175). Other factors such as genetic inheritance, family history of psychiatric disorder, early adversity, social support, and educational achievement can also affect the likelihood of PTSD after exposure to trauma.[2]

With the 1994 publication of DSM-IV, the diagnostic criteria were updated to describe the circumstances most likely to result in PTSD as "a traumatic event in which . . . the person experienced, witnessed, or was confronted with an event or events that involved actual or threatened death or serious injury, or a threat to the physical integrity of self or others, [and] the person's response involved intense fear, helplessness, or horror" (424). Symptoms that are typically manifested after such a trauma include recurrent, uncontrollable recollections of the traumatic event, such as dreams or flashbacks; persistent avoidance of stimuli associated with the trauma through techniques such as withdrawal from social contact, emotional numbing, and a restricted range of emotions; and persistent symptoms of increased arousal that are indicated by factors such as difficulty sleeping, irritability or outbursts of anger, difficulty concentrating, hypervigilance, and an exaggerated startle response. To qualify for formal diagnosis, the sufferer must experience "clinically significant distress or impairment in social, occupational, or other important areas of functioning" (429).

Among the first to write about such symptoms in Civil War veterans, Herbert Hendin and Ann Pollinger Haas surmised, in a somewhat cursory analysis, that Ambrose Bierce suffered from what today would be diagnosed as PTSD. Bierce's war record unquestionably documents that over a four-year period from 1861 to 1865 he was repeatedly exposed to the threat of violent death or dismemberment and often witnessed such violence to others. An impressionable and naïve youth of eighteen when he enlisted, he fought in some of the bloodiest battles of the war, including Shiloh, Stones River, Chickamauga, Franklin, and Nashville. In one of his first engagements, during the Battle of Laurel Hill on 11 July 1861, he distinguished himself for his bravery in carrying a wounded comrade to safety in the midst of heavy enemy fire. Receiving a nearly fatal shotgun wound to the head at Kennesaw Mountain, Georgia, on 23 June 1864, Bierce survived a two-day railway journey to Chattanooga, where he was hospitalized and then furloughed home. After returning to the front in September, he continued to experience what he described as recurring "fits of fainting, sometimes without assignable immediate cause, but mostly when suffering exposure, excitement or excessive fatigue" ("Four Days in Dixie" SS 51).

Roy Morris points to one of Bierce's minor short stories, "The Other Lodgers," as echoing the author's state of mind at the time he returned to active duty after his injury. Clearly, this tale, which was one of the last that he was to publish, also suggests the long-term psychological effects of the war on Bierce, who, writing more than forty years afterwards, uses the genre of the ghost story to blunt the impression of the stressful memories related to his wounding. In this story, Colonel Levering recalls spending a night at Atlanta's Breathitt House Hotel in September 1864. Levering, who at the time of the visit has "not entirely recovered from a gunshot wound in the head, received in an altercation," is "worn out by two days and a night of hard railway travel" and so lies down fully clothed on the mattress of his darkened room and goes to sleep. Waking up in the middle of the night, he discovers "at least a dozen other lodgers" on the floor of his room—"obviously all dead!" and laid out "on their backs, disposed orderly along three sides of the room, their feet to the walls" (SF 1026). At first unable to cry out, as if he is having a nightmare, Levering eventually jumps up and runs to the office to complain. When he does, however, he finds the night clerk "just sitting and staring," motionless, "with a colorless face and the whitest, blankest eyes [he] ever saw." When the clerk mysteriously disappears before his eyes, "a kind-faced gentleman" who claims to "'look after the premises'" appears to explain the situation. He informs the agitated colonel that the hotel, now unoccupied, had been used as a hospital during the recent siege of Atlanta and that Levering's room had been "'the dead-room'" where corpses were kept. The clerk also "'has been dead a few weeks'" according to the man. Although the gentleman offers to take Levering back to the room to investigate the situation, the colonel instead flees, "bolting out of the door into the street" (1027).

In addition to the dating and location of the story's action, the references to Levering's head injury and his train ride to the "hospital" imbue the tale with an obvious autobiographical cast. Further, the explicit description of the positioning of the dead bodies, coupled with the colonel's acknowledgment of the nightmarish quality of his experience, echoes Bierce's description of the corpses in one of his own recurring nightmares. In recounting this dream in his essay "Visions of the Night," he writes of finding a score of dead male bodies "naked and arranged symmetrically" around a central "tank of white marble." Continuing his description of this gruesome scene, he notes that "[t]he feet were outward" and "[e]ach lay upon its back" (CW 10: 126). Bierce recalls first having had this nightmare in his early youth. The fact that he also had the dream repeatedly as an adult, and at least subconsciously links it to his Civil War experiences in his writings, suggests a connection between Bierce's war trauma and his early childhood trauma, a psychic loss that he experienced as a fear of death associated with maternal separation or unavailability. This process by which separate traumas become linked has been documented in the literature of PTSD. In such cases, by what is termed a "two trauma mechanism," the initial trauma, which can be either single or multiple, continues to grow from internal and external stimuli even though it has been defensively walled off by the mind. When a later trauma then occurs that is similar to the original one in terms of representing a real, potential, or imagined separation or loss, it can cause the person to draw upon the earlier reality to cope with the later one.[3] In Bierce's case, his unresolved traumatic loss in childhood, whether real or imagined, resulted in emotional numbing and withdrawal, as well as other attachment deficiencies that also increased his vulnerability for combat-related PTSD as an adult and possibly exacerbated its effects. Both dispositional and contextual attachment-related processes have been found to shape daily responses to the trauma of war, causing more severe war-related PTSD in chronically insecure and avoidant people.[4]

After his wounding, Bierce's weakened physical condition and associated restlessness eventually moved him to resign his military commission in early 1865, but not before he escaped from a four-day ordeal in which he was held prisoner by the Confederates. At the time he mustered out of the army, he had been mentioned in "dispatches for gallantry about fifteen or sixteen times" (McWilliams, *Ambrose Bierce* 58). Bierce continued to suffer from lingering physical effects from his head wound for the rest of his life. In the memoir "Four Days in Dixie," he acknowledges that he experienced fainting spells "for many years," and his pension application documents his "'violent headaches and nausea,'" for which he was still receiving benefits as late as 15 November 1912 (SS 51; Morris 277n4).

In spite of his traumatic combat experiences, Bierce had thrived on the stimulation of military service, the purpose that the war gave him, and the self-esteem that he garnered from adhering to the dictates of his culture's hero-system. Perhaps understandably, he had difficulty readjusting to civilian life, which he had left as a youth and now came back to as an adult. Having cut his always tenuous ties with family and friends, he had no home to which he wished to return. "Like other young veterans before and after him, he embarked on a series of abortive careers in a restless effort to establish himself" (Grenander, *Ambrose Bierce* 26). In his first such job, he worked as a treasury agent in Alabama from April until September 1865, and during this time period he suffered his first documented attacks of asthma. These attacks recurred particularly during times of emotional stress throughout the rest of his life.

Asthma is a complex disease with many contributing physical factors that often co-occurs with anxiety disorders in youths and adults.[5] It is unclear whether Bierce's asthma originated in the stress of his wartime experience or in his early childhood experience. Recent studies indicate that the psychological environment of the child, and especially parenting difficulties, may play a role in its development.[6] Asthma can have a delayed onset or exist in a "hidden" or less severe state that goes undetected. Thus, Bierce may have experienced symptoms of "hidden asthma" as a child on an intermittent or short-term basis that were never documented. The fact that his condition was aggravated to full-blown asthma as the war ended may be linked, at least in part, to the psychological trauma related to his wounding and to the additional stress he experienced when he left the military and had to begin a new life without the support of family, friends, or comrades.

As a way to reconnect with General William B. Hazen, who had served as a father figure to him during the war, Bierce accepted a civilian post as an engineering attaché to Hazen, who had been ordered by the War Department to carry out a mapping and surveying expedition of forts in the western United States. Setting out in July 1866, Bierce's asthma began to clear up in this new healthier environment and perhaps also because he was in better spirits now that he was again working for Hazen. At the older man's recommendation, Bierce also applied for a commission as a captain in the regular army; however, when he instead was offered only a second lieutenancy, Bierce declined the commission and about the same time was brevetted a major in recognition of his war service.[7] Once again jobless and adrift, in 1867 he took a position as a night watchman for the United States Mint in San Francisco, a city in which he was to work for much of the rest of his life. Soon promoted to memorandum clerk, Bierce impressed his new "associates with his military carriage, dignity, geniality, and charm—but, above all, by his outspoken irreverence; for he lost no opportunity to lacerate their pious sensibilities with gibes at subjects they held sacred" (Grenander, *Ambrose Bierce* 30). This "outspoken irreverence" for the institutions, attitudes, and belief systems of American society, as well as for the failings of human nature in general, was to characterize Bierce increasingly from this time forward. As Joanna Montgomery Byles explains, war can serve as a "collective phenomenon," an enemy upon which one can organize and project anxieties (210). Now that Bierce no longer had such a sanctioned enemy to fight, he arguably began to attack human society in general, in essence inventing a new enemy as a means to manage his internal anger and aggression.

About this time, Bierce also began a course of self-education, reading extensively to prepare himself for his career as a writer. "It is my ambition to write books," he declared, "and to do this well you must be acquainted with the language and be a master at the use of words" (qtd. in Grenander, *Ambrose Bierce* 30). Although Bierce was to devote himself mainly to shorter forms instead, he found his true calling as a writer, and he worked professionally at this craft from 1867 to 1909. His canon, admittedly uneven in quality, includes poetry, short stories, fables, epigrams, essays, and satires, as well as a vast output of journalism that has never been collected. "Basilica" and "A Mystery," his first poems, were published in the *Californian* in the fall of 1867. Deciding poetry was not his true calling, he quickly shifted to prose, publishing a few essays in the *Californian* and the *Golden Era* before formally launching his career as a journalist in mid-1868 by joining the staff of the *San Francisco News Letter and California Advertiser.* In December of that year, Bierce assumed editorial responsibilities for the *News Letter,* including the writing of a regular column called "The Town Crier." It was through this column that he established his early professional reputation as a caustic wit and cynic. These characteristics of his writing also adhered to his public persona, which combined with his rigid physical bearing and emotional aloofness to create the mistaken impression that he was misanthropic. As Lawrence I. Berkove contends, "The assumption that Bierce was unfeeling and cynical his whole life long is untenable when the evidence is evaluated. He was far more complicated than such a simplistic view. . . . Bierce often was irascible and hard, but it was case-hardness, an exterior severity developed to protect something softer within" (xiv). In explaining this distinction, Bierce himself claimed, "A cheap and easy cynicism rails at everything. The master of the art accomplishes the formidable task of discrimination" (CW 8: 357). His acerbic style, however, also increasingly shielded his personal insecurities and frequent bouts with depression, concealing his sincere concern for his fellow human beings and for society as a whole.

Berkove points with good reason to a "Town Crier" column that appeared in the *News Letter* of 29 April 1871 to support his argument for a more complex and sympathetic view of Bierce.[8] In this column, Bierce writes about a young woman who was moved to commit suicide because of her gender confusion. "The account can be read as mocking her, but to do so would neglect both its empathetic portrayal of her despair and the question she asks, 'Why did not God make me a man?'" (Berkove 8). Significantly, the ending jibe directed at the woman's mother, who is frying doughnuts in the next room as the woman takes her life, undercuts the legitimate pathos by injecting ghoulish wit into the tragedy: "Ah! Poor old wretch! Your doughnuts shall sizzle and sputter and swim unheeded in their grease; but the beardless jaw that should have wagged filially to chew them is dropped in death; the stomach which they should have distended is crinkled and dry for ever!" (qtd. in Berkove 160). Even this early in his career, then, Bierce was writing about death and perhaps unconsciously developing the defensive strategies that he would later use to project his own familial demons onto others in fictional form, while masking his pain with a veneer of grisly humor that often dismayed his readers.

Bierce's adult attachment deficiencies suggest the combined imprint of his unresolved childhood and combat traumas. He met and married his wife, Mary Ellen "Mollie" Day in 1871, and they spent the first few years of their marriage in England, where she took "no part in his London roistering" and had little in common with his "rowdy friends" (Fatout 112). Day, their first son, was born there in December 1872, as was their second son Leigh in the spring of 1874. Choosing to return to the United States without her husband so that she might be close to her family in San Francisco, Mollie waited six months before telling Bierce of her pregnancy with their third child. Although the birth of this child, their only daughter, Helen, brought him back to California in 1875, his relationship with both his wife and children continued to be characterized by distance, both psychological and geographical. Paul Fatout reports that Bierce "was not an integral part of home affairs" (123). Because of his asthma, he increasingly lived apart from his family, coming home usually for the weekend. Evidencing the disrupted sleep patterns characteristic of PTSD, he frequently slept during the day even when at home, closeting himself away from his family to write through the night (Morris 187). Although his publisher Walter Neale insists that Bierce was not an alcoholic, he admits that "at times he drank copiously, and even got drunk" (59).

Carey McWilliams explains that Bierce's "manner with his children was most characteristic of the man generally. He was very severe, a Spartan parent, in the matters which he thought were important" (*Ambrose Bierce* 148). In particular, he encouraged his sons to be "individualistic, self-reliant" and irreverent, but he also "abominated vulgarity" and held his wife and daughter to a higher moral standard because of "the active hatred he entertained for a 'common' woman" (148–49). Given his experience of the world and sophistication in other matters, Bierce's views of sex and women were surprisingly sophomoric, suggesting he never recovered from his childhood experience of maternal loss. "He questioned the morals of actresses, allied feminism with immorality, and suspected any woman who attracted public notice. He was even unwilling to allow a woman to use her mind. Goodness meant nothing less than artless perfection never blown upon by a breath of detraction. His good woman—innocent, modest, secluded, and ornamental—perched on a pillar that might be toppled by a whisper" (Fatout 144). In an extreme statement that appeared in the 28 October 1882 edition of the San Francisco *Wasp,* Bierce invokes figurative death imagery to describe the fate of any woman who aspires to a public role: "It matters not who she may be nor what her purpose—ambition, art, gain, charity—the woman who has been a public show is a peach with the bloom rubbed off. To a man of sentiment and sensibility she has no longer any value. She is a cup of wine gone stale—a story that is told—a song that is sung. She is dead; let her be decently buried out of sight in the arms of a fool" (qtd. in Fatout 144).

Restless after returning from London, and feeling unfulfilled in an editorial position at the *Argonaut,* he took part in an ill-fated mining venture in the Black Hills before rededicating himself to writing. Working first as editor of the *Wasp* from 1881 to 1886, he joined the staff of William Randolph Hearst's *Examiner* in 1887. Bierce remained on Hearst's payroll until 1909, first in San Francisco and later in Washington, D.C., but the relationship between the two men was complicated by Bierce's difficult personality and unrealistic expectations. Bierce respected the publisher's business acumen, as well as the freedom of expression and generous salary that Hearst extended to him. In his own words, he acknowledged that Hearst "did not once direct nor request me to write an opinion that I did not hold, and only two or three times suggested that I refrain for a season from expressing opinions that I did hold, when they were antagonistic to the policy of the paper, as they commonly were" ("A Thumb-Nail Sketch" SS 202). Nevertheless, Bierce also maintained that, although "Mr. Hearst is always generous," he is "[n]ever just" (204). According to Neale, the writer often "tried to force Hearst to quarrel with him. However, Hearst would not quarrel, but would ignore Bierce's insulting letters and continued to pay him . . . whether or not Bierce would write a line or obey an order" (95). On several occasions, "Hearst personally lured him back into the fold after the columnist had angrily resigned over some real or imagined slight" (Morris 199).

Hearst's forgiveness was "a trait that Bierce, for one, neither exhibited nor understood" (Morris 199). The writer's interpersonal relationships, in general, were often conflicted by his own quick anger and inability to forgive slights, whether real or not. As his reputation grew, he enjoyed the regard of a number of aspiring protégés, several of whom became close friends. Eventually, however, he argued and broke with most of them. Neale, who claims that he never once heard Bierce laugh, observes that he "was seldom given to a display of affection, although none could have known him well without being aware that he craved the love of his kind. Some hold that he loved his friends devotedly—while he loved them. To be sure, he succeeded in alienating them . . . ; yet, in his way he loved them, I verily believe" (60–61). Increasingly, he suffered from the isolating effects of his behavior.

Bierce's rigid attitudes, emotional detachment, and unrealistic expectations affected all of his relationships, but they particularly led to tragic repercussions for himself and his family. His final separation from his wife, which occurred around 1888, was the result of his wrongly suspecting her of infidelity based on the evidence of correspondence between her and another man. Rebuffing numerous attempts by friends and family to resolve this misunderstanding, Bierce remained fixed in his position and thereafter avoided all contact with Mollie, who did not divorce her husband until shortly before her death in 1905 and then only because she incorrectly believed he wished his freedom. Bierce's failure to file for divorce himself suggests his abiding love despite his inability to compromise his protective shield and give himself the opportunity to develop a healthy partnership with her.

Shortly before his parents' separation, fifteen-year-old Day, in an eerie echo of Bierce's own break with his parents, had left home after arguing with his father about his decision to quit school and become a journalist. Barely a year later, on 27 July 1889, the youth was killed in a duel with his best friend over a woman to whom he was engaged but who had eloped instead with the friend. Upon viewing his son's body at the undertaker's, Bierce supposedly whispered, "You are a noble soul, Day. You did just right" (qtd. in Morris 207). He never explained these words—if, in fact, he actually spoke them about his favorite son, who had an uncanny resemblance to Bierce both in looks and in temperament. Although staggered by these twin losses, Bierce "seldom spoke of Day's death afterwards and then only to a few friends. Of his wife he never spoke: not even to friends" (McWilliams, *Ambrose Bierce* 195). Subsequently, Bierce's younger son Leigh also chose journalism for a career, and although Bierce was pleased with this decision, he nevertheless quarreled with the young man over his choice of a wife. Still estranged from his son when Leigh died in 1901 of pneumonia complicated by the effects of alcoholism, Bierce steadfastly refused to see Leigh's wife thereafter, although he did make financial arrangements for her. Until his wife's death, Bierce also continued to provide for her financially, using their daughter Helen as an intermediary. Even though he maintained amicable relations with Helen, they saw each other only infrequently, and the fact that she married and divorced three times before her death suggests that she did not escape psychic repercussions from her childhood environment.

In 1888, about the time he permanently separated from his wife, Bierce wrote in the *San Francisco Examiner* that "[m]arriage, being a human institution . . . is a failure" (qtd. in Fatout 166). Similarly, in discussing parenting with Neale, he once remarked that he could "'plainly see that children could be better reared outside of the environs of the homes in which they are brought up—with a few exceptions, but very few'" (127). Public statements such as these, in the face of his lifelong silence about his own family turmoil, reflect Bierce's inability consciously to acknowledge his personal role in the failures of his relationships with his parents, wife, and children. His fiction nevertheless points to the unconscious guilt that he bore for these losses. Bierce's avoidant pattern of adult attachment, his parenting behavior, his often harsh views of humanity in general, and his preoccupation with death, in not only his Civil War fiction but his other tales as well, indicate the deep and abiding effects of both the emotional trauma that he experienced in childhood and the trauma of his combat experience.

It is perhaps significant that during the period in which he separated from his wife and both of his sons died, Bierce's literary production was at its height, suggesting that he found his only consolation in his writing. From about 1887 to 1893, with increasing frequency, Bierce chose to supplement his "Prattle" column, which was the long-running successor to "The Town Crier," with fiction and nonfiction on more serious subjects than had characterized his writings previously (Berkove 23). That this writing was filled with violent death imagery points to the extent of the writer's grief and its earliest connection with his own pre-Oedipal experience, as well as to the long-term traumatic effects of the Civil War, which was so often the focus of his stories during this time. Juliet Mitchell theorizes that "[t]raumatic language is a verbal version of the visual language of dreams;

words are metaphors, similes, and symbolic equations; they have the status of inner but not internal objects; they become expressions of feeling rather than of meaning" (132). Emotionally isolated as he was, writing may have served therapeutic purposes for Bierce, enabling him to give voice to his pain and animate his repressed feelings of guilt and anger for a positive purpose. His writing, thus, may have kept his anxiety and depression from deepening into a static state that may have resulted in even more serious psychological consequences.

Bierce's obsessive absorption with war in general and the Civil War in particular provides the strongest evidence that he never resolved the traumatic memories related to his military service. "No subject was of greater interest to Bierce throughout his adult life than was warfare. . . . For more than forty years he gave it frequent study, almost daily" (Neale 70). His first memoir of his war experiences, "What I Saw of Shiloh," was not published until 1874, six years after he took his first professional writing position, and it was not until 1881 that he added the stirring conclusion to this piece. The retrospective and ambivalent tone of the essay and its graphic imagery of death reflect the psychic toll that "the phantoms of [this] blood-stained period" had on Bierce (SS 24–25). All of Bierce's Civil War writings have a retrospective cast, and even when the tone is overtly humorous, an underlying tension reflects the longstanding and still unresolved pain that may have worked to isolate Bierce from family and friends.

In "George Thurston," the narrator, who is a topographic engineer like Bierce, recollects the dramatic suicide of his fellow staff officer, Lieutenant George Thurston. The narrator depicts Thurston as being both physically stiff and emotionally aloof, and he observes that the men "did not like him; he was unsocial" (SF 420). These characteristics, which Bierce also shared, and the inclination of Thurston to adhere himself to the narrator as he works imply the kindred nature of the two men. Thurston, who has the habit of standing recklessly in harm's way with his arms folded, evades death by enemy fire on two occasions. However, like Herman Brayle in "Killed at Resaca," Thurston seemingly is intent on killing himself, although his motivation, unlike that of Brayle, is never explained. The reason for his crossed arms remains equally puzzling. The narrator surmises that the man's "stiffish attitude and folded arms" might reflect the fact that "[w]hen one is tranquilly looking death in the eye and refusing him any concession one naturally has a good opinion of one's self" (422). The quartermaster, however, contends that it may be the lieutenant's way of stealing himself against a constitutional inclination to run away in the face of danger. Whether cowardly or courageous, the enigmatic Thurston goes to his death with his secrets inside him and his arms folded when he plunges from a high rope swing that the men had rigged for their amusement.

Since the reader is never able to probe the inner recesses of the title character's mind, the state of the narrator, who witnesses the traumatic event and then describes it retrospectively, deserves perhaps more attention than typically has been accorded him. The beginning of the tale, as Richard Luke Kocher observes, includes a curious emphasis on the narrator's topographic duties that has no direct relevance to the subsequent account of Thurston's demise. In particular, with a full-paragraph description that connects the historical precedents of British topography to the techniques associated with his own map-making responsibilities during wartime, the narrator explains:

> In some of the dark corners of England and Wales they have an immemorial custom of "beating the bounds" of the parish. On a certain day of the year the whole population turns out and travels in procession from one landmark to another on the boundary line. At the most important points lads are soundly beaten with rods to make them remember the place in after life. They become authorities. Our frequent engagements with Confederate outposts, patrols, and scouting parties, had, incidentally, the same educating value; they fixed in my memory a vivid and apparently imperishable picture of the locality—a picture serving instead of accurate field notes, which, indeed it was not always convenient to take, with carbines cracking, sabers clashing and horses plunging all about. These spirited encounters were observations entered in red. (SF 420–21)

The sheer length of this passage, as well as its placement early in the narrative, points to its centrality in discerning the full import of the climactic incident of Thurston's death that concludes the tale.

As a seasoned soldier, the narrator has become an "authority" on war and considers himself inured to combat scenes of graphic death and dismemberment. His duties, after all, constitute "a business in which the lives of men counted as nothing against the chance of defining a road or sketching a bridge" (SF 420). He certainly, if asked, would have deemed himself above being affected by such "an ignoble death" as was to be the fate of "[t]his intrepid man, George Thurston" (422). And yet, in spite of his ingrained cynicism, this hardened officer was moved to cry out as he watched Thurston swing ever higher and higher. Even more telling is his admission that he now "[a]t this distance of many years . . . can distinctly recall that image of a man in the sky, its head erect, its feet close together, its hands" outside the imprint in his mind as "[a]11 at once, with an astonishing suddenness and rapidity, it turns clear over and pitches downward." In what "could have been but an instant, yet . . . seemed an age," the narrator relives this bizarre scene in the present tense, finally recalling "an indescribable sound—the sound of an impact that shakes the earth, and these men, familiar with death in its most awful aspects, turn sick" (423). In an ironic twist of fate, this absurd and astonishing image of unexpected death becomes an observation fixed "in red" in the narrator's and his comrades' memories. In this image, death strikes "with an unfamiliar weapon." As the narrator acknowledges, "We did not know that he had so ghastly resources, possibilities of terror so dismal" (423). In the vivid details of this flashback memory of Thurston's death, Bierce communicates the depths of the narrator's trauma as he continues to struggle with the fear of death that overwhelmed him that day. Thus, as Kocher claims, it is the narrator, and not the title character, who is Bierce's real focus in "George Thurston." In the end, the narrator, like Bierce, is as isolated as Thurston, whose "stiffish attitude" may have concealed his fears of cowardice in the face of death while simultaneously alienating him from other men. His crossed arms, thus, would seem to symbolize his "desperate attempt to hold himself together psychologically, while at the same time" they serve to "separate him from the other men," such as the narrator, "who must suffer individually the same fears that he himself experienced" (Kocher 137). While Thurston's suffering ends with his death, the narrator's continues. Through this story, Bierce argues that it is not only impossible to become a true "authority" on war, but also that the only escape from the grip of unrelenting traumatic memories lies in death.

Perhaps Bierce's most retrospective tale, as well as the one that best supports the argument that the author suffered from PTSD, is "The Major's Tale," which was originally published in the 5 January 1890 edition of the *San Francisco Examiner.* Reminiscing back to his days as a staff officer just before the Battle of Nashville in December 1864, a veteran named Broadwood recounts a practical joke that he and some of his comrades had played on a certain Lieutenant Haberton, a noted "lady-killer" who "never tired of relating his amatory exploits" despite the chagrin of his listeners (SF 707). In the midst of this hoax, which involved another soldier dressing up as a southern belle to secure Haberton's affections, a Confederate shell crashed into the building, bringing a premature end to the subterfuge. For the purpose of this study, the details of this playful deception matter little. Rather, it is again the narrator and his disposition that draw the reader's attention.

Bierce emphasizes his speaker's distance from the recollected account in the rambling opening sentences of the story. To prepare his audience for the recollection he is about to share, Broadwood reflects:

> In the days of the Civil War practical joking had not, I think, fallen into that disrepute which characterizes it now. That, doubtless, was owing to our extreme youth—men were much younger than now, and evermore your very young man has a boisterous spirit, running easily to horse-play. You cannot think how young the men were in the early sixties! Why, the average age of the entire Federal Army was not more than twenty-five; I doubt if it was more than twenty-three, but not having the statistics on that point (if there are any) I want to be moderate: we will say twenty-five. (SF 706)

Continuing in the same vein, the narrator's nostalgic tone deepens as he elaborates before concluding, "Depend upon it, my friends, men of that time were greatly younger than men are to-day, but looked much older. The change is quite remarkable" (SF 706). As David M. Owens adroitly observes, the speaker's rhetorical style "is that of an after-dinner speaker telling an anecdote at a formal reunion many years after the fact" (121). With such introductory remarks, Bierce, who was in his late forties when he wrote the tale, seems to align Broadwood with his own age, perspective, and sensibilities. This narrating veteran stands apart from the present generation while he simultaneously seeks to amuse them by recalling, not a scene of heroic glory on the battlefield, but rather a harmless incident of nonsense and camaraderie. His decision to share a humorous memory rather than a sobering one is perhaps calculated by the speaker as doubly safe—one that will not bring discomfort either to himself or to his audience. The titular narrator in "The Major's Tale" also suggests other more direct autobiographical connections to Bierce, who, in addition to carrying the same brevetted rank, served as a staff officer to General Samuel Beatty during the Battle of Nashville. This battle was the last major engagement in which Bierce fought before resigning his commission, making it a fitting focus for such a sentimental remembrance.

About halfway through the tale, however, the veteran interrupts his lighthearted recollection with a somber digression that undercuts the ostensible humor by injecting a disturbing memory. Almost as if the images come without his bidding, he visualizes the somber reality of what is about to befall these same men, as well as the traumatic impact upon himself, who alone survived:

> On that bleak December morning a few days later, when from an hour before dawn until ten o'clock we sat on horseback on those icy hills, waiting for General Smith to open the battle miles away to the right, there were eight of us. At the close of the fighting there were three. There is now one. Bear with him yet a little while, oh, thrifty generation; he is but one of the horrors of war strayed from his era into yours. He is only the harmless skeleton at your feast and peace-dance, responding to your laughter and your footing it featly, with rattling fingers and bobbing skull—albeit upon suitable occasion, with a partner of his choosing, he might do his little dance with the best of you. (SF 709)

This grim vision reverberates unexpectedly in the midst of the speaker's otherwise playful address, creating the impression of an intrusive flashback, as well as the death-in-life experience common to sufferers of severe posttraumatic stress.[9] Immediately after uttering these words, Broadwood picks up the threads of his narrative, which he then completes without again faltering. The "harmless skeleton" thus refrains from falling back into his accustomed dance of death and so concludes the "peace-dance" without further misstep, projecting the practiced, untroubled façade of the Civil War veteran-hero that he knows will satisfy his nineteenth-century audience's expectations while also suppressing his own pain.

Bierce, much like Broadwood, considered himself "A Sole Survivor." As the final of eleven memoirs that he collected under the heading "Bits of Autobiography" in the first volume of his *Collected Works,* Bierce reprinted an essay by this title that he had originally published in the 18 October 1890 edition of the *Oakland Daily Evening Tribune.* In what he saw as a fitting conclusion to his reflections on his life, Bierce incorporates as his own experience the same traumatic memory from the Battle of Nashville that the fictional Broadwood recalls:

> Six men are on horseback on a hill—a general and his staff. Below, in the gray fog of a winter morning, an army, which has left its intrenchments, is moving upon those of the enemy—creeping silently into position. . . . [T]he risen sun has burned a way through the fog, splendoring a part of the beleaguered city.
>
> "Look at that, General," says an aide; "it is like enchantment."
>
> "Go and enchant Colonel Post," said the general, without taking his field-glass from his eyes, "and tell him to pitch in as soon as he hears Smith's guns."
>
> All laughed. But to-day I laugh alone. I am the Sole Survivor. (CW 1: 385–86)[10]

Significantly, the aura of enchantment again blankets the land this morning of Bierce's final engagement, just as it did the countryside of West Virginia in his early days as a soldier. Coming full circle, now so many years afterwards, Bierce still remains unable to pierce the fog and reconcile his ambivalent memories of the war. Closing this piece with a civilian recollection of a London dinner party for seven, all of whom are now dead but himself, he claims that his role of Sole Survivor has become his favorite over time. "It has become habitual to me; I rather like it," he insists (CW 1: 401). Having learned to accept and even relish his role as the emotionally benumbed but "harmless skeleton," Bierce sits alone. With only one dance remaining, he ponders his fate while closing the literary feast represented by his writings, many of which draw so poignantly from his own traumatic experiences to reveal the true workings and cost of war.

Bierce's Final Dance of Death

To be a Gringo in Mexico—ah, that is euthanasia!
—Ambrose Bierce

In concluding his "Bits of Autobiography," Bierce depicts himself as a "Sole Survivor," sitting alone at the "feast of unreason" that the eleven memoirs grouped in this section of his *Collected Works* represent (CW 1: 401). Such an image reflects a candid recognition of his emotional isolation, as well as his conviction that the world, which he so doggedly satirized in his writings, was largely governed by chance. Never able "to reconcile reason and feeling, yet unable to resign himself to the remorseless operation of nature's processes, and unwilling to extirpate from himself all sense of sympathy and compassion, Bierce pursued skepticism to the point of Pyrrhonism. Thus the desperate situations in which he places his protagonists represent, allegorically, the insoluble dilemmas with which he himself grappled" (Berkove 50). His inability to reconcile his ambivalent feelings for war—his reasoned disdain for the destruction that war wrought versus his emotional nostalgia for the youthful idealism and adventure it also represented—was, thus, emblematic of what he came to see as the tragedy of the human condition.

Although Bierce's early idealism was largely destroyed by his Civil War experiences and his increasingly stoic outlook, it would be an overstatement to say that this philosophy was forged solely through his own personal tragedies, whether they occurred before, during, or after the war. Over the course of his professional career as a journalist, he also made it his business to study and report on the world around him, which provided a wealth of information in addition to his own lived experience, all of which he used to draw his conclusions about human society. His subjects, which he approached from both local and national angles, included such issues as religion, the railroad, labor strikes, the legal system, imperialism, politics, and, of course, war. While death was not his *only* character, real or otherwise, as Edmund Wilson has claimed, no other motif appeared so prominently and consistently in his most enduring work, as perhaps would be expected of a writer who considered life largely a state of war.

In his later years, especially after moving to Washington, D.C., in early 1900, Bierce began to weary of the issues against which he had long railed in his columns. "He was repeating himself and even giving ground, and his writings and correspondence are tinted by a growing somberness quite different from the combative irreverence of his early years," although he continued to write sporadically (Berkove 29). As a sign of his resignation, "he now variously referred to himself as the Curmudgeon Philosopher, the Sentimental Bachelor, and the Bald Campaigner. These tags were certainly part of the self-depreciating humor he had begun many years ago when he called his column 'Prattle,' but now they also reflected self-knowledge, a recognition and acceptance of the aspects of his character revealed by the tags" (Joshi, Berkove, and Schultz 973). Although acquiescing to the popular opinion of his character, Bierce nevertheless continued to strive for social criticism that was framed by conviction and reason, even though it might be laced with generous touches of sentiment as well. Death continued to haunt him in these final writings, whether they took fictional or nonfictional forms.

In the summer of 1903, Bierce, who had always steadfastly refused to attend reunions of Civil War veterans, made his first of at least three tours of his former battlefields, an experience of revisiting old ghosts that he subsequently reflected upon, first in a letter dated 3 October 1903 that he wrote for the eighteenth reunion of the Ninth Indiana Volunteers,[1] and then in a revised version, an essay entitled "The Passing Show," which appeared in the 22 November 1903 issue of the *New York American*. The fact that Bierce again revised this account in 1912 as he incorporated it into volume 11 of his *Collected Works* (under the title "A Bivouac of the Dead") suggests its significance in his final attempts to find closure about the war and its meaning to his life. His account of this journey back to the "dreamland" of Cheat River territory documents his visit to the national cemetery in Grafton, West Virginia, where over twelve hundred Federal dead are now buried, including some of his earliest comrades in Company C of the Ninth Indiana, most of whom he discovered had been "duly registered, so far as identified" and then buried after giving their lives in the "'green and salad days' of the great rebellion" (SS 2). He ponders the fact that "more than a half of the green graves . . . are marked 'Unknown,'" and then specifically points out the "forgotten graves" where eighty to a hundred Confederates repose, "neglected and obscure" despite the fact that "[t]hey were honest and courageous foeman, having little in common with the political madmen who persuaded them to their doom and the literary bearers of false witness in the aftertime" (2–3). These unidentified and forgotten men give him pause in remembering all that has transpired both during and after the war and yet still not healed the country's or its soldiers' divisions. Further, his concern for their anonymity suggests his own fears that he, too, will be forgotten after he dies.

A later story from this final period, "A Resumed Identity," continues Bierce's efforts to come to terms with his war ghosts and the related issue of lost identity as he faced old age and his own mortality. In this tale, the clearly autobiographical protagonist believes himself to be a twenty-three-year-old lieutenant on the staff of General William B. Hazen. Attributing his sense of disorientation to the effects of a minor, glancing wound he thinks he has just suffered, he fears that "the uncanny silence" of the night means that the Federal troops have lost the Battle at Stones River and now "are moving on Nashville." Walking forward with apprehension, the soldier grows increasingly puzzled by the "cultivated fields showing no sign of war and war's ravages" (SF 1037). At daybreak, he meets Dr. Stilling Malson, a physician of Murfreesboro who is returning from visiting a patient. Malson, who suspects the soldier is suffering from "lost identity and the effect of familiar scenes in restoring it," assures the man that he himself has "'met no troops'" and questions why he is dressed in civilian clothes rather than a uniform. Provoked to anger by his inability to make sense of the situation, the soldier tells Malson he may "'go to the devil!'" and then strides "away, very much at random, across the dewy fields" (1038–39).

Soon experiencing an unaccountable sense of fatigue that causes him to sit down on a rock to rest, the soldier casually examines himself and discovers that he has aged to the point of being a "physical wreck." His hands are "lean and withered," and his face is "seamed and furrowed" (SF 1039). He also realizes that it is summer, rather than December, and wonders if he has in the intervening months suffered amnesia as an effect of his injury and now somehow escaped from the hospital where he was being treated. The full reality of his fate—that he has lost over forty years of his life as a consequence of war—becomes clear to the man and the reader only when he discovers a nearby "monument of hewn stone" that is now "brown with age, weather-worn at the angles, spotted with moss and lichen" (1039). Reading the inscription on this old monument, the lieutenant learns that it is dedicated to the memory of the soldiers of Hazen's Brigade "'who fell at Stone River, Dec. 31, 1862.'" Collapsing in dismay beside a nearby pool of water, the man observes "the reflection of his face, as in a mirror." Finally realizing his loss in the full horror of the past he has so imperfectly escaped, he falls "face downward, into the pool and yield[s] up the life that had spanned another life" (1040).

According to David M. Owens, this monument had special significance to Bierce. The first Civil War battlefield monument to be erected, it is bounded by a wall of native Indiana limestone that was constructed in early 1863 by Hazen's men to honor the nearly one-third of the brigade who were casualties at Stones

River. "Sixty-nine of Hazen's soldiers are buried within the small plot enclosed by the wall," and the monument also bears an inscription that commemorates the lives of those who were killed at Shiloh, where Bierce had first fought under Hazen (Owens 62). While on his way to Galveston, Texas, with his friend Percival Pollard, Bierce made his second battlefield tour in October 1907, at which time he stopped at Stones River. Wandering through this long-tranquil field at the age of sixty-five, and pointing out to Pollard the monument to Hazen's brigade, he perhaps sought to lay to rest the ghosts of old comrades that still haunted him as he approached the end of his own life. "A Resumed Identity" first appeared in the September 1908 issue of Hearst's *Cosmopolitan,* less than a year after this return to Stones River, suggesting that Bierce's return to the site moved him to reflect on his mixed feelings about both the battles that took these lives and his own enduring sense of lost identity after the war.

Preoccupied with putting his affairs in order, Bierce tendered his final resignation to Hearst in 1909 so that he could dedicate his full attention to preparing his *Collected Works,* which his friend Walter Neale's company published in twelve volumes between 1909 and 1912. The intensity of Bierce's devotion to preparing his *Collected Works* suggests his strong desire to create a lasting legacy, so he could avoid the anonymous fate of so many soldiers who had preceded him in death. In this way, he sought to satisfy what Otto Rank claimed was the human need for self-immortality. Rank believed this need was part of man's irrational nature, a position with which Bierce, no doubt, would have concurred. However, Rank also believed that for the artist, unlike the neurotic, this endeavor resulted in constructive self-realization that served to minimize the fears of life and death through creative expression of the will.[2] The double-motif so characteristic of much of Bierce's work can be seen to represent the struggle between the neurotic and artistic aspects of the self, a struggle mirrored in Bierce's own life.

Precluded from securing a sense of continuity and self-realization through close bonds with his family, through a theological belief in life after death, or through a transcendental identification with Nature, Bierce felt compelled to achieve artistic validation through the publication of his collected writings. The reception of the *Collected Works,* however, was overwhelmingly negative, both critically and commercially, and much of the blame was attributed to Bierce's failings as an editor. Determining his journalism in all regards inferior to his literary works, the writer excluded the former from the collection, while incorporating all manner of the latter with no regard for their substance or aesthetics. His failure to validate himself through this collection probably increased his vulnerability to death anxiety, and without the constructive outlet of his writing to refocus and relieve this additional stress, he became more detached as his depression deepened.

The accounts of Bierce's biographers are remarkably aligned on this point. C. Hartley Grattan observes that, in Bierce's final years, "dissatisfaction and discontent ate at his mind. He felt that he was played out. With nothing more to say and with his creative powers gone, he found life a burden. Though his health was as good as could be expected, and although he occasionally came upon new experiences and pleasures—particularly on his trips to California in 1910 and 1912—he could not throw off his depression" (73). Roy Morris writes that, during Bierce's trip to California in the summer of 1912, "[f]riends had the definite sense that he was taking leave of them forever; to one, he confided that he was 'sleepy for death'" (246). At this time, he also made his last visit to the gravesites of his former wife and two sons, telling the sexton that he was "going into Mexico" and leaving him money to tend the plot. McWilliams confirms that "[t]here was a finality about this last trip. Every task had been attended; his affairs were in order" (*Ambrose Bierce* 314). Later this same year, he made a final visit to see his daughter Helen, who was then living in Bloomington, Illinois, and he left with her a large collection of his personal papers before returning to Washington. During this two-week visit, although cheerful, "he seemed vaguely uneasy and was determined that he would 'go away'" (McWilliams, *Ambrose Bierce* 315). He told her that "[t]his fighting in Mexico interests me. I want to go down and see if these Mexicans can shoot straight" (qtd. in McWilliams, *Ambrose Bierce* 316).

The record of the writer's correspondence in 1913 confirms and gives shape to the vague comments about Mexico that Bierce voiced to the sexton and others in the summer of 1912. On 10 September, he wrote to Helen, "If I am to hear from you again for a long time you'll have to answer this letter pretty soon. I am going away. My plans are not very definite, but they include a journey into—and possibly across—South America. I have arranged for a pretty long absence. If we have trouble with Mexico before I leave I shall probably go there instead—or at least first" (MM 240). In a 19 September letter he continued to finalize his affairs by advising the Neale Publishing Company that he had assigned his copyrights and royalties to his longtime secretary and personal friend Carrie Christiansen. Writing just two days later to Eleanor Sickler, he responds to her concerns about his intentions to travel to Mexico and South America by writing, "My plan, so far as I have one, is to go through Mexico to one of the Pacific ports, if I can *get* through without being stood up against a wall and shot as an American. . . . Naturally, it is possible—even probable—that I shall not return. These be 'strange countries,' in which things happen; that is why I am going. And I am seventy-one!" (241). Elaborating a bit further on 21 September, he suggests the affinity of his projected journey with his past by writing to another friend that "[b]efore 'visiting' Mexico (if I can get in) I am going over my old battlefields of a half-century ago—Chickamauga, Chattanooga, Murfreesboro, Franklin, Nashville, Shiloh, and so forth" (242). Again on 1 October, in a now famous letter to his niece Lora, he wrote of his hopes: "Good-bye—if you hear of my being stood up against a Mexican stone wall and shot to rags please know that I think that a pretty good way to depart life. It beats old age, disease, or falling down the cellar stairs. To be a

Gringo in Mexico—ah, that is euthanasia!" (243).[3] Bierce clearly anticipated that this journey to revolutionary Mexico might be his final adventure, one to which he looked forward as a means to a "good death" that might also make sense of his life and give it enduring meaning. By participating in another country's war of self-division, he could reconnect to memories from his youthful participation in his country's internal war and so perhaps heal, or at least forget the pain of, his own conflicted self.

The suggestion that his trip was planned as a final journey to death rather than just a dangerous journey that might end in death is strengthened not only by Bierce's depressed state of mind and the elaborate preparations that he made for it but also by other comments the writer had made about ending his life before he became ill or a burden to others. Neale explains that "[t]ime and again Bierce seriously discussed with me and with others his fixed determination to kill himself unless he should die a natural death in the meanwhile, and estimated that he would do so at about seventy, saying that he doubted if he should defer the act much beyond that age" (430). Further, according to Neale, one of Bierce's close associates gave Bierce a revolver as a present sometime in 1912, at which time the writer said that he would use it "when the time should come for him to blow out his brains. That would be the manner of his passing: a shot through the brain: that was the soldier's way, the decent method" (431). Bierce seems to have determined to die as a soldier, whether by battle or by his own hand.

Much mystery still surrounds Bierce's disappearance in late 1913 and presumed death in early 1914. What is known, for sure, is that, after he left Washington alone on 12 October, he spent approximately three weeks in a final tour of his old Civil War battlegrounds. Stopping at the St. Charles Hotel in New Orleans on 23 October, he suffered a severe asthma attack. When he had recovered sufficiently, he was interviewed by a reporter for the New Orleans *States,* who wrote that Bierce told him, "'I'm on my way to Mexico, because I like the game. . . . I like the fighting; I want to see it.'" He spoke also of the possibility of continuing on to South America before returning to the United States, but, at the same time, he stressed his lack of ties or commitments at home: "There is no family that I have to take care of; I've retired from writing and I'm going to take a rest" (qtd. in Morris 253). From Laredo, on 6 November, he sent a copy of the article to his niece Lora in which he added a puzzling postscript, telling her, "You need not believe *all* that these newspapers say of me and my purposes. I had to tell them *something*" (qtd. in Morris 254). Writing from San Antonio just two days earlier to his daughter, however, he had written, "I mean to go into Mexico; that is all that you need to know. There is good fighting all along the border and everywhere. Maybe I shall see some of it—as an 'innocent bystander'" (MM 243). Still recovering from his asthma bout, he again wrote Helen on 4 November to say he had been detained but was preparing to leave "for Laredo and I don't know where else." Continuing, he admitted, "My future is uncertain (there can not be much of it, anyhow) but I am a bit better satisfied with myself than when idling away my life in Washington to no purpose" (244). For some reason, instead of entering Mexico from Laredo he decided to proceed on to El Paso, apparently crossing the border there. A letter dated 16 December from Juarez "relates that he had just ridden in from Chihuahua to post it. It was sharp weather but he was enjoying the life. There was much talk of 'Jornada del Muerto,' the journey of death, and the roads were dotted with groups of refugees. There was a distinctly military atmosphere about the place and it pleased him" (McWilliams, *Ambrose Bierce* 324). One final letter, dated 26 December from Chihuahua, insinuates that he may have abandoned his intention to go on from Mexico to South America, although he does not explain why. He writes, "I . . . told you that I intended to go [to the Andes] by the way of Mexico, which I am doing, though it looks now as if 'the Andes' would have to wait" (MM 245). He closes the postscript to this letter with the enigmatic words, "As to me, I leave here tomorrow for an unknown destination" (246). Silence followed. Despite an official inquiry that was made at the request of Bierce's daughter, no body was ever recovered, and no subsequent sighting of Bierce has ever been substantiated.

Based on this information, various scenarios have been devised about Bierce's fate and how he met it. Most believe that he died in Mexico in January 1914, whether in battle, from illness, or perhaps even at the hand of Pancho Villa himself. Without stating his source, Paul Fatout, for one, claims that in Juarez, Bierce "was cordially received and given credentials as an observer attached to Villa's army marching to Chihuahua" (317). If Bierce did join Villa's rebel forces, his 26 December 1913 letter implies that he was with Villa's army when it left Chihuahua to move on to Ojinaga, where an especially fierce battle was fought on 11 January 1914. On the basis of admittedly circumstantial evidence, M. E. Grenander believes Bierce was probably killed during this battle, at the end of which all of the dead bodies were burned to prevent the spread of typhus. "Salvador Ibarra, one of General Ortega's officers [at Ojinaga], recalled seeing Bierce going into the battle, but not afterward. Captain Emil Holmdahl, another rebel officer, heard later that 'an old gringo' had been shot during the fighting" (*Ambrose Bierce* 74). Others surmise that he either never went to Mexico or that he left there to journey to the Grand Canyon, where he killed himself.[4] Given Bierce's final letters and the elaborate ruse that would have been involved in such a deception, it seems more likely that he did go to Mexico and die there; however, ultimately more important than the specifics involved is the care with which Bierce took to fashion his own death, as well as the lasting impression that he sought to make with such a dramatic and mysterious departure.

Bierce's motivation for ending his life and the plan he developed to do so can perhaps best be understood within the context of Robert Jay Lifton's concept of revolutionary immortality. Taking his starting point with Rank's assertion of the human urge to immortality, Lifton makes this need comprehensible by placing it in a larger context of the revolutionary's quest for symbolic immortality. He defines revolutionary immortality as "a shared sense of participating in permanent revolutionary fermentation, and of transcending individual death by 'living on' indefinitely within the continuing revolution" (*Revolutionary Immortality* 7). Thus, the revolutionary vision represents a symbolic quest for rebirth and renewal, and through such a vision, the individual can overcome "the anxiety associated both with biological death and with collective forms of desymbolization" (27). In the last decade of his life, facing old age and infirmity, Bierce increasingly looked back on his youthful soldiering with his heart rather than his mind, as his repeated trips to his Civil War battlegrounds reflect. Unable to forget the form and identity that his fervent dedication to the Union cause had given his life, his intellectual disdain for war receded as he again sought a revolutionary cause that would offer him the opportunity to gain power over death through death. As a revolutionary in Mexico, Bierce found a socially created family to replace his failed biological family. To compensate for his inability to believe in a theological solution to death, he also could embrace the revolutionary vision of a secular utopia with "images closely related to the spiritual conquest of death and even to an afterlife" (Lifton, *Revolutionary Immortality* 8). Further, through the promise of transformation that the revolution would effect, he was again able to believe in the natural world as a place of experiential transcendence. In short, through his journey to Mexico to die, Bierce sought to return to the enchanted dreamland of his youth and achieve the promise of immortality that is only possible in such a romantic setting. It was in this spirit that Bierce entered Mexico to find a "good death." That talk of his death has continued unabated for nearly one hundred years suggests that he succeeded in fashioning a final dance of death that would unify his life's story, magnify his writings, and make them both live on beyond him. In the story of his own death, he left his readers the best ghost story of all. It was at once his tragedy and his triumph.

Notes

Introduction

1. In 1877, Bierce collaborated with his friends William A. Rudolfson and Thomas A. Harcouth to write *The Dance of Death* under the joint pseudonym of William Herman.

2. C. Hartley Grattan, *Bitter Bierce: A Mystery of American Letters* (1929); Franklin Walker, *Ambrose Bierce: The Wickedest Man in San Francisco* (1941); Paul Fatout, *Ambrose Bierce: The Devil's Lexicographer* (1951); Roy Morris, Jr., *Ambrose Bierce: Alone in Bad Company* (1995).

3. Although the publication date of *Tales of Soldiers and Civilians* is 1891, it was not actually released until 1892. M. E. Grenander was the first to recognize this discrepancy in her essay "Ambrose Bierce and *In the Midst of Life*." *In the Midst of Life* is the title that Bierce gave to the revised and expanded edition of *Tales of Soldiers and Civilians* that he published in 1898.

4. See especially Russell Duncan and David J. Klooster, eds., *Phantoms of a Blood-Stained Period: The Complete Civil War Writings of Ambrose Bierce* (2002); Robert L. Gale, *An Ambrose Bierce Companion* (2001); and three works edited by S. T. Joshi and David E. Schultz: *Ambrose Bierce: An Annotated Bibliography of Primary Sources* (1999); *A Much Misunderstood Man: Selected Letters of Ambrose Bierce* (2003); and *A Sole Survivor: Bits of Autobiography* (1998). In addition, Joshi, Lawrence I. Berkove, and Schultz have recently published a three-volume scholarly edition of Bierce's short fiction, *The Short Fiction of Ambrose Bierce: A Comprehensive Edition* (2006).

5. Most notable of these readings are Grenander's interpretation of "The Death of Halpin Frayser" (*Ambrose Bierce* 106–14), James G. Powers's "Freud and Farquhar: An Occurrence at Owl Creek Bridge?" and Peter Stoicheff's "'Something Uncanny': The Dream Structure in Ambrose Bierce's 'An Occurrence at Owl Creek Bridge.'" For the first study of Bierce's "The Death of Halpin Frayser" from a post-Freudian perspective, see Allan Lloyd Smith, "*Can Such Things Be?:* Ambrose Bierce, the 'Dead Mother,' and Other American Traumas," which was published in 2004.

6. Even insightful critics and scholars sometimes fail to recognize the importance of responsible biography in the case of Bierce, whose writings have tended to be shorted in the press for sensationalism. For instance, in *A Prescription for Adversity: The Moral Art*

of Ambrose Bierce, Berkove overreacts to this tendency by sweepingly dismissing the relevance of *all* psychoanalytic approaches to Bierce or his works, claiming that they encourage readers to see the author as "psychologically disordered" and his writings as "evidence of his warped personality" (141). While Berkove's frustration is perhaps understandable, this position is indefensible.

7. This position was inspired by Shoshana Felman's argument about Edgar Allan Poe in "On Reading Poetry: Reflections on the Limits and Possibilities of Psychoanalytic Approaches."

Chapter 1

1. See especially Rank, *Beyond Psychology;* Rollo May, *The Meaning of Anxiety;* Robert Jay Lifton, *The Broken Connection: On Death and the Continuity of Life;* and Norman O. Brown, *Life against Death: The Psychoanalytical Meaning of History.*

2. It should be noted that Becker usually fails to include female referents in his writings. Unless specifically noted otherwise, however, the applicability of his argument to females as well as males should be inferred.

3. Freud first used the term "Oedipus complex" in 1910 in "A Special Type of Object Choice by Men."

4. For a more extreme interpretation of the development of death anxiety in children, see Joseph C. Rheingold, *The Mother, Anxiety, and Death: The Catastrophic Death Complex.* Rheingold argues that fear of annihilation is not part of the child's natural experience but rather is engendered by maternal deprivation.

5. For related information on childhood death in Puritan America, see David E. Stannard, *The Puritan Way of Death: A Study in Religion, Culture, and Social Change,* as well as Margaret M. Coffin, *Death in America: The History and Folklore of Customs and Superstitions of Early Medicine, Funerals, Burials, and Mourning.*

6. See especially Margaret S. Mahler, Fred Pine, and Anni Bergman, *The Psychological Birth of the Human Infant.*

7. See John Bowlby, *Separation: Anxiety and Anger.*

8. See George Buelow, Mark McClain, and Irene McIntosh, "A New Measure for an Important Construct: The Attachment and Object Relations Inventory"; Lynne Murray, "Intersubjectivity, Object Relations Theory, and Empirical Evidence from the Mother-Infant Interactions"; and Rebecca Smith Behrends and Sidney Jules Blatt, "Internalization and Psychological Development throughout the Life Cycle."

9. Carey McWilliams first discovered this epitaph and suggests that it was written by Bierce in her 1932 essay, "Ambrose Bierce and His First Love: An Idyll of the Civil War." See also Fatout, *Ambrose Bierce: Devil's Lexicographer* (29).

10. For a synopsis of previous responses to *The Parenticide Club,* see Berkove, *Prescription for Adversity* (141–43).

11. For a complete copy of both of these letters, see Bierce (MM 16–17).

Chapter 2

Epigraph from Bierce's elegy "William F. Smith" (CW 5: 306).

1. Consider, for instance, the horrifying male Ambrosio in Matthew Gregory Lewis's *The Monk* and Montoni in Ann Radcliffe's *The Mysteries of Udolpho, a Romance,* as well as the horrifying female in Charlotte Bronte's *Jane Eyre* and in Bram Stoker's *The Lair of the White Worm.*

2. See *Art of Darkness* (99–107), where Williams defines the five criteria of male gothic and compares them to the opposing characteristics of female gothic.

3. Joshi's resourceful effort to resolve the complexities of the plot in "What Happens in 'The Death of Halpin Frayser,'" represents his second attempt to unravel the tale. See also his discussion of "The Death of Halpin Frayser" in "Ambrose Bierce: Horror as Satire" (161–62).

4. See Smith, "*Can Such Things Be?*"

5. See also Leeann Whites, *The Civil War as a Crisis in Gender: Augusta, Georgia, 1860–1890,* and Bertram Wyatt-Brown, *Southern Honor: Ethics and Behavior in the Old South.*

6. Nina Silber writes of this phenomenon in "Intemperate Men, Spiteful Women, Jefferson Davis."

7. In "What Happens in 'The Death of Halpin Frayser,'" Joshi claims that Frayser's crimes are literally enacted rather than merely psychically experienced. In his interpretation, Frayser lives with his mother as husband and wife under the name Larue after she follows him to California and then actually murders her before losing his memory of these events from their traumatic effects on him. While such an overt, physical enactment of Frayser's Oedipal crisis is not incorporated here, it is not precluded from the realm of possibility.

8. See Bierce's *Black Beetles in Amber* and *Shapes of Clay.* Bierce subsequently revised and enlarged both of these collections of poems as volumes 4 and 5 of his *Collected Works.*

9. For a complete copy of this poem, see CW 4: 342–44.

Chapter 3

1. *In the Midst of Life* was a revised and expanded edition of Bierce's original 1891 [1892] collection entitled *Tales of Soldiers and Civilians.*

2. "The Boarded Window," originally published in the 12 April 1891 edition of the *Examiner,* also features a panther. In this tale, the panther enters through an open window and directly attacks and kills a woman, who has mistakenly already been pronounced dead and prepared for burial by her husband, who sleeps through her attack.

3. For Rank's theory, see his *The Trauma of Birth.*

4. Joshi speculates that Jenner is actually insane rather than Irene, basing his conclusion on the fact that Jenner "had been incensed at Irene's rejection of his proposal to the point that he wished to strangle her." Although he does not develop the argument in terms of its psychological implications, Joshi claims that, "[w]hen Jenner sees the shining eyes at his window, he may be playing out some subconscious desire to kill Irene—and he in fact does so" ("Ambrose Bierce: Horror as Satire" 150).

Chapter 4

Epigraph by Friedrich Schiller is quoted by Robert A. Rogers in *A Psychoanalytic Study of the Double in Literature* (3).

1. Jung makes this argument in "The Relations between the Ego and the Unconscious." For a concise presentation of Jung's concept of individuation, see Jolande Jacobi, *The Psychology of C. G. Jung* (105–9).

2. Stephen Damian Nacco defines Bierce's condition as synaesthesia in his unpublished dissertation, "The Double Motif in the Short Stories of Ambrose Bierce" (28).

3. As Nacco observes, Gordon Rattray Taylor describes this literary figure as the "bad mother" or the evil counterpart for the Virgin Mary. See Taylor, *Sex in History* (124).

Chapter 5

The epigraph is an often quoted line from Herman Melville's "Shiloh: A Requiem," one of the poems in his Civil War collection *Battle-Pieces and Aspects of the War,* which was published in 1866 (90).

1. See Fatout, *Devil's Lexicographer* (31) and Morris, *Ambrose Bierce* (15–16).

2. For information on substitute attachments, see Mary D. Salter Ainsworth, "Attachments across the Life Span."

3. See also Morris, *Ambrose Bierce* (16–17).

4. See especially Frank S. Caprio, "A Study of Some Psychological Reactions during Prepubescence to the Idea of Death"; Melanie A. Klein, "A Contribution to the Theory of Anxiety and Guilt"; Bronislaw Malinowski, *Magic, Science, and Religion and Other Essays;* Rheingold, *Mother, Anxiety, and Death;* Wilhelm Stekel, *Conditions of Nervous Anxiety and Their Treatment;* and Gregory Zilboorg, "Fear of Death."

5. For further elaboration on the concepts of anxiety and fear of death see Rollo May, *The Meaning of Anxiety,* and Paul Tillich, "Existential Philosophy" and *The Courage to Be.*

6. See, for instance, Edmund Wilson, *Patriotic Gore* (xv–xvi).

7. See especially Duncan and Klooster's edition of Bierce's Civil War writings, *Phantoms of a Blood-Stained Period,* as well as Owens, *Devil's Topographer.*

8. In its thematic concern with the potentially lethal results of irrational fear, "A Tough Tussle" is related to some of Bierce's gothic tales (e.g., "The Man and the Snake" and "The Suitable Surroundings").

9. In *Just What War Is: The Civil War Writings of De Forest and Bierce,* Michael W. Schaefer observes that, by "devoting most of his energies to describing not what the battle really looked like but rather the impressions his imagination generated from it at the time, Bierce suggests that the truth about combat has little to do with surface details or historical perspectives but is instead chiefly a matter of the individual's unavoidably subjective responses to it" (104).

Chapter 6

The epigraph, with various minor rewordings, is a remark said to have been made by General Robert E. Lee to his subordinate James Longstreet on 13 December 1862 as they watched the Battle of Fredericksburg. It was first reported by John Esten Cooke in *A Life of Gen. Robert E. Lee,* which was published in 1871. See Ralph Keyes, *The Quote Verifier: Who Said What, Where, and When* (239).

1. Bierce also uses this motif of the lone rider on horseback in "A Son of the Gods," a story in which a nameless young officer, who is described as a "military Christ," makes a sacrificial ride to draw fire from the enemy forces and disclose their location (SF 602).

2. See McWilliams, *Ambrose Bierce* (53–54).

3. For a copy of the poem, see McWilliams, "Ambrose Bierce and His First Love" (255).

4. Evidence suggests that Marshall fabricated the ratio-of-fire statistics to substantiate his central findings in *Men against Fire;* however, his understanding of the effects of combat on soldiers is still widely recognized. In his introduction to a recent edition of Marshall's 1947 text, Russell W. Glenn observes, "Though flawed as a historian, Marshall was an astute student in war" (7).

Chapter 7

Epigraph from William Tecumseh Sherman, *Memoirs of General W. T. Sherman* (301).

1. For instance, see F. J. Logan, "The Wry Seriousness of 'Owl Creek Bridge.'" Logan claims, "Farquhar is not brave, he is foolhardy; he is not sensitive, he is callous . . . ; and he is not highly intelligent. He is, . . . rather stupid" (103).

2. Most presume that Farquhar's illusion, which in terms of subjective time takes much longer, transpires objectively in an instance, but at least one critic claims that it conceivably may take as long as fifteen minutes, consistent with the time required for

brain death to occur. Blume develops this argument in "'A Quarter of an Hour': Hanging as Ambrose Bierce and Peyton Farquhar Knew It."

3. See *The Trauma of Birth* for Rank's seminal theory connecting the fear of death with the psychological trauma of birth. Bierce also uses this motif in his gothic tale "The Eyes of the Panther."

4. See Freud, *The "Uncanny."* For a full development of the "uncanny" implications in Bierce's tale, see Peter Stoicheff, "'Something Uncanny': The Dream Structure in Ambrose Bierce's 'An Occurrence at Owl Creek Bridge.'"

5. See Kelli A. Larson, "Bierce's 'Chickamauga': A Lesson in History" (17, 20) and Owens, *Devil's Topographer* (96–97). For additional information on the Glenn family, see also Peter Cozzens, *This Terrible Sound: The Battle of Chattanooga* (139–40) and Glenn Tucker, *Chickamauga: Bloody Battle in the West* (139).

6. Grenander was the first to contrast the sense impressions of the child in "Chickamauga" with those of Farquhar in "An Occurrence at Owl Creek Bridge" (*Ambrose Bierce* 95–96).

Chapter 8

The epigraph is one of the epigrams that Bierce published in volume 8 of his *Collected Works* (369).

1. See especially Mitchell Berkun, "Inferred Correlation between Combat Performance and Some Field Laboratory Stresses"; Ben Shalit, *The Psychology of Conflict and Combat;* and Dave Grossman, *On Killing: The Psychological Cost of Learning to Kill in War and Society.*

2. Emanuel Miller describes this state in *The Neuroses in War.*

3. In *Just What War Is,* Schaefer observes that most of Bierce's war stories focus on men in isolated situations, which he argues is consistent with the author's "propensity in all his fiction for centering his attention on the isolated, alienated individual consciousness" (105).

4. Bierce also uses the motif of suicide in three other Civil War stories: "George Thurston," "An Affair of Outposts," and "One Officer, One Man."

5. Da Costa first documented his findings in a 1862 War Department communication entitled "On Irritable Heart." For more information on Da Costa's study, see Charles F. Wooley, *The Irritable Heart of Soldiers and the Origins of Anglo-American Cardiology: The U.S. Civil War (1861) to World War I (1918).*

6. In *The Experimental Fictions of Ambrose Bierce,* Cathy N. Davidson notes the similarities between these two tales, observing that "The Story of a Conscience" in a number of ways mirrors and inverts "Parker Adderson, Philosopher" (69).

7. See Edwin Shneidman, *Definition of Suicide,* for discussion of this and other examples of the cognitive aspects of suicide (136–42).

8. See Linderman, *Embattled Courage* (147–49).

9. See Erich Fromm, *The Anatomy of Human Destructiveness.*

10. In *Broken Connection,* Lifton argues for the need to incorporate death into a psychological understanding of life, especially among those who have experienced traumatic, life-threatening situations. James J. Reid begins with Lifton's idea of the life-death continuum and then uses Fromm's scale of aggressive subtypes to examine case studies of soldiers who evidenced aggressive or sadistic traits during the Crimean War, the American Civil War, and the Franco-Prussian War. In discussing the American Civil War, Reid uses Bierce's depiction of Jerome Searing as a literary example of such traits ("Psychological Factors: Soldiers in an Era of Warfare" 415–21).

11. For a comprehensive analysis of Grayrock's dream vision, see Woodruff, *Short Stories of Ambrose Bierce* (71–76).

12. In *The Devil's Topographer,* for instance, Owens argues, "It is equally plausible that William, now becoming the inheritor of the bird's legacy, simply does likewise and deserts the army, perhaps returning through the terrain of his dream to the Enchanted Land of his brother" (35).

Chapter 9

The epigraph comes from Walt Whitman's elegy for Abraham Lincoln, "When Lilacs Last in the Dooryard Bloom'd," which was first published in 1865 (356).

1. See Herbert Hendin and Ann Pollinger Haas, "Posttraumatic Stress Disorders in Veterans of Early American Wars"; Eric T. Dean, *Shook over Hell;* and Reid, "Psychological Factors."

2. See Marilyn Bowman, "Individual Differences in Posttraumatic Stress Disorder. Problems with the DSM-IV Model"; Chris R. Brewin, Bernice Andrews, and John D. Valentine, "Meta-Analysis of Risk Factors for Posttraumatic Stress Disorder in Trauma-Exposed Adults"; and Emily Ozer, Suzanne Best, Tami Lipsey, and Daniel Weiss, "Predictors of Posttraumatic Stress Disorder and Symptoms in Adults: A Meta-Analysis."

3. Clancy D. McKenzie and Lance S. Wright document this theory in *Delayed Posttraumatic Stress Disorders from Infancy: The Two Trauma Mechanism.*

4. See Mario Mikulincer, Phillip R. Shaver, and Neta Horesh, "Attachment Bias of Emotion Regulation and Posttraumatic Adjustment."

5. See Renee D. Goodwin, "Asthma and Anxiety Disorders."

6. See Mary D. Klinnert, Harold S. Nelson, Marcella R. Price, Allen D. Adinoff, Donald Y. M. Leung, and David A. Mrazek, "Onset and Persistence of Childhood Asthma:

Predictors from Infancy"; and Astrida Seja Kaugars, Mary D. Klinnert, and Bruce G. Bender, "Family Influences on Pediatric Asthma."

7. In his biography of Bierce, Morris explains that "[b]y order of Congress the adjutant general had been directed to promote some 6,600 selected Civil War veterans to the next rank above their last wartime positions. For some reason, never explained, Bierce was promoted not to captain, as would have been the correct rank, but to major" (116).

8. In 1873, Bierce republished this untitled column in his first book, *The Fiend's Delight.* For ease of reference, Berkove reproduces the column as Appendix A in *Prescription for Adversity* (159–60).

9. For an in-depth study of the death-dominated lives of survivors of mass death, see Lifton, *Death in Life: Survivors of Hiroshima.*

10. Owens, who was the first to connect this passage to "The Major's Tale," definitively sets the scene as occurring at Nashville on the morning of 16 December 1864, confirming Bierce's close affinity to Broadwood in this link to his final battle. See *Devil's Topographer* (121–22).

Chapter 10

The epigraph is an often quoted line from a letter Bierce wrote to his niece Lora on 1 October 1913 (MM 243).

1. This letter is known now as "Battlefields and Ghosts."

2. See Rank, "The Double as Immortal Self" in *Beyond Psychology* (62–101).

3. In the novel *The Old Gringo,* Carlos Fuentes bases his fictionalized account of Bierce's death on this letter.

4. See, for instance, Morris, *Ambrose Bierce* (247–68), and Neale, *Life of Ambrose Bierce* (429–47).

Bibliography

Aaron, Daniel. *The Unwritten War: American Writers and the Civil War.* New York: Knopf, 1973.

Ainsworth, Mary D. Salter. "Attachments across the Life Span." *Bulletin of the New York Academy of Medicine* 61 (1985): 792–812.

American Psychiatric Association. *Diagnostic and Statistical Manual of Mental Disorders (DSM-III).* Washington, DC: APA, 1980.

———. *Diagnostic and Statistical Manual of Mental Disorders (DSM-IV).* Washington, DC: APA, 1994.

Ames, Clifford R. "Do I Wake or Sleep? Technique as Content in Ambrose Bierce's Short Story, 'An Occurrence at Owl Creek Bridge.'" *American Literary Realism* 19 (1987): 52–67.

Beatty, John. *Memoirs of a Volunteer, 1861–1863.* Ed. Harvey S. Ford. New York: Norton, 1946.

Becker, Ernest. *The Denial of Death.* New York: Free, 1973.

Behrends, Rebecca Smith, and Sidney Jules Blatt. "Internalization and Psychological Development throughout the Life Cycle." *Psychoanalytical Study of the Child* 40 (1985): 11–39.

Berkove, Lawrence I. *A Prescription for Adversity: The Moral Art of Ambrose Bierce.* Columbus: Ohio State UP, 2002.

Berkun, Mitchell. "Inferred Correlation between Combat Performance and Some Field Laboratory Stresses." Research Memo (Fighter II). Arlington: Human Resources Research Office, 1958.

Bierce, Ambrose. *Black Beetles in Amber.* San Francisco: Western Authors, 1892.

———. *The Collected Works of Ambrose Bierce.* 12 vols. New York: Neale, 1909–12.

———. *In the Midst of Life: Tales of Soldiers and Civilians.* New York: Putnam's, 1898.

———. *The Letters of Ambrose Bierce.* 1922. Ed. Bertha Clark Pope. New York: Gordian, 1967.

———. *A Much Misunderstood Man: Selected Letters of Ambrose Bierce.* Ed. S. T. Joshi and David E. Schultz. Columbus: Ohio State UP, 2003.

———. *Phantoms of a Blood-Stained Period: The Complete Civil War Writings of Ambrose Bierce.* Ed. Russell Duncan and David J. Klooster. Amherst: U of Massachusetts P, 2002.

———. *Poems of Ambrose Bierce.* Ed. M. E. Grenander. Lincoln: U of Nebraska P, 1995.

———. *Shapes of Clay.* San Francisco: Wood, 1903.

———. *The Short Fiction of Ambrose Bierce: A Comprehensive Edition.* Ed. S. T. Joshi, Lawrence I. Berkove, and David E. Schultz. 3 vols. Knoxville: U of Tennessee P, 2006.

———. *A Sole Survivor: Bits of Autobiography.* Ed. S. T. Joshi and David E. Schultz. Knoxville: U of Tennessee P, 1998.

———. *Tales of Soldiers and Civilians.* San Francisco: Steele, 1891 [1892].

———. *The Unabridged Devil's Dictionary.* Ed. David E. Schultz and S. T. Joshi. Athens: U of Georgia P, 2000.

Bierce, Ambrose, Thomas A. Harcouth, and William A. Rudofson (Herman, William). *The Dance of Death.* San Francisco: Keller, 1877.

Bloom, Harold. *The Anxiety of Influence: A Theory of Poetry.* New York: Oxford UP, 1973.

Blume, Donald T. *Ambrose Bierce's Civilians and Soldiers in Context: A Critical Study.* Kent: Kent State UP, 2004.

———. "'A Quarter of an Hour': Hanging as Ambrose Bierce and Peyton Farquhar Knew It." *American Literary Realism* 34 (2002): 146–57.

Bowlby, John. "The Growth of Independence in the Young Child." *Royal Society of Health Journal* 76 (1956): 587–91.

———. *Separation: Anxiety and Anger.* Vol. 2. *Attachment and Loss.* New York: Basic, 1973.

Bowman, Marilyn. "Individual Differences in Posttraumatic Stress Disorder: Problems with the DSM-IV Model." *Canadian Journal of Psychiatry* 44 (1999): 21–32.

Brazil, John R. "Beyond the Bitterness: Ambrose Bierce in Text and Context." *American Literary Realism* 13 (1980): 225–37.

Brewin, Chris R., Bernice Andrews, and John D. Valentine. "Meta-Analysis of Risk Factors for Posttraumatic Stress Disorder in Trauma-Exposed Adults." *Journal of Consulting and Clinical Psychology* 68 (2000): 748–66.

Bronte, Charlotte. *Jane Eyre.* 1847. Ed. Jane Jack and Margaret Smith. Oxford: Clarendon, 1969.

Brooks, Cleanth, and Robert Penn Warren. *Understanding Fiction.* 1943. 3rd ed. Englewood Cliffs: Prentice, 1979.

Brown, Norman O. *Life against Death: The Psychoanalytical Meaning of History.* Middletown: Wesleyan UP, 1959.

Buelow, George, Mark McClain, and Irene McIntosh. "A New Measure for an Important Construct: The Attachment and Object Relations Inventory." *Journal of Personality Assessment* 60 (1996): 604–23.

Byles, Joanna Montgomery. "Psychoanalysis and War: The Superego and Projective Identification." *Journal for the Psychoanalysis of Culture and Society* 8 (2003): 208–13.

Caprio, Frank S. "A Study of Some Psychological Reactions during Prepubescence to the Idea of Death." *Psychoanalytic Review* 24 (1950): 495–505.

Clinton, Catherine., and Nina Silber, eds. *Divided Houses: Gender and the Civil War.* New York: Oxford UP, 1992.

Coffin, Margaret M. *Death in Early America: The History and Folklore of Customs and Superstitions of Early Medicine, Funerals, Burials, and Mourning.* Nashville: Nelson, 1976.

Coleman, Penny. *Flashback: Posttraumatic Stress Disorder, Suicide, and the Lessons of War.* Boston: Beacon, 2006.

Cooke, John Esten. *A Life of Gen. Robert E. Lee.* New York: Appleton, 1871.

Cozzens, Peter. *This Terrible Sound: The Battle of Chickamauga.* Urbana: U of Illinois P, 1992.

Davidson, Cathy N. *The Experimental Fictions of Ambrose Bierce: Structuring the Ineffable.* Lincoln: U of Nebraska P, 1984.

De Forest, John William. *A Volunteer's Adventures: A Union Captain's Record of the Civil War.* Ed. James H. Coushore. New Haven: Yale UP, 1946.

Dean, Eric T., Jr. *Shook over Hell: Post-traumatic Stress, Vietnam, and the Civil War.* Cambridge: Harvard UP, 1997.

Dimeo, Steven. "Psychological Symbolism in Three Early Tales of Invisibility." *Riverside Quarterly* 5 (1971): 20–27.

Duncan, Russell, and David J. Klooster, eds. *Phantoms of a Blood-Stained Period: The Complete Civil War Writings of Ambrose Bierce.* By Ambrose Bierce. Amherst: U of Massachusetts P, 2002.

Durkheim, Emile. *Suicide: A Study in Sociology.* Ed. George Simpson. Trans. John A. Spaulding. New York: Free, 1951. (Originally published in 1897 as *Le suicide.*)

Edel, Leon. *Writing Lives: Principia Biographica.* New York: Norton, 1984.

Farrell, James J. *Inventing the American Way of Death, 1830–1920.* Philadelphia: Temple UP, 1980.

Fatout, Paul. *Ambrose Bierce: The Devil's Lexicographer.* Norman: U of Oklahoma P, 1951.

Faust, Drew Gilpin. *This Republic of Suffering: Death and the American Civil War.* New York: Knopf, 2008.

Feifel Herman, ed. *New Meanings of Death.* New York: McGraw, 1977.

Felman, Shoshana. "On Reading Poetry: Reflections on the Limits and Possibilities of Psychoanalytical Approaches." *The Purloined Poe: Lacan, Derrida, and Psychoanalytic Reading.* Ed. John P. Muller and William J. Richardson. Baltimore: Johns Hopkins UP, 1988. 133–56. Originally published in *The Literary Freud: Mechanisms of Defense and the Poetic Will.* Ed. Joseph Smith. Vol. 4. New Haven: Yale UP, 1980. 119–48.

Fishler, Priscilla H., Michael B. Sperling, and Arthur C. Carr. "Assessment of Adult Relatedness: A Review of Empirical Findings from Object Relations and Attachment Theories." *Journal of Personality Assessment* 55 (1990): 499–520.

Fitch, Michael Hendrick. *The Chattanooga Campaign.* Madison: Wisconsin State History Commission, 1911.

Fornari, Franco. *The Psychoanalysis of War.* Trans. Alenka Pfeifer. Bloomington: Indiana UP, 1975.

Frank, Joseph Allan, and George A. Reaves. *"Seeing the Elephant": Raw Recruits at the Battle of Shiloh.* New York: Greenwood, 1989.

Frazer, James George, Sir. *The Golden Bough: A Study in Magic and Religion.* 1922. Abr. ed. New York: Macmillan, 1958.

Freud, Sigmund. *The Interpretation of Dreams.* 1900. *The Standard Edition of the Complete Psychological Works of Sigmund Freud.* Ed. and trans. James Strachey. Vols. 4–5. London: Hogarth, 1953.

———. "A Special Type of Object-choice Made by Men." 1910. *The Standard Edition of the Complete Psychological Works of Sigmund Freud.* Ed. and trans. James Strachey. Vol. 11. London: Hogarth, 1957. 163–75.

———. *The "Uncanny."* 1919. *The Standard Edition of the Complete Psychological Works of Sigmund Freud.* Ed. and trans. James Strachey. Vol. 17. London: Hogarth, 1955. 217–52.

Fromm, Erich. *The Anatomy of Human Destructiveness.* New York: Holt, 1973.

Fry, Carrol L., and Wayne A. Chandler. "An Epiphany at Owl Creek Bridge: Intimations of Immoralities in Ambrose Bierce's Fiction." *Studies in Weird Fiction* 24 (1999): 8–14.

Fuentes, Carlos. *The Old Gringo.* Trans. Margaret Sayers Peden and Carlos Fuentes. New York: Farrar, 1985.

Gabriel, Richard A. *No More Heroes: Madness and Psychiatry in War.* New York: Hill, 1987.

Gale, Robert L. *An Ambrose Bierce Companion.* Westport: Greenwood, 2001.

Glenn, Russell W. Introduction. *Men against Fire: The Problem of Battle Command.* By Samuel L. A. Marshall. Norman: U of Oklahoma P, 2000. 1–8.

Goodwin, Renee D. "Asthma and Anxiety Disorders." *Asthma: Social and Psychological Factors and Psychosomatic Syndromes.* Ed. E. S. Brown. Advances in Psychosomatic Medicine. Vol. 24. Basel, Switzerland: Karger, 2003. 51–71.

Grattan, C. Hartley. *Bitter Bierce: A Mystery of American Letters.* 1929. New York: Cooper, 1966.

Gray, J. Glenn. *The Warriors: Reflections on Men in Battle.* New York: Harper, 1959.

Grenander, M. E. *Ambrose Bierce.* Twayne's United States Authors Series, 180. Boston: Twayne, 1971.

———. "Ambrose Bierce and *In the Midst of Life.*" *Book Collector* 20 (1971): 321–31.

———. Introduction. *Poems of Ambrose Bierce.* By Ambrose Bierce. Lincoln: U of Nebraska P, 1995. xiii–xli.

Grossman, Dave. *On Killing: The Psychological Cost of Learning to Kill in War and Society.* Boston: Little, 1995.

Habibi, Don Asher. "The Experience of a Lifetime: Philosophical Reflections on a Narrative Device of Ambrose Bierce." *Studies in the Humanities* 29 (2002): 83–108.

Hallam, Clifford. "The Double as Incomplete Self: Toward a Definition of the *Doppelgänger.*" *Fearful Symmetry: Doubles and Doubling in Literature and Film.* Papers in the Fifth Annual Florida State University Conference on Literature and Film. Gainesville: UP of Florida, 1982. 1–31.

Harnik, J. "One Component of the Fear of Death in Early Infancy." *International Journal of Psychoanalysis* 11 (1930): 485–91.

Hendin, Herbert, and Ann Pollinger Haas. "Posttraumatic Stress Disorders in Veterans of Early American Wars." *Psychohistory Review* 12 (1985): 25–30.

Hoppenstand, Gary. "Ambrose Bierce and the Transformation of the Gothic Tale in the Nineteenth-century American Periodical." *Periodical Literature in Nineteenth-Century America.* Ed. Kenneth M. Price and Susan Belasco Smith. Charlottesville: UP of Virginia, 1995. 220–38.

Howells, William Dean. "Editha." 1905. *Norton Anthology of American Literature.* Ed. Nina Baym. Vol. 1. New York: Norton, 1998. 258–67.

Jackson, Charles O., ed. *Passing: The Vision of Death in America.* Contributions in Family Studies, 2. Westport: Greenwood, 1977.

Jacobi, Jolande. *The Psychology of C. G. Jung.* 7th ed. Trans. Ralph Manheim. New Haven: Yale UP, 1968.

Jones, Ernest. *On the Nightmare.* New ed. New York: Liveright, 1951.

Jones, Edgar, and Simon Wessely. *Shell Shock to PTSD: Military Psychiatry from 1900 to the Gulf War.* Maudsley Monographs, 47. Hove, East Sussex, Great Britain: Psychology, 2005.

Joshi, S. T. "Ambrose Bierce: Horror as Satire." *The Weird Tale: Arthur Machen, Lord Dunsany, Algernon Blackwood, M. R. James, Ambrose Bierce, H. P. Lovecraft.* By S. T. Joshi Austin: U of Texas P, 1990. 143–67.

———. "What Happens in 'The Death of Halpin Frayser.'" *Studies in the Fantastic* 2 (Winter 2008), 94–101.

Joshi, S. T., Lawrence I. Berkove, and David E. Schultz, eds. *The Short Fiction of Ambrose Bierce: A Comprehensive Edition.* By Ambrose Bierce. 3 vols. Knoxville: U of Tennessee P, 2006.

Joshi, S. T., and David E. Schultz, eds. *Ambrose Bierce: An Annotated Bibliography of Primary Sources.* Westport: Greenwood, 1999.

——, eds. *A Much Misunderstood Man: Selected Letters of Ambrose Bierce.* Columbus: Ohio State UP, 2003.

——, eds. *A Sole Survivor: Bits of Autobiography.* By Ambrose Bierce. Knoxville: U of Tennessee P, 1998.

Jung, Carl G. "The Relations between the Ego and the Unconscious." 1934. *The Collected Works of C. G. Jung.* Ed. Herbert Read, Michael Fordham, and Gerhard Adler. Trans. R. F. C. Hull. 2nd ed. Vol. 7. Princeton: Princeton UP, 1966. 123–241.

Kane, Harnett Thomas. *Spies for the Blue and Gray.* Garden City: Hanover, 1954.

Kaugars, Astrida Seja, Mary D. Klinnert, and Bruce G. Bender. "Family Influences on Pediatric Asthma." *Journal of Pediatric Psychology* 29 (2004): 475–91.

Keyes, Ralph. *The Quote Verifier: Who Said What, Where, and When.* New York: St. Martin's, 2006.

Kimmel, Michael. *American Manhood: A Cultural History.* New York: Free, 1996.

Kirkpatrick, Lee A. "Attachment and Religious Representations and Behavior." *Handbook of Attachment: Theory, Research, and Clinical Applications.* Ed. Jude Cassidy and Phillip R. Shaver. New York: Guilford, 1999. 803–22.

Klein, Melanie A. "A Contribution to the Theory of Anxiety and Guilt." *International Journal of Psychoanalysis* 29 (1948): 114–23.

Klinnert, Mary D., Harold S. Nelson, Marcella R. Price, Arllen D. Adinoff, Donald Y. M. Leung, and David A. Mrazek. "Onset and Persistence of Childhood Asthma: Predictors from Infancy." *Pediatrics* 108.4 (2001): E69.

Kluckhohn, Clyde, and Henry A. Murray, eds. *Personality in Nature, Society, and Culture.* New York: Knopf, 1953.

Knepper, George W. Introduction. *Travels in the Southland, 1822–1823: The Journal of Lucius Verus Bierce.* Ed. George W. Knepper. Columbus: Ohio State UP, 1966. 3–43.

Kocher, Richard Luke. "Fear and Dilemma in the War Stories of Ambrose Bierce." Unpublished doctoral dissertation, University of Southern California, Los Angeles, 1978.

Kristeva, Julia. *Powers of Horror: An Essay on Abjection.* Trans. Leon S. Roudiez. New York: Columbia UP, 1982.

——. *Revolution in Poetic Language.* Trans. Margaret Waller. New York: Columbia UP, 1984.

Lacan, Jacques. *Ecrits: A Selection.* 1966. Trans. Alan Sheridan. New York: Norton, 1977.

Larson, Kelli A. "Bierce's 'Chickamauga': A Lesson in History." *Midwestern Miscellany* 27 (1999): 9–22.

Lewis, Matthew Gregory. *The Monk.* 1796. Ed. Howard Anderson. Oxford: Oxford UP, 1990.

Liechty, Daniel, ed. *Death and Denial: Interdisciplinary Perspectives on the Legacy of Ernest Becker.* Westport: Praeger, 2002.

Lifton, Robert Jay. *The Broken Connection: On Death and the Continuity of Life.* 1979. New York: Basic, 1983.

———. *Death in Life: Survivors of Hiroshima.* New York: Random, 1968.

———. *Revolutionary Immortality.* New York: Random, 1968.

Linderman, Gerald F. *Embattled Courage: The Experience of Combat in the American Civil War.* New York: Free, 1987.

Linenthal, Edward Tabor. *Changing Images of the Warrior Hero in America: A History of Popular Symbolism.* New York: Mellon, 1982.

Logan, F. J. "The Wry Seriousness of 'Owl Creek Bridge.'" *American Literary Realism* 10 (1977): 101–13.

Loyd, Dennis. "'All is Hushed at Shiloh': A Reminiscence." *Border States* 8 (1991): 7–14.

Lundberg, David. "The American Literature of War: The Civil War, World War I, and World War II." *American Quarterly* 36 (1984): 373–88.

Mahler, Margaret S., Fred Pine, and Anni Bergman. *The Psychological Birth of the Human Infant.* New York: Basic, 1975.

Malinowski, Bronislaw. *Magic, Science, and Religion and other Essays.* New York: Macmillan, 1925.

Mariani, Giorgio. "Ambrose Bierce's Civil War Stories and the Critique of the Martial Spirit." *Studies in American Fiction* 19 (1991): 221–28.

Marshall, Samuel L. A. *Men against Fire: The Problem of Battle Command.* New York: Morrow, 1947.

Masserman, Jules. *Principles of Dynamic Psychiatry.* Philadelphia: Saunders, 1961.

May, Rollo. *The Meaning of Anxiety.* New York: Ronald, 1950.

McKenzie, Clancy D., and Lance S. Wright. *Delayed Posttraumatic Stress Disorders from Infancy: The Two Trauma Mechanism.* Amsterdam, Netherlands: Harwood, 1996.

McLean, Robert C. "The Deaths in Ambrose Bierce's 'Halpin Frayser.'" *Papers on Language and Literature* 10 (1974): 394–402.

McPherson, James M. *Battle Cry of Freedom: The Civil War Era.* New York: Oxford UP, 1988.

———. *For Cause and Comrades: Why Men Fought in the Civil War.* New York: Oxford UP, 1997.

McWilliams, Carey. *Ambrose Bierce: A Biography.* New York: Boni, 1929.

———. "Ambrose Bierce and His First Love: An Idyll of the Civil War. *Bookman* 75 (1932): 254–59.

Melville, Herman. *Battle-Pieces and Aspects of the Civil War.* 1866. Ed. Sidney Kaplan. Amherst: U of Massachusetts P, 1972.

Mikulincer, Mario, Phillip R. Shaver, and Neta Horesh. "Attachment Bias of Emotion Regulation and Posttraumatic Adjustment." *Emotion Regulation in Families: Pathways to*

Dysfunction and Health. Ed. Douglas K. Snyder, Jeffry A. Simpson, and Jay N. Hughes. Washington, DC: APA, 2006. 77–99.

Miller, Emanuel. *The Neuroses in War.* New York: Macmillan, 1940.

Mitchell, Juliet. "Trauma, Recognition, and the Place of Language." *Diacritics* 28 (1998): 121–33.

Morris, Roy, Jr. *Ambrose Bierce: Alone in Bad Company.* New York: Oxford UP, 1995.

Murray, Lynne. "Intersubjectivity, Object Relations Theory, and Empirical Evidence from the Mother-Infant Interactions." *Infant Mental Health Journal* 12 (1991): 219–32.

Nacco, Stephen Damian. "The Double in the Short Stories of Ambrose Bierce." Unpublished doctoral dissertation, Fordham University, New York, 1991.

Neale, Walter. *Life of Ambrose Bierce.* New York: Neale, 1929.

Owens, David M. *The Devil's Topographer: Ambrose Bierce and the American War Story.* Knoxville: U of Tennessee P, 2006.

Ozer, Emily, Suzanne Best, Tami Lipsey, and Daniel Weiss. "Predictors of Posttraumatic Stress Disorder and Symptoms in Adults: A Meta-Analysis." *Psychological Bulletin* 129 (2003): 52–73.

Poe, Edgar Allan. "The Philosophy of Composition." 1846. *The Complete Works of Edgar Allan Poe.* Ed. James A. Harrison. Vol. 14. New York: AMS, 1965. 193–208.

Porte, Joel. "'In the Hands of an Angry God': Religious Terror in Gothic Fiction." *The Gothic Imagination: Essays in Dark Romanticism.* Ed. G. R. Thompson. Pullman: Washington State UP, 1974. 42–64.

Powers, James G. "Freud and Farquhar: An Occurrence at Owl Creek Bridge?" *Studies in Short Fiction* 19 (1982): 278–81.

Radcliffe, Ann. *The Mysteries of Udolpho, a Romance.* 1794. Ed. Bonamy Dobrée. London: Oxford UP, 1966.

Rank, Otto. *Beyond Psychology.* 1941. New York: Dover, 1958.

———. *The Double: A Psychoanalytic Study.* 1914. Ed. and trans. Harry Tucker, Jr. Chapel Hill: U of North Carolina P, 1971.

———. *The Trauma of Birth.* 1929. Mineola: Dover, 1994. (Originally published in 1924 as *Das Trauma der Geburt.*)

Reid, James J. "Psychological Factors: Soldiers in an Era of Warfare." *Crisis of the Ottoman Empire: Prelude to Collapse, 1839–1878.* Stuttgart, Germany: Steiner, 2000. 386–455.

Rheingold, Joseph C. *The Mother, Anxiety, and Death: The Catastrophic Death Complex.* Boston: Little, 1967.

Richter, Jean Paul. *Siebenkäs,* 1796.

Rogers, Robert A. *A Psychoanalytic Study of the Double in Literature.* Detroit: Wayne State UP, 1970.

Rubens, Philip M. "The Gothic Foundations of Ambrose Bierce's Fiction." *Nyctalops* 14 (1978): 29–31.

Schaefer, Michael W. *Just What War Is: The Civil War Writings of De Forest and Bierce.* Knoxville: U of Tennessee P, 1997.

Shalit, Ben. *The Psychology of Conflict and Combat.* New York: Praeger, 1988.

Sherman, William Tecumseh. *Memoirs of General W. T. Sherman.* 1875. New York: Library of America, 1990.

Shneidman, Edwin. *Definition of Suicide.* 1985. Northvale: Aronson, 1994.

Silber, Nina. "Intemperate Men, Spiteful Women, Jefferson Davis." *Divided Houses: Gender and the Civil War.* Ed. Catherine Clinton and Nina Silber. New York: Oxford UP, 1992. 283–305.

Silverman, Kaja. *Male Subjectivity at the Margins.* New York: Routledge, 1992.

Smith, Allan Lloyd. "*Can Such Things Be?* Ambrose Bierce, the 'Dead Mother,' and Other American Traumas." *Spectral America: Phantoms and the National Imagination.* Ed. Jeffrey Andrew Weinstock. Madison: U of Wisconsin P, 2004. 57–77.

Solomon, Eric. "The Bitterness of Battle: Ambrose Bierce's War Fiction." *Midwest Quarterly* 5 (1964): 147–65.

Stannard, David E. "Death and the Puritan Child." *Death in America.* Ed. David E. Stannard. Philadelphia: U of Pennsylvania P. 1975. 9–29.

———. *The Puritan Way of Death: A Study in Religion, Culture, and Social Change.* New York: Oxford UP, 1977.

Stein, William Bysshe. "Bierce's 'The Death of Halpin Frayser': The Poetics of Gothic Consciousness." *ESQ* 18 (1972): 115–22.

Stekel, Wilhelm. *Conditions of Nervous Anxiety and Their Treatment.* New York: Liverwright, 1949.

Stoicheff, Peter. "'Something Uncanny': The Dream Structure in Ambrose Bierce's 'An Occurrence at Owl Creek Bridge.'" *Studies in Short Fiction* 30 (1993): 349–58.

Stoker, Bram. *The Lair of the White Worm.* London: Rider, 1911.

Talley, Sharon. "Anxious Representations of Uncertain Masculinity: The Failed Journey to Self-Understanding in Ambrose Bierce's 'The Death of Halpin Frayser.'" *Journal of Men's Studies* 14 (2006): 161–72.

———. "Childhood and the Fear of Death in Ambrose Bierce's *The Parenticide Club* and 'Visions of the Night.'" *American Imago* 66.1 (Spring 2009): 41–69.

Taylor, Gordon Rattray. *Sex in History.* New York: Harper, 1954.

Thomson, Douglass H. "Ambrose Gwinett Bierce (1842–1914)." *Gothic Writers: A Critical and Bibliographical Guide.* Ed. Douglass H. Thomson, Jack G. Voller, and Frederick S. Frank. Westport: Greenwood, 2002. 60–68.

Tillich, Paul. *The Courage to Be.* New Haven: Yale UP, 1952.

———. "Existential Philosophy." *Journal of the History of Ideas* 5 (1944): 44–70.

Tucker, Glenn. *Chickamauga: Bloody Battle in the West.* New York: Bobbs, 1961.

Walker, Franklin. *Ambrose Bierce: The Wickedest Man in San Francisco.* San Francisco: Colt, 1941.

Whites, Leeann. *The Civil War as a Crisis in Gender: Augusta, Georgia, 1860–1890.* Athens: U of Georgia P, 1995.

Whitman, Walt. "When Lilacs Last in the Dooryard Bloom'd." 1865. *The Complete Poems.* London: Penguin, 1996. 351–59.

Williams, Anne. *Art of Darkness: A Poetics of Gothic.* Chicago: U of Chicago P, 1995.

Wilson, Edmund. *Patriotic Gore.* New York: Oxford UP, 1962.

Woodruff, Stuart C. *The Short Stories of Ambrose Bierce: A Study in Polarity.* Pittsburgh: U of Pittsburgh P, 1964.

Wooley, Charles F. *The Irritable Heart of Soldiers and the Origins of Anglo-American Cardiology: The U.S. Civil War (1861) to World War I (1918).* History of Medicine in Context. Aldershot, Hampshire, England: Ashgate, 2002.

Wyatt-Brown, Bertram. *Southern Honor: Ethics and Behavior in the Old South.* New York: Oxford UP, 1982.

Zilboorg, Gregory. "Fear of Death." *Psychoanalytic Quarterly* 12 (1943): 465–75.

Index

Adinoff, Allen D., 141n6
"Affair of Outposts, An" (Bierce), 140n4
aggression, subtypes of, 105, 141n9
Ainsworth, Mary D. Salter, 138n2
Akron, OH, 4, 6, 54, 55
American Psychiatric Association, 114
American Revolution, 21, 63
"Ancestral Bond, The" (Bierce), 48
Andrews, Bernice, 141n2
Argonaut (magazine), 119
asthma, 116–17, 141–42nn5–6. *See also* Bierce, Ambrose Gwinett: postwar life
Atlanta Campaign, 74
Atlanta, GA, 115
attachment: definition of, 5; relation to object-relations theory, 5, 136n8; theories of, xv, 5, 55, 56, 136n6–7, 138n2, 141n4. *See also* Bierce, Ambrose Gwinett: childhood and youth, Civil War experiences, postwar life
authorship: and anxiety of influence, 27, 28; and quest for immortality, 46–47, 130

"Basilica" (Bierce), 118
Battle-Pieces and Aspects of the War (Melville), 138
"Battlefields and Ghosts" (Bierce), 142n1
Beatty, General Samuel, 125
Beatty, John, 104
Becker, Ernest, 136n2; and fear of death, xv, 2, 3, 17, 37; and hero-system, xv, 57; and Oedipal project, 2; and narcissism, 57, 61, 77, and responses to death, 87
Behrends, Rebecca Smith, 136n8
Bender, Bruce G., 142n6
Bergman, Anni, 136n6
Berkove, Lawrence I., xiv, xv, 10, 135n4, 48, 59, 118, 142n8; and biographical approaches to Bierce, 135–36n6; and interpretation of *The Parenticide Club*, 7, 9, 137n10
Berkun, Mitchell, 140n1
Best, Suzanne, 141n2
Bierce, Adelia (sister), 5
Bierce, Albert (brother), 10, 59
Bierce, Ambrose Gwinett
—childhood and youth, xv, xvi, 3, 6, 11, 14–15; birth, 3; attachment issues, 5–6, 11, 54, 55, 56, 57; depression, 55; dreams of, 1, 11, 14–15, 45; enrollment in military school, 55; fear of death, 3, 11; life in Warsaw, 53–54; relationship with parents, 1, 5, 6, 7, 10–11; religious influences, 3, 6, 13; move from home, 53; move to Akron, 54; search for parental role models, 53–54
—Civil War experiences: xiii, xvi, xvii, 56, 127; attachment issues, 73, 74; combat stress, 53, 98–99, 114, 116, 118; discharge, 56, 116; engagement to Bernice Wright, 73–76; enlistment, fearlessness in combat, 53, 73; head

Civil War experiences (cont.)
wound, 56, 59, 76, 99, 114–15, 116; letter to Clara Wright, 74–76, 98–99; prisoner of war, 76–77; promotion through ranks, 56, 73; recognition for bravery, 56; relationship with General William B. Hazen, 56–57, 130; service as topographical engineer, 56; war as psychic defense for, 55, 59–60
—postwar life: asthma, 37, 38, 116, 117, 119, 132; attachment issues, 116, 118, 120, 121; attitude toward women, 119; Black Hills mining venture, 119; brevetted rank, 117, 125, 142n7; cynicism, 118; commentary on relationship with parents, xv; disappearance and death, 132–34; divorce, 120; *doepplegänger* experience, 45–46; fear of literary failure or anonymity, 27–28, 41–42, 130; as journalist, 118, 119, 121, 127–28; in London, 45–46, 118–19, 126–28 ; marriage, 118–19, 120, 121; as "misanthrope," 59, 60, 118; move to Washington, D.C., 120, 128; obsession with war, 59, 122; as parent, 119, 121; as poet, 27–28, 118; preparation of *Collected Works*, 130; relationship with General William B. Hazen, 117; and Posttraumatic Stress Disorder, xvii, 114, 116, 119, 121, 124; relationship with William Randolph Hearst, xvii, 119–20; in San Francisco, 117–18, 119; and Stoicism, xiv, 127; vanity, 73; visits to Civil War battlefields, 128, 130, 132, 134
—writing: xiii, xv, xvi–xvii, 59, 60, 99, 117–18, 122, 127; works by (*see individual works alphabetically by title*)
Bierce, Arthur (brother), 5
Bierce, Aurelia, (sister), 5
Bierce, Day (son), 119, 120–21
Bierce, Helen (daughter), 119, 121, 131, 132
Bierce, Laura Sherwood (mother), 3, 4
Bierce, Leigh (son), 119, 121
Bierce, Lora (niece), 131, 132, 142
Bierce, Lucius (uncle), 4, 54–55, 56
Bierce, Marcus Aurelius (father), 3, 4–5, 6
Bierce, Mary Ellen ("Mollie," wife), 118, 119, 120
birth, trauma of, 138n3; and fear of death, 23, 24, 37, 88–89, 136n4, 140n3 (*see also* object-loss anxiety)
Bits of Autobiography. See *Sole Survivor: Bits of Autobiography, A*
"Bivouac of the Dead, A" (Bierce). *See* "Passing Show, A"
Black Beetles in Amber (Bierce), 137n8
Blatt, Sidney Jules, 136n8
Bloom, Harold, 25, 28
Bloomington, IL, 131
Blume, Donald T., xiv–xv, 79, 80–81, 140n2
"Boarded Window, The," 138n2
Book of Common Prayer, 29
Bowlby, John, 55, 136n7
Bowman, Marilyn, 141n2
Bradford, William, 3
Brazil, John R., xiv, 59
Brewin, Chris R., 141n2
Bronte, Charlotte, 137n1
Brooks, Cleanth, 87
Brotherton family, 90
Brown, John, 55
Brown, Norman O., 2, 136n1
Buelow, George, 136n8
Byles, Joanna Montgomery, 59, 117

Californian (magazine), 118
Can Such Things Be? (Bierce), xvi, 47
Caprio, Frank S., 138n4
Carrick's Ford, WV, 63
Chattanooga, TN, 76, 90, 115, 131
Cheat Mountain, WV, 60, 62, 63, 128
"Chickamauga" (Bierce), xvii, 84, 90–95, 140n5–6

Chickamauga, Battle of, 56, 64, 90, 91, 92, 94–95, 114, 140n5
Chickamauga, GA, 131
Chihuahua, Mexico, 133
Christiansen, Carrie, 131
Civil War, U.S., 20, 58; anxiety before battle in, 66; civilian casualties in, 84; courage in, 65, 69, 70–71; definition of espionage in, 81, 86, 102, 103; desertion during, 109; as first modern war, 59, 66, 97, 104; and declining morale, 75; and importance of mail, 75; and lack of psychological care, 101; raw recruits in, 62; and resentment toward civilians, 89–90; respect for flags in, 65; snipers in, 104, 141n8; veterans, 113–14; women's roles in, 71–72
Cleopatra, 35
Cleveland, TN, 74
Coffin, Margaret M., 136n5
"Cold Greeting, A" (Bierce), xvi, 47
Collected Works of Ambrose Bierce, The, xvii, 6, 126, 127, 128, 130, 137n8, 140
Cooke, John Esten, 139
Cornwall, CT, 3
Cosmopolitan (magazine), 130
Cozzens, Peter, 91, 140n5
"Crime at Pickett's Mill, The" (Bierce), xvii, 75, 93, 99
Cumberland Mountains, TN, 102

Da Costa, Jacob Mendes, 101
"Damned Thing, The" (Bierce), xvi, 38–42, 43
Dance of Death (Bierce), xiii, 135n1
Darwin, Charles, 48
Davidson, Cathy N., xiv, 18, 34, 35, 36, 80, 94, 140n6
Davis, Jefferson, 20, 137n6
Dean, Eric T., 114, 141n1
death
—by suicide, xv, xvii, 31–32, 50, 97–111, 113, 118, 122, 140n4, 141n10, 142n8; affective elements in, 98; altruistic, 100–101; cognitive elements in, 98, 103, 141n7; definition of, 98; as metacritical act, 110–11; guilt as a factor in, 102 (*see also* "Affair of Outposts, An"; "George Thurston"; "One Officer, One Man")
—fear of: xv, 97–98; in children, 2, 13, 136n4–5; and the Civil War, 61; in context of war, xv, xvi–xvii, 58, 78, 98; and the mother, 3, 13, 17; repression of, xviii, 2, 17, 57; universal, xviii, 57 (*see also* birth, trauma of; Generative Death Anxiety; object-loss anxiety)
—human responses to, 87
—knowledge of: 2–3
"Death of Halpin Frayser, The" (Bierce), xv, xvi, 15,17–28, 29, 30, 43, 48, 54, 60, 93, 137n3–4, 137n7
De Forest, John William, 69
Diagnostic and Statistical Manual of Mental Disorders (DSM-III, DSM-IV), 114
Dimeo, Steven, 41–42
doppelgänger, xvi, 43, 49, 107; origin of term, 43 (*see also* double)
double, xvi, 130; artist's use of, 46–47; Bierce's use of, 43–52; early belief in concept of, 44; latent form of, 48; manifest form of, 48; object form of, 52; psychoanalytic theory and, 44–45, and the uncanny, 45 (see also *doppelgänger*)
dreams: and fear of death, 1, 12–15, 19, 22, 24–26; Bierce's definition of, 11; Freud's definition of, 11–12; and language, 121–22 (*see also* "Death of Halpin Frayser, The"; "Eyes of the Panther, The"; "Mocking-Bird, The"; "Occurrence at Owl Creek Bridge, An"; "Visions of the Night")
Duncan, Russell, 135n4, 139n7
Durkheim, Emile, 100–101

Edel, Leon, xvii–xviii
"Editha" (Howells), 72
Edwards, Jonathan, 4
El Paso, TX, 133
Elkhart County, IN, 55
Elkhart, IN *Review*, 73
euthanasia, 127, 132
Examiner. See *San Francisco Examiner*
"Eyes of the Panther, The" (Bierce), xvi, 35–38, 39, 54, 138n2, 140n3

Fairbrother, G. W., 54
Fatout, Paul, 3, 4, 5, 46, 54, 73, 119, 133, 135n2, 136n9, 138n1
Faust, Drew Gilpin, 83–84, 104
Feifel, Herman, 57
Felman, Soshana, 136n7
Fiend's Delight, The (Bierce), 142n8
Fitch, Michael Hendrick, 90
Fornari, Franco, xv, 55
"Four Days in Dixie" (Bierce), xvii, 76–77, 116
Frank, Joseph Allan, 63
Franklin, Battle of, 114
Franklin Springs, KY, 55
Franklin, TN, 131
Frazer, Sir James George, 44
Fredericksburg, Battle of, 139
Freud, Sigmund, xv, 2, 11, 44, 45, 136n3, 140n4; application of theories to Bierce's works, xv, 18–19, 51, 52, 135n5, 137n7
Fromm, Erich, 105, 141n9–10
Fuentes, Carlos, 142n3
Fun (magazine), 45

Gale, Robert L., 135n4
Galveston, TX, 130
Ganzer Syndrome, 99, 140n2
Gatewood, Jeff, 76
Gaylesville, AL, 76
Generative Death Anxiety (GDA), xv, 1–2, 87
"George Thurston" (Bierce), xvii, 122–24; 140n4
"Ghost of Mine, That" (Bierce), xvi, 45–46, 47
Glenn, Eliza, 90, 91, 92
Glenn family, 90, 140n5
Glenn, John, 91, 92
Glenn, Russell W., 139n4
Golden Era (magazine), 118
Goodwin, Renee D., 141n5
gothic, xvi, 4, 11, 17, 26, 29, 36, 39, 42, 43, 61, 139n8, 140n3; male, 17–18, 24, 27, 137n2; and religion, 15
Grafton, WV, 102, 128
Grant, General Ulysses S., 65
Grattan, C. Harley, 3, 73, 130, 135n2
Gray, J. Glenn, 67, 68
Grenander, M. E., xiv, xv, 18, 27, 32, 133, 135n3 135n5, 140n6
Grossman, Dave, 105, 140n1

Haas, Ann Pollinger, 114, 141n1
Habibi, 87
Harcouth, Thomas A., 135n1
Harnik, J., 37
Hazen, General William B., 56–57, 69, 75, 90, 117, 129, 130
Hazen's Brigade, 75, 129–30
Hearst, William Randolph, xvii, 119–20, 130
Hendin, Herbert, 114, 141n1
Herman, William (joint pseudonym of Bierce, William A. Rudolfson, and Thomas A. Harcouth), 135n1
heroism, xvii; and fear of death, 57, 58, 87, 97, 107; human urge to, 3, 33, 57–58, 89; in context of Civil War, xvi, 53, 56, 58–59, 69, 70, 73, 80–81, 100
hero-system, xvii; in context of Civil War, 61–62, 66, 67, 69, 71, 72, 81, 83–84, 87, 101, 111, 116; role of society as, xv, 57–58, 59, 103, 113
Holmdahl, Captain Emil, 133

Hood, Tom, 45–46, 47
Horesh, Neta, 141n4
Howard, Major General Oliver, 75
Howells, William Dean, 72
"Hypnotist, The" (Bierce), 9
"Humility" (Bierce), 27

Ibarra, Salvador, 133
Imaginary Order, 14, 19
immortality, human need for, xvii, 44, 46–47, 57, 77, 130, 133, 142n2
immortality, revolutionary, xvii, 133–34
"Imperfect Conflagration, An" (Bierce), 9
In the Midst of Life (Bierce), xvi, 30, 35, 38, 42, 135n3, 137n1. See also *Tales of Soldiers and Civilians*
Indiana Hospital for the Insane, 114
Indianapolis, IN, 55
"Inhabitant of Carcosa, An" (Bierce), 15

Jackson, Charles O., 4
Jane Eyre (Bronte), 137n1
Jones, Ernest, 14
Joshi, S. T., 18, 135n4, 137n3, 137n7, 138n4
Jacobi, Jolande, 138n1
Juarez, Mexico, 133
Jung, Carl, 43–44, 138n1

Kane, Harnett Thomas, 86
Kaugers, Astrida Seja, 142n6
Kelly family, 90
Kennesaw Mountain, GA, 56, 76, 103, 115
Kentucky Military Institute, 55
Keyes, Ralph, 139
"Killed at Resaca" (Bierce), xvii, 69–72, 73, 83, 99, 101–2, 122
Kimmel, Michael, 21
Kierkegaard Soren, 2
Klein, Melanie, A., 138n4
Klinnert, Mary D., 141n6, 142n6
Klooster, David J., 135n4, 139n7
Kocher, Richard Luke, 122–23, 124
Kristeva, Julia, xvi, and abjection, 14; and theories of language and the unconscious, 14, 18, 21

Lacan, Jacques, xvi; and theories of language and the unconscious, 12, 13, 18
Lair of the White Worm, The (Stoker), 137n1
Laredo, TX, 132, 133
Larson, Kelli, A., 90, 140n5
Laurel Hill, Battle of, 63, 114
Laurel Hill, WV, 63
Lee, General Robert E., 69
Leung, Donald Y. M., 141n6
Lewis, Matthew Gregory, 137n1
Liechty, Daniel, 1
Lifton, Robert Jay: xvii, 100, 103, 133–34, 136n1, 141n10, 142n9
Lincoln, Abraham, 55, 84, 141
Linderman, Gerald F., 61, 65, 70–71, 71–72, 83, 89–90, 141n8
Lipsey, Tami, 141n2
"Little of Chickamauga, A" (Bierce), xvii. 94–95
Logan, F. J., 139n1
London, England, 45, 46, 118, 119, 126
London Sketch-Book, 64
Longstreet, General James, 139
"Love of Country, The" (Bierce), 6

Macabre, the: Bierce's use of, 6, 8, 29, 68
Mahler, Margaret S., 136n6
"Major's Tale, The" (Bierce), xiii, xvii, 124–26; 142n10
Malinowski, Bronislaw, 138n4
"Man and the Snake, The" (Bierce), xvi, 32–35, 139n8;
Mariani, Giorgio, 59
Marshall, Samuel L. A, 79, 139n4
Masserman, Jules, 97–98
May, Rollo, 136n1, 138n5
McClain, Mark, 136n8

McIntosh, Irene, 136n8
McKenzie, Clancy D., 141n3
McLean, Robert C, 18
McPherson, James M., 58, 61, 65, 66, 78, 79, 84, 90
McWilliams, Carey, xiii, 73, 73–74, 119, 131, 136n9, 139n2–3
Meigs County, OH, 3
Melville, Herman, 53, 138
Mexican Revolution of 1910, 131–34
Mexican-American War, 64, 91
Mikulincer, Mario, 141n4
Miller, Emanuel, 140n2
Mitchell, Juliet, 121
"Mocking-Bird, The" (Bierce), xvii, 99, 107–11, 113, 141n11–12
"Modern Warfare" (Bierce), 104
"Moonlit Road, The" (Bierce), 15
Monk, The (Lewis), 137n1
Morris, Roy, Jr., 5, 6, 115, 131, 135n2, 138n1, 138n3, 142n4, 142n7
"Moxon's Master" (Bierce), xvi, 49
Mrazek, David A., 141n6
Murfreesboro, TN, 129, 131
Murray, Lynn, 136n8
"My Day of Life" (Bierce), 27–28, 137n9
"My Favorite Murder" (Bierce), 7
"Mystery, A" (Bierce), 118
Mysteries of Udolpho, a Romance, The (Radcliffe), 137n1

Nacco, Stephen Damian, 47, 48, 51 138n2–3
narcissism, 2, 57, 61, 77
Nashville, Battle of, 114, 124, 125, 126
Nashville, TN, 129, 131
Neale Publishing Company, 130, 131
Neale, Walter, 54, 73, 119, 120, 121, 130, 132, 142n4
Nelson, Harold S., 141n6
New Orleans, LA, 132
New Orleans *States*, 132
News Letter. See *San Francisco News Letter and California Advertiser*
Nietzsche, Friedrich, 2
Ninth Indiana Volunteers, 55, 56, 64, 68, 128
Ninth Indiana Regiment. *See* Ninth Indiana Volunteers
Northern Indianian, 53, 54

Oakland Daily Evening Tribune, 126
object-loss anxiety, 3, 17, 24–25, 26, 37, 38, 51, 55, 92
object relations: definition, 5; theory, xv; and relation to attachment theory, 5
"Occurrence at Owl Creek Bridge, An" (Bierce), xv, xvii, 84–90, 93, 135n5, 139n1–2, 140n3–4, 140n6
Oedipal project, xvi, 2, 18, 19, 24, 27, 28
Oedipus complex, 2, 19, 136n3
Ojinaga, Mexico, 133
"Oil of Dog" (Bierce), 7–9
Old Gringo, The (Fuentes), 142n3
"On a Mountain" (Bierce), xvi, 62–63, 64, 99
"One Officer, One Man" (Bierce), 140n4
"One of the Missing" (Bierce), xvii, 99, 103–7
"One of Twins" (Bierce), xvi, 49–52, 53, 54
Ortega, General Toribio, 133
"Other Lodgers, The" (Bierce), xvii, 115–16
Ossawatomie, KS, 55
Owens, David M., xv, 56, 60, 71, 84, 90, 125, 129, 139n7, 140n5, 141n12, 142n10
Ozer, Emily, 141n2

Parenticide Club, The (Bierce), xvi, 1, 6–10, 11, 29, 38, 137n10
"Parker Adderson, Philosopher" (Bierce), xvii, 69, 77–81, 83, 87, 102, 140n6
parricide, xvi, 1, 6–7, 38
"Passing Show, The" (Bierce), 128–29
Philippi, WV, 63
Pickett's Mill, Battle of, 75, 99
Pickett's Mill, GA, 75
Pine, Fred, 136n6

Pittsburg Landing, TN, 64, 65
Poe, Edgar Allan, 136n7; and theory of concentrated special effect, 29
Poe family, 90
poetry, motif of, 21–22, 24, 25, 26
Pollard, Percival, 130
Porte, Joel, 15
Posttraumatic Stress Disorder [PTSD], xvii, 114, 141n1–4. *See also* stress, posttraumatic; stress, combat
Pottawatomie Creek, KS, 55
Powers, James G., 135n5
"Prattle" (Bierce), 121, 128
pre-Oedipal phase, 3, 13, 21
Price, Marcella R., 141n6
Puritans, 3–4, 136n5
Pyrrhonism, 127

Radcliffe, Ann, 137n1
Rank, Otto, xvi, xvii, 2, 37, 44, 45, 46, 130, 133, 136n1, 138n3, 140n3, 142n2
Real Order, 13–14
reason, fallability of, 30, 31–32, 34–35
Reaves, George A., 63
Reconstruction, 20
Reed family, 91
Reid, James J., 105, 141n1, 141n10
Resaca, Battle of, 69, 74–75
Resaca, GA, 69
"Resumed Identity, A" (Bierce), 129, 130
Rheingold, Joseph C., 136n4, 138n4
Rubens, Philip M., 17
Rogers, Robert, xvi, 47–48, 52, 138
Rosecrans, General Williams, 90
Rudolfson, William A., 135n1

San Antonio, TX, 132
San Francisco, CA: 117, 118, 119, in "A Cold Greeting," 47; in "One of Twins," 52; in "The Death of Halpin Frayser," 23
San Francisco Examiner, 11, 30, 32, 35, 38, 119, 121, 124, 138n2
San Francisco News Letter and California Advertiser, 118
satire, Bierce's use of, 6, 7, 117
Schaefer, Michael W., 139n9, 140n3
Schiller, Friedrich, 43, 138
Schultz, David E., 135n4
Semiotic Order, 21, 22, 24–25, 27
Shalit, Ben, 140n1
Shapes of Clay (Bierce), 137n8
sharpshooters. *See* Civil War, U.S., snipers in
Shaver, Phillip R., 141n4
Sherman, General William Tecumseh, 75, 83, 103, 139
"Shiloh: A Requiem" (Melville), 138
Shiloh, Battle of, 56, 63–68, 114, 130
Shiloh Church, TN, 63, 84, 131
Shneidman, Edwin, 98, 110, 141n7
Sickler, Eleanor, 131
Silber, Nina, 137n6
Silverman, Kaja, xvi, 19
Smith, Allan Lloyd, 135n5, 137n4
Smith, General A. J., 125
Snodgrass family, 90
Socrates, 2
Solomon, Eric, 59
Sole Survivor: Bits of Autobiography, A (Bierce), 126, 127, 137n4
"Son of the Gods, A" (Bierce), 139n1
Spanish-American War of 1898, 72
Spencer, Herbert, 48, 49
Spinoza, 2
St. Charles Hotel (New Orleans), 132
Stannard, David E., 3–4, 136n5
Stein, William Bysshe, 18
Stekel, Wilhelm, 138n4
Stoicheff, Peter, 88, 135n5, 140n4
Stoker, Bram, 137
Stone, Rev. Timothy, 4
Stones River, Battle of, 56, 64, 70, 114, 129–30
Stones River, TN, 70, 130
"Story of a Conscience, The" (Bierce), xvii, 99, 102–3, 140n6

stress, combat, 65–66, 97, 98–99, 103, 105, 113, 140n1; early studies of, 101, 140n5 (*see also* posttraumatic stress; Posttraumatic Stress Disorder)
stress, posttraumatic, xv, xvii, 113, 125, 142n9 (*see also* Posttraumatic Stress Disorder; stress, combat)
suicide. *See* death, by suicide
"Suitable Surroundings, The" (Bierce), xvi, 30–32, 139n8
Symbolic Order, 12, 13, 14, 19, 22
synaesthesia, 46, 138n2

"Taking Oneself Off" (Bierce), 111
Tales of Soldiers and Civilians, xiv–xv, 107; publication date, 135n3, 137n1 (see also *In the Midst of Life*)
Taylor, Gordon Rattray, 138n3
"Three and One Are One" (Bierce), 6
"Thumb-Nail Sketch, A" (Bierce), 120
Tillich, Paul, 138n5
"To a Dejected Poet" (Bierce), 27
"Tough Tussle, A" (Bierce), xvi, xvii, 60–63, 99–100, 108, 139n8
"Town Crier, The" (Bierce), 118, 121
Town Topics (magazine), 38
Tucker, Glenn, 140n5

Uncanny, the, 45, 88, 140n4
Unheimliche, das. See Uncanny, the
United States Mint, 117

Valentine, John D., 141n2
Villa, Francisco ("Pancho"), 133
"Visions of the Night" (Bierce), xvi, 1, 11–15, 27, 30, 43, 45, 61, 88, 115
Vittetoe family, 91

Walker, Franklin, 135n2
war: civilian guilt, 86; fatalism as response to, 78; psychoanalytic theories of, 55, 59, 117; as spectacle, 67
War of 1812, 64
Warren, Robert Penn, 87
Warsaw, IN, 6, 53, 54, 74, 76
Washington, D.C., 120, 128, 131, 132, 133
Wasp (magazine), 59, 119
Weiss, Daniel, 141n2
"What I Saw of Shiloh" (Bierce), xvi, 64–68, 99, 110, 122
"When Lilacs Last in the Dooryard Bloom'd" (Whitman), 141
Whites, Leeann, 137n5
Whitman, Walt, 113, 141
Wilder, Colonel John T., 94
"William F. Smith" (Bierce), 137
Williams, Anne, 13, 17–18, 137n2
Williams, Jo, 76
Williams, L. H., 54
Williams, Reuben, 54
Wilson, Edmund, 128, 139n6
Windsor, Ontario, 55
Woodruff, Stuart C., xiii–xiv, 34, 62, 141n11
Wooley, Charles F. 140n5
Wright, Bernice ("Fatima," "Tima"), 73–76
Wright, Clara, xvii; 74–76, 78, 98
Wright, Lance, 141n3
Wyatt-Brown, Bertram, 137n5

Zilboorg, Gregory, xv, 2–3, 37, 57, 86, 138n4

Ambrose Bierce and the Dance of Death was designed and typeset on a Macintosh computer system using InDesign software. The body text is set in 10/13 Kepler and display type is set in Blackmoor. This book was designed and typeset by Chad Pelton, and manufactured by Thomson-Shore, Inc.